Blender 3D: Architecture, Buildings, and Scenery

Create photorealistic 3D architectural visualizations of buildings, interiors, and environmental scenery

Allan Brito

PUBLISHING

BIRMINGHAM - MUMBAI

Blender 3D: Architecture, Buildings, and Scenery

First published: May 2008

Production Reference: 1220508

Published by Packt Publishing Ltd.
32 Lincoln Road
Olton
Birmingham, B27 6PA, UK.

ISBN 978-1-847193-67-4

www.packtpub.com

Cover Image by Allan Brito (allanrbs@gmail.com)

Credits

Author

Allan Brito

Reviewer

Yorik van Havre

Senior Acquisition Editor

David Barnes

Development Editor

Swapna V. Verlekar

Technical Editor

Meeba Renny Abraham

Editorial Team Leader

Akshara Aware

Project Manager

Abhijeet Deobhakta

Indexer

Rekha Nair

Proofreaders

Dirk Manuel

Chris Smith

Production Coordinator

Shantanu Zagade

Cover Work

Shantanu Zagade

About the Author

Allan Brito is a Brazilian architect specialized in information visualization, who lives and works in Recife, Brazil. He works with Blender 3D to produce animations and still images, for visualization and instructional material.

Besides his work with Blender as an artist, he also has substantial experience teaching 3D modeling, animation, and multimedia at Mauricio de Nassau College.

He is an active member of the community of Blender users, writing about Blender 3D and its development for websites in Brazilian Portuguese (http://www.allanbrito.com) and English (http://www.blendernation.com).

This is his second book about Blender 3D; the first one was Blender 3D — Guia do Usuário, which was published in Brazil. It's a guide on how to use Blender, covering from the basics to character animation.

He can be reached through his website at http://www.blender3darchitect.com, where he covers the use of Blender 3D and other tools for architectural visualization.

I would like to thank my family for supporting me during the production of this book, specially my wife Érica and of course Mutsumu and Nanna, who are my Father and Mother-in-law.

About the Reviewer

Yorik van Havre is an architect from Belgium, who currently lives in Brazil, where he works as a freelance architect. Blender is part of his everyday work. He regularly writes articles and tutorials about Blender, architecture, and architecture software, and is actively involved in several communities and free software projects.

Table of Contents

Preface

Blender was developed as an in-house application by the Dutch animation studio NeoGeo (not to be confused with the Neo-Geo game console) and Not a Number Technologies (NaN). It was primarily authored by Ton Roosendaal, who had previously written a ray tracer called Traces for the Amiga in 1989. The name "Blender" was inspired by a song by Yello, from the album Baby.

What This Book Covers

Chapter 1 covers architectural visualization and Blender, and some other techniques and assets that we will need in the course of the book. It also covers Blender and the requirements of software and hardware to start using it, along with the benefits of using computers to create Architectural Visualization.

Chapter 2 deals with all the basic aspects related to Blender and the basics to get deep into more specific questions about modeling and rendering architectural visualizations and scenarios. It's very important to understand how object manipulation, creation, and editing work in Blender, as this helps us to work a lot faster and create better models and visualizations. It helps us to use the interface, set up the interface, select objects, work with modes, transform objects, create objects, copy objects, work with the camera, and with rendering basics.

Chapter 3 helps us to start working with modeling tools and techniques in Blender. This will give us a better basis to deal with specific aspects related to architectural and landscape modeling. This also gives us a start with: how to create objects with Blender, what meshes are and how to edit them, the advantages of using meshes instead of solids, how to transform objects, how to extrude vertices, edges, and faces, how to work with modifiers, how to work with groups, and how to model with the proportional editing.

Chapter 4 teaches us to create models for architecture visualization. We see some techniques to create walls, floors, roofs, and other specific architectural elements. Some of these elements are pretty simple to create, but some require special tricks or adjustments in the modeling to be created. The main topics covered here are planning the modeling, how to model with precision, organizing our scenes in layers, creating walls, creating openings, creating floors and linings, and how to start a model from a CAD file.

Chapter 5 shows us how to add more details into our models, like windows, doors, and stairs. A great level of realism is achieved in architectural visualization by adding details to models, like window frames and more. Some of the concepts learned in this chapter are rotation/scale pivots, arrays to create multiple copies, applying a mirror modifier to create symmetrical models, and level of detail for models.

Chapter 6 points out how important it is to use furniture in our models and scenes, to give all environments more details and realism. It also covers certain interesting topics such as: how to build your own furniture library, to reuse in future projects, how to model a chair, and how to model a sofa.

Chapter 7 explains what materials are, and how they can give more realism to our scenes. It also shows us How to create materials, how to organize materials, how to import materials between scenes, setting up a material color, determine how the material reacts to light, using raytracing materials, how to create transparent materials, and how to create materials with reflections.

Chapter 8 talks about working with textures, to give our materials more realism. Certain issues covered here are how to choose and organize textures, applying and setting up a bitmap texture, how to map a texture around a model, using normal maps, and creating UV Layouts, to create more complex textures.

Chapter 9 illustrates how the light system works in Blender, and when to use a particular light type. All light types share common parameters like energy and influence area. What makes every light type unique is how they generate shadows and their unidirectional or directional nature.

Chapter 10 focuses on how to use the Radiosity and Ambient Occlusion options, to create better illumination for our scenes. With the Radiosity options, we can generate a lightweight solution to create shadows and interactions between elements. The light is distributed at the scene following a physics-based energy distribution, with the light rays bouncing at the objects' faces.

Chapter 11 deals with more sophisticated illuminations, which have the Ambient Occlusion option. With this tool we can simulate a global illumination environment, creating a smooth lighting solution.

Chapter 12 shows us how to improve our images with the advanced features offered by YafRay. With these features we can produce images using global illumination options, like photons and light reflection on surfaces. It describes how to choose YafRay as render engine for Blender, set up the basic parameters of YafRay, use the YafRay GI settings, set up a scene using the SkyDome method of YafRay, and set up a scene using the Full GI method of YafRay.

Chapter 13 features the techniques and tools used to create animation in Blender. This is focused on camera animation, which requires a lot less work than character animation is, but not less adjustments. It covers certain topics such as what animation, and how to plan the process to avoid problems and issues during the creation of the animation, different types of planning for animation, like animatic and storyboards, the types of keyframes in Blender and how to use them to make animations, setting up the animation with three special windows in Blender; Timeline, NLA Editor, and the IPO Curve Editor, and how to create interactive animations and make a standalone application with them.

Chapter 14 teaches us how to avoid the long render times in Blender, and switch to Gimp at the end of the work for the post-production process. Some adjustments can be done in Gimp with a lot less effort than Blender, especially for colour correction. It explains how to use Gimp tools to make color corrections, correct errors caused by displaced geometry with the stamp and heal tools, use layers to composite the image with real photos, add text to the rendered images, and add watermarks to the images, to protect your work

Conventions

In this book, you will find a number of styles of text that distinguish between different kinds of information. Here are some examples of these styles, and an explanation of their meaning.

New terms and **important words** are introduced in a bold-type font. Words that you see on the screen, in menus or dialog boxes for example, appear in our text like this: "At the **Scene Panel**, we can find a combo box, which allows us to choose the render engine used to process the scene."

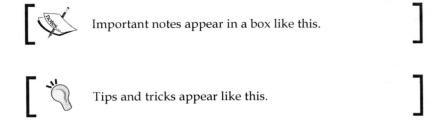

Important notes appear in a box like this.

Tips and tricks appear like this.

Reader Feedback

Feedback from our readers is always welcome. Let us know what you think about this book, what you liked or may have disliked. Reader feedback is important for us to develop titles that you really get the most out of.

To send us general feedback, simply drop an email to feedback@packtpub.com, making sure to mention the book title in the subject of your message.

If there is a book that you need and would like to see us publish, please send us a note in the **SUGGEST A TITLE** form on www.packtpub.com or email suggest@packtpub.com.

If there is a topic that you have expertise in and you are interested in either writing or contributing to a book, see our author guide on www.packtpub.com/authors.

Customer Support

Now that you are the proud owner of a Packt book, we have a number of things to help you to get the most from your purchase.

Errata

Although we have taken every care to ensure the accuracy of our contents, mistakes do happen. If you find a mistake in one of our books, we would be grateful if you would report this to us. By doing this you can save other readers from frustration, and help to improve subsequent versions of this book. If you find any errata, report them by visiting http://www.packtpub.com/support, selecting your book, clicking on the **let us know** link, and entering the details of your errata. Once your errata are verified, your submission will be accepted and the errata added to the list of existing errata. The existing errata can be viewed by selecting your title from http://www.packtpub.com/support.

Questions

You can contact us at questions@packtpub.com if you are having a problem with some aspect of the book, and we will do our best to address it.

1

Introduction to Blender and Architectural Visualization

As you know, every project that involves some kind of construction — such as building a house, movie sets, or virtual sets — needs a project. These projects are made up of a lot of documents and technical drawings that help in the construction of these buildings and movie sets. For the construction crew, these technical drawings and documents are just fine. But when you need to make a presentation of these projects to people who can't read technical drawings, things can get a little difficult.

Architectural Visualization

The traditional way to show architectural projects is with perspective views of the project made by hand and painted with watercolor or airbrushes. A perspective view of a project works like a picture of something that still doesn't exist. It's far easier to understand a picture of a building or environment than make decisions based on reading a technical drawing. These kinds of presentations look really great, but are expensive to create, and require a long time for production of each view. That's where the computer-generated architectural visualization comes in — to make everything easier for everyone involved with the project.

The benefits of using computer-generated visualization for architecture led to them quickly becoming a standard for these kinds of presentations. Today, almost every project for buildings, sets, or anything involving construction has a 3D-visualization for project development or to show the concept to someone who wouldn't understand a presentation based on technical drawings. The use of 3D-models bring more options even in the project stage, since it's possible to quickly visualize all the environments and parts while it's being planned, and to make changes to improve the organization and oversee every aspect of the project.

Even if its main benefit is being faster and cheaper to produce, the computer-generated architectural visualization has another benefit. And it's one that can't be beaten by traditional art work! Yes, we are talking about animation. With animation, the project can be presented in a much richer environment than on paper.

How about Blender 3D?

What is Blender 3D ? And how is it related to Architectural Visualization?

Well, Blender 3D is an open-source 3D graphics suite, capable of modeling, rendering and animating 3D environments. Like many other open-source projects, Blender is completely free! Everyone can download and use it immediately in commercial projects. It's not a shareware with limited tools, or time constraints; you can use it freely. In the past few years, the Blender user base has grown significantly. Everyday, more and more students and professionals switch to Blender, as its tools get better in every new release.

One of the aspects that calls attention to Blender is its size—it is only 10 MB. That's right! Only 10 MB and we can even run it directly from a portable drive. Another great aspect of Blender is that we can use various Operating Systems such as Linux, Windows, and Mac OS X, leaving us the choice of which one to use.

When we start using Blender to model and render, we will see that lightweight does not mean lack of power. A lot of quality work has been done with Blender in the last few months, such as the first Open Movie made entirely with Blender, called *Elephants Dream*, which has awesome scenario designs.

[

Elephants Dream

If you want to download the movie, along with the production files, visit http:// www.elephantsdream.org.
]

As we go through this book, we will see that Blender is a great tool, designed to give artists a lot of productivity and fast access to tools and menus. This means that Blender is strongly based on keyboard shortcuts, and not menus. For advanced users, this would be easy, although it can be difficult for new users. However, don't worry; with some practice and the examples that we will cover in this book, it will be possible to understand quickly all of the aspects and tricks involving 3D modeling and animation to create great Architectural Visualizations and Scenarios with Blender.

Download Blender

To download Blender, we must access the Blender Foundation website at
`http://www.blender.org`, and choose the download page. There, we can find
a lot of download options such as mirrors and compilations for different
Operating Systems.

The Blender Foundation is responsible for the coordination and development of
Blender and its support, since it's a community project, and not a product from the
Foundation. It coordinates the efforts to develop and improve Blender, such as the
Blender website and development forums.

Hardware and Software Requirements for Blender

Blender doesn't require a powerful hardware setup for anyone who just wants to
start using it. (Just to get started with tools such as 3ds, max, or Maya, you need a
very powerful computer.)

Is there anything special about the hardware needed for Architectural Visualization?

Well, if you want to produce photorealistic renderings, then I strongly recommend
you ensure your system has plenty of RAM and CPU power, since these kind of
rendering require a lot of processing. However, if you just want to create renderings
that look more like a sketch, or something that doesn't look photorealistic, it won't
be necessary to use a powerful computer, since this kind of rendering demands
less resources.

The Blender Foundation recommends the following minimum requirements:

- Three-button mouse
- Open GL Graphics Card with 16 MB RAM
- 300 MHz CPU
- 128 MB RAM
- 1024 x 768 pixels Display with 16-bit color
- 20 MB free hard disk Space

However, there is more. If you really want to get maximum performance, there is a more powerful configuration:

- 2 GHz dual core CPU
- 2 GB RAM
- 1920 x 1200 pixels Display with 24-bit color
- Three-button mouse
- Open GL Graphics Card with 128 or 256 MB RAM

There isn't much to say about the software, only that you can run Blender on almost any operating system available. The following is the list of systems that support Blender:

- Windows 98, ME, 2000, XP or Vista
- Mac OS X 10.2 and later
- Linux i386, x86_64/amd64 or PPC
- FreeBSD 6.2 i386 and later
- Irix 6.5 mips3
- Solaris 2.8 sparc

Other Tools for Visualization

Although it is a very powerful 3D graphics suite, Blender can't handle all the processes of creating Architectural Visualization alone. We will need some extras tools such as Gimp, for post processing, and image editing. There are some tasks such as texture editing and creation that need a more specialized tool, and for that, Gimp is the best choice.

Another great tool that we will be using is YafRay, which can make awesome renders using a Global Illumination engine that Blender doesn't have. The integration between Blender and YafRay is really great, and even provides direct access to the YafRay engine from the Blender interface.

The visualization workflow requires the use of a whole set of tools. Blender is just one of them, but we could say that it is the tool responsible for the creation of the images and animations. Along with Blender, the following tools can help a visualization artist to create a good presentation:

- **CAD**: Everything starts with a CAD file, which has the technical drawings for a project. The following tools are used for CAD Drawing: QCAD, VariCAD, AutoCAD, and ArchiCAD.
- **3D Modeling and Rendering**: Here is where Blender comes in.

- **Image processing**: We may need to make adjustments or corrections to the files after generating images with Blender. We could use tools like Gimp or Photoshop to make these adjustments.

- **Presentation**: After the editing process, we could use some other tool to make a presentation. If we choose to print the perspectives, Inkscape could be a good choice to make a sheet or folder. Another option is to use a slideshow to present the perspectives, which can be done with Open Office Impress.

CAD and 3D-Architectural Modeling

To work with Architectural Visualization we will need to understand how Blender deals with files from CAD software such as AutoCAD, ArchiCAD, QCAD, and other tools. The most common file format used to exchange CAD drawings is **DXF** (**Drawing Exchange Format**). So if your CAD software can save your drawings in the DXF file format, Blender will be able to import it. Since most CAD packages can do that, it makes Blender highly compatible. Another common file format to use is the 3DS, from the old 3D Studio. If you want to make some 3D-modeling in your own CAD software, the 3DS file format is also a good choice. Besides these file formats, Blender can read a lot of 3D formats such as Maya OBJ, LightWave LWO, and a lot more.

3D Models from the Internet

Creating architectural visualizations and scenarios with computers may be a very quick task if you only need to model and work on walls, floors, and other basic elements. What can really change the look of our scenes are the details. The secret for a good scene is the amount of detail and objects that it contains. A good visualization for an office space is filled with desks, computers, chairs, and objects placed over the desks. However, don't worry—we don't have to model all of the objects every time. For that, we have to create a good library of objects, which we will be able to use for our scenes. These include cars, people, vegetation, and all other objects that can be interesting.

The easiest way to gather all these files is from the Internet. Places such as 3D Cafe (http://www.3dcafe.com), allow anyone to download 3D models for free.

The following is a list of places to find models for Blender:

- http://resources.blogscopia.com/: Furniture models in the native Blender file format.

- http://www.e-interiors.net: Lost of pictures and free models of furniture. Most files are in 3DS or DXF file formats.

- `http://www.linedstudio.com`: More furniture models and scenes already in Blender native file format.
- `http://blender-archi.tuxfamily.org/Models`: A collection of models to be used in Blender for Architectural Visualization, all in the Blender native file format.

Visualization with Blender

If you want to find some good examples of Architectural Visualization made with Blender, there are some websites that you can visit. Most of them are related to some external render engine which can be integrated with Blender. However, their communities of artists are a great example of what Blender can do for visualization.

For this book, we chose to use YafRay, which is the external renderer that best integrates with Blender. There is even a standard menu, which we can use to render a scene with YafRay. We could use some other great external renderers as well:

- Indigo Render: `http://www.indigorenderer.com`
- Kerkythea: `http://www.kerkythea.net`
- Sunflow: `http://sunflow.sourceforge.net/`
- Pov-Ray: `http://www.povray.org/`
- `YafRay: http://www.yafray.org`

Take a look into the gallery of these renderers and you will find some great examples of Architectural Visualization made with Blender. Also, we can't forget about the Blender Gallery (`http://www.blender.org/features-gallery/gallery/images/`), which is updated monthly. This gallery has nothing but images from Blender, and almost every month some great new new visualization images hit the gallery.

As an example of what we will cover throughout the rest of this book, here is an image of a dining room made with Blender, and rendered with YafRay.

Summary

In this chapter, we took a glance at Architectural Visualization and Blender and some other techniques and assets that we will need along the book. We learned the following:

- What is architectural visualization?
- What is Blender, and the software and hardware required to start using it.
- The benefits of using computers to create Architectural Visualization
- How Blender is related to CAD software.
- How important a good model library is, and where to find some good free 3D-models to use.
- The workflow of Architectural Visualization and where Blender is located in this pipeline.

2
Blender 3D: Quick Start

This chapter will deal with all the basic aspects related to Blender, which we will be using before getting the entire book. We must first learn the basics before getting deeper into more specific questions about modeling and rendering Architectural Visualizations and Scenarios. It's very important to understand how object manipulation, creation, and editing works in Blender. This way, we will be able to work a lot faster, and create better models and visualizations.

If you have already worked with Blender, it's probably better to just have a quick overview of this chapter, and skip to the next one.

Interface

One of the most important parts of any software application is its interface, and with Blender, it is no different. But the Blender interface is unique, because it's all based on OpenGL graphics built in real time. Hence, we can say that Blender has no interface. What we can find is a default interface that can be arranged to fit your needs in almost any way. It's even possible to zoom all the items in the menus and buttons. Let's take a look at the interface.

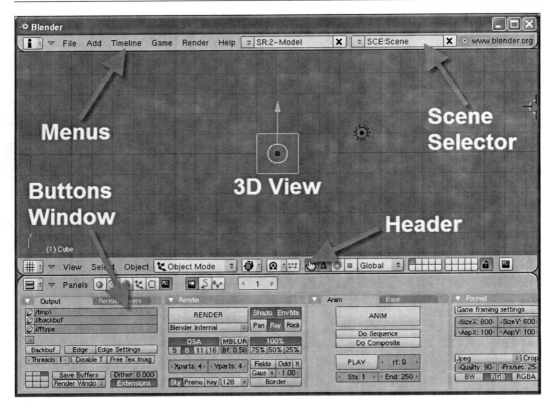

The default Blender interface is always divided into:

- **3D View:** This is the section of the interface where you visualize of all of your objects. If we are in the modeling process, this window should always be visible.

- **Buttons Window**: Here, we will find almost all of the tools and menus, with options to set up things such as modifiers, materials, textures, and lights. We can change the options available in this window with some small icons that contextualize the buttons with specific tasks such as materials, shading, editing, and others.

- **Header**: All windows in Blender have a **header**, even if it's not visible at the time we create the window. The content of the Header can change, depending on the Window Type. For example, in the header for the 3D View, we can find options related to visualization, object manipulation, and selection.

- **Menus**: These menus works just like in any other application, with options to save files, and import and export models.

- **Scene Selector**: We can create various scenes in Blender, and this selector allows us to choose and create these scenes. Since we will be modeling and dealing with scenery, this will be an important tool for us.

Although, these parts constitute the default interface of Blender, we can change all of the aspects of the interface. There are even some modified screens, adapted to some common tasks with Blender, for us to choose. To access these modified screen sets, we must click on the selector located to the left of **Scene Selector.**

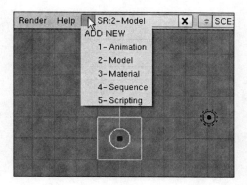

There are screen sets prepared for working with **Animation, Model, Material, Sequence, and Scripting**. Each of these sets has a different interface organization, optimized for its specific task. A nice way to switch between these sets is by using a keyboard shortcut, which is *CTRL* plus left-arrow or right-arrow. Try this shortcut, and you will switch between sets very quickly.

If you make any changes in the interface of Blender, and want to overwrite the default interface, just press *CTRL+U* and your current interface will become the new default. This way, every time Blender is started, your new interface will be shown. The same option can be selected via the File menu with the option called Save Default Settings. To restore the standard default interface, just use the option Load Factory Settings, in the File menu.

Windows and Menus

Blender has a lot of different windows that can do a lot of nice things. Two of the most common windows are the **3D View** and the **Buttons** Window, but there are a lot more. With the **Window** selector we can choose among several types such as **File Browser, Text Editor, Timeline,** and others. The window type selector is always located in the left corner of each window.

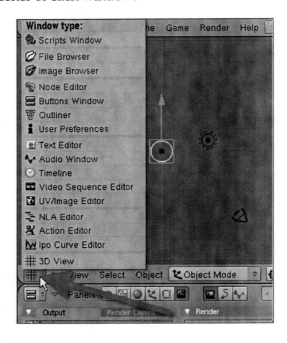

Let's see what's the function of each window:

- **Scripts Window**: This window groups some nice scripts written in Python, to add some extra tools and functionalities to Blender. It works much like plug-ins in other 3D Packages. There are scripts to help in a lot of different tasks including modeling, animation, and importing models. Some of these scripts are very helpful in architectural modeling, such as Geom Tool and Bridge Faces. In most cases, the **Scripts** will appear in the right place at the **Blender menus.** Use this window only if you want to browse all scripts available in your **Blender Scripts** folder.

- **File Browser:** With this window we can browse the files in a specific folder. This window automatically appears when we try to save or open a file.

- **Image Browser:** Here, we can view the image files in a specific folder. This window is very useful in searching for textures.

- **Node Editor**: With this window, it's possible to build node sets, and create complex materials and textures.

- **Buttons Window**: We already have talked about this window. But it is useful to remember that after the 3D View, this is one of the most important windows, because here, we can set up options for almost any tool or functionality in Blender.

- **Outliner:** This window shows us a list of the objects in your scene, and lists the relations between them. Here, we can see if an object is related to some other object in a hierarchical way.

- **User Preferences:** As the name suggests, here we can change a lot of Blender configurations, such as file paths, themes, **Auto Save,** and other options.

- **Text Editor:** This window allows us to write and open text files, to make comments, and place some notes. We can also open and run Python scripts here.

- **Timeline:** This is the place where we create animations. This window gives us nice tools to add key frames and build animations.

- **Video Sequencer Editor:** Here, we can build and compose images and video files. It's a very nice window that can replace a video editor in some respects. We can easily create a complex animation with a lot of shots, and sequence them together using this window. And we can use the Node Editor to create complex compositions and effects.

- **Audio Window:** Here, we can open and compose audio files in sequences. It works much like the **Video Sequencer Editor,** but for audio files.

- **UV/Image Editor:** With this window, we can edit and set up images and textures. There is even a paint application, which we can use to edit, and make some adjustments to, textures and maps. This is a very important window for us, since a lot of the texture work we will be doing will involve the use of UV **Textures** that require a lot of adjustments using the **UV/Image Editor.**

- **NLA Editor**: Here, we can visualize and set up non-linear animations. This window is more related to animations and key frame visualization.

- **Action Editor:** This window has some nice options to set up actions, relating to character animation.

- **IPO Curve Editor:** In this window, we can create and set up your animations in a more visual manner, using curves. It's possible to add, edit, and delete key frames. Even for animations that do not require much work with characters, and object deformations like the ones we will be creating, it still requires a lot of work in the set up of curves, to create good animations.

Now we know what each of those windows do, and some of them such as the **Buttons and Script Window** will be very important for your visualization tasks.

Multiple Windows

A great feature in Blender is the possibility to split the interface and use various window types at the same time. The way to do this is very simple. When you place the mouse cursor at the border of a window, the cursor will change into a double arrow. Just right-click and choose **Split Window** from the menu, and a division will be created.

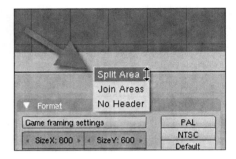

There are two kinds of divisions that we can create: vertical and horizontal divisions.

- **Vertical**: Click on the upper or lower border of a window to create a vertical division.
- **Horizontal**: Click on the right or left border of a window, to create a horizontal division.

After choosing Split Window, just place your mouse cursor where you wish the division to be created, and left-click with your mouse.

Merge Windows

It's possible to merge two different windows with the same menu. There is an option called Join Areas, which will appear when you click with your left mouse button, on the border of a window. After doing that, a big arrow will show which two windows will be joined together.

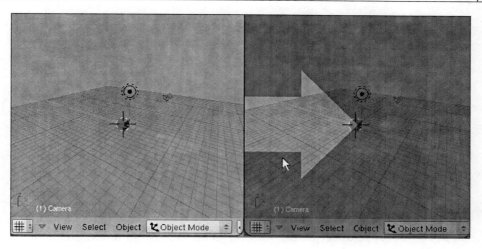

When you have chosen the windows to be joined, just left-click with your mouse to confirm. You can only join windows that share the entire border with each other. Windows that only share a part of their borders can't be joined together.

Header

Every window in Blender has a **Header**, which holds some options related to the window. These Headers are shown as a horizontal bar that is attached to a window. The Headers can be placed at the upper border, or the lower border of a window. At the default Blender interface, we can see tree Headers that are attached to the Buttons Window, 3D View, and User Preferences window.

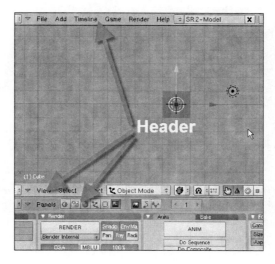

Let's see some examples of the options available on some of the Blender windows:

- **Text Editor:** The Header for this window has some options to edit and manipulate text. There are also options to view the line numbers, change fonts and edit tabulation.

- **IPO Curve Editor:** The Header for this window provides options such as, zoom a specific area of the curve graphic, copy the curves to the clipboard, choose which type of curves to visualize, and more.

As we can see, for each window type, the Header shows different and contextualized options related only to that window types.

Add or Remove a Header

To add or remove a Header from a window, we use the same menu that creates divisions in a window. When you left-click with your mouse over the border of a window, you will have two options. If a Header already exists, an option called No Header will appear, and if a Header doesn't exist, another option called **Add Header** will appear.

We can choose the position of the Header and place it at the top or bottom of a window. To do that, we must right-click an existing Header, and a small menu will appear. With this menu, we can choose the position of the Header. There is an option to remove a specific Header.

Active Window

A very important concept for the Blender interface is the active window. When we are dealing with an interface divided by a lot of windows and window types, and we activate a specific tool or command, in which window will it be executed? Well, the answer is: in the active window.

Only one window can be active, and what makes a specific window, the active one, is the mouse cursor location. When the mouse cursor is over a window, it automatically becomes the active window. We can even notice a small change in the color of the window, to a darker gray.

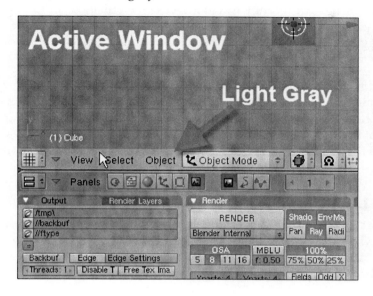

To understand this, let's do a small test that will show how the active window concept works. For this, we will use the home button on the keyboard. When we press this button, a command hat adjust the zoom level will be adjusted to fit the visualization to all visible objects. Well, just place the mouse cursor over the Buttons window and press home, and you will see that nothing happens. This is because all the menus and buttons there are already zoomed to fit all the Windows. But, if you place your mouse cursor over the 3D View and press home, you will see that the visualization for that window will be adjusted, and we will see all the objects placed in the 3D View. Note that for this example work, we must use the default Blender interface.

 Every time your 3D View is too crowded, or you've messed around with the zoom too much, and lost your objects, just press home and the visualization will be adjusted. This is valid even for the menus and the organization of the interface.

Keyboard Shortcuts

Now that we know the Blender interface, and how it works, it's time to start working with the keyboard shortcuts. One of the most interesting aspects of Blender is that it's built to give artists, different ways to increase the efficiency of their production time. The way to do that is to focus on keyboard shortcuts, and Blender does that a lot. This may be difficult for new users, but for more experienced users, it's a real productivity gain.

There are shortcuts for almost every tool or command in Blender, and we will use some of them in this book. With some practice and continuous work, we will become more and more familiar with the shortcuts. So don't worry if you find yourself writing down a few of them at the beginning. Just focus on the modeling and 3D work, and soon you will find that you naturally remember the most commonly- used shortcuts.

3D Visualization

When we start to work in a 3D environment, knowing how to navigate, and how to adjust the view to fit our needs is very important. At this point, having a three button mouse is very important, since a lot of the navigation process is done with the middle mouse button, or the mouse wheel.

Let's start with the orthographic views, which are: Top, Front, Right, Left, Bottom, and Back View. All of those views can be activated via the numeric keypad. To use these shortcuts, we must make the 3D View the active window, by placing your mouse cursor over the window. Then just press the follwing keys to activate those views:

Key	Action
8	Rotate View Up
7	Top View
CTRL+7	Bottom View
6	Rotate View Right
5	Swap orthographic and perspective view
4	Rotate View Left
3	Right View
CTRL+3	Left View
2	Rotate View Down
1	Front View
CTRL+1	Back View
0	Camera View
Home	Fit the zoom to all objects

As we can see, there are some more options besides the orthographic views, such as options to rotate the view. These are the options to manipulate the view with the keyboard, but we can use the mouse to get even more control over the visualization. Here is a list with some combinations of mouse buttons and keys, to control visualization:

Key	Action
Wheel + CTRL	Zoom in / Zoom Out
Wheel + SHIFT	Pan View
Wheel	3D Orbit View
Scroll Wheel Forward	Zoom in
Scroll Wheel Backwards	Zoom out

All these options are very important for manipulating and visualizing your scenes, and only with a bit of practice will it be possible to become familiar with all of the commands.

Wheel or Middle Mouse Button?

Remember that, when we use the term Wheel in the table above, it could well be the middle mouse button, if your mouse doesn't have a Wheel. However, you won't be able to use the Scrolling options with only a middle mouse button,. To use the Zoom and Pan options, you will have to use the *CTRL* or *SHIFT* keys to manipulate the view.

Selecting Objects

The process of selecting objects is very important for manipulating and visualizing objects in any 3D package. To select objects in Blender, we have options to use the mouse, or to select objects by name. If we want to select a single object, just click with the right mouse button over this object, and it will be selected. To add another object to the selection, just press *SHIFT*, and click with the right mouse button on another object.

Mouse buttons

In Blender, the mouse buttons work in a different way. In most 3D applications, the left mouse button selects one object. But with Blender, the right mouse button selects objects. If you find this confusing, you can change it in your user preferences.

The *A* Key is a very important tool when we are selecting objects, because it can unselect all objects that are selected, or remove objects from a selection. If there isn't any object selected, all objects are selected when we press the *A* key. This is valid even when we are dealing with the selection of vertices, edges, and faces on objects.

To select multiple objects we have the Box Select too. This works with the B Key. When we press the B key, with the 3D View as the active window, we will be able to draw a selection box around a group of objects. After pressing the *B* Key, just press your left mouse button down and drag a marquee around the objects that you want to select. When all the objects are inside the marquee, just release the mouse button, and they will all be selected.

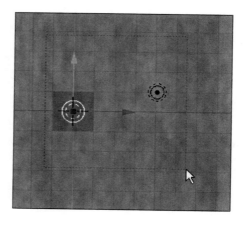

If you want to remove the objects from selection, just press the *A* Key, and all selected objects will be removed from selection.

If we press the *B* key twice, it will turn on the Pencil Select. The mouse cursor will turn into a circle, which we can use to "paint" the selection. Just press the left mouse button and drag the cursor to select anything that touches the selection circle. If you press the right mouse button, and drag the cursor over any selected object, it will remove this object from the selection.

We can control the size of the selection circle with the + and – keys on the numeric keypad. Scrolling the mouse wheel, if you have one, will also change the size of the selection circle as well.

This type of selection doesn't work in Object Mode. We will talk more about work modes later in this chapter.

Selecting by Name

When we start to work with more complex scenes, the number of objects on your screen will increase dramatically. Simple tasks such as selecting one specific object will become more difficult, because we will first have to find this object on the screen. That's why, some times, it is a good practice to rename objects, so it is easier to find them by name later.

In Blender, to select objects by name, we can use a window called Outliner. This window will show a list of objects, and we can choose the objects that will be selected by name from this list.

The outline window can be displayed in two ways: the Oops Schematic, and **the Outliner**. To change between them, use the View menu at the Outliner window header.

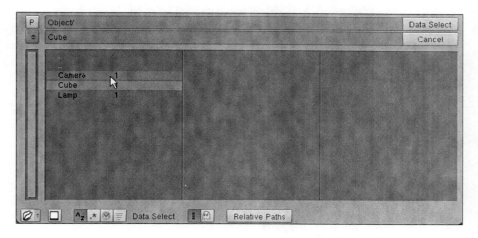

To select an object, the process is simply to left-click on the object name. If you want to select more than one object, just hold down the *SHIFT* key while you click.

Besides the ability to select objects by name, we also have a few extra controls in the Outliner. On the right, we can find three small icons, which allow us to control a few properties of objects:

- **Eye**: With the Eye icon, we can control the visibility of the object. If the eye is open, the object is visible, and if it's closed, the object is hidden. Right-click on this icon to open or close the eye.

- **Cursor**: If this cursor is turned off, we won't be able to select the object in the 3D View. To turn the cursor on or off, right-click on this icon.

- **Landscape**: With this control, we can determine if the object will show up in the render.

Renaming Objects

We can rename any object in Blender to make the selection process easier, and your scenes more organized. Before you rename anything, it is important to remember that every object in Blender must have a unique name. If we try to give two objects the same name, Blender will automatically add a suffix to the name of the second object. This suffix will be a sequential number, in the order of creation.

For example, if we have an object called "Box", and we try to give the name "Box" to another object, it will be automatically renamed "Box.001".

To rename an object we must use the Panel called Editing. This can be accessed with the shortcut F9 or by clicking on the small icon identified in the image below.

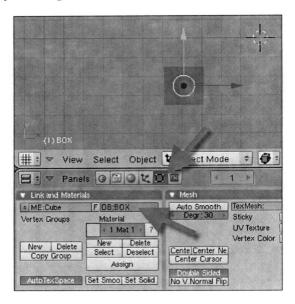

Before renaming an object, we must first select this object. Then click in the text box to rename the object. When we select one object, we can see the object name in the lower left corner of the 3D View. Try to give names to objects that better identify the function of the object, such as "**left wall**" or "**window glass**". It will be a great help when we need to select objects in complex scenes.

We can use the Outliner to rename objects too. Hold down the *CTRL* key, and right-click on the name of an object to rename it.

3D Cursor

When we first get started with Blender, it's possible to notice a small icon in the 3D View window that looks like a target. This is the 3D Cursor, which is an important component in Blender as it determines the place where the objects are created. To place this cursor at another point in the 3D View, just click with your left mouse button anywhere in the screen.

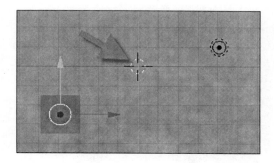

Another function of the 3D Cursor is to become the center for object transformations. When we need to rotate an object, using a specific point as center of the rotation, we can use the 3D Cursor as the center point.

Cursor Snap

To work with the 3D Cursor and selected objects, we can use a Snap option to place the cursor in some specific places. If we press *SHIFT+S*, the menu with the Snap options will be displayed. There are a few options in the menu, as explained below:

- **Selection | Grid:** This option aligns the selected objects with the grid lines.
- **Selection | Cursor:** With this option, we can align a selected object with the 3D Cursor. This way, the selected object will be moved, so it's centre point is placed at the center of the cursor.
- **Cursor | Grid:** This option aligns the 3D Cursor with the grid lines.
- **Cursor | Selection:** This option will move the 3D cursor to the centre of the selected object.
- **Selection | Center:** With this option, we can move the selected objects to the geometric center of the selection.

With these options, it is easier for us to place the 3D cursor and the selected objects in specific places. We will use this option a lot when we deal with modeling for architecture, since it's a great tool for precision modeling. Every time you need to place the 3D cursor at a specific place, remember to use the Cursor Snap. In chapters 4, 5, and 6 we will talk more about other methods of snapping.

Modes

To edit and manipulate objects in Blender, we must understand how to work with the Modes. These modes determine what we want to do with an object. To manipulate and transform an object, we have the **Object Mode,** and to edit and model we have the **Edit Mode**. To select these modes, we use a combo box located in the Header of the 3D View.

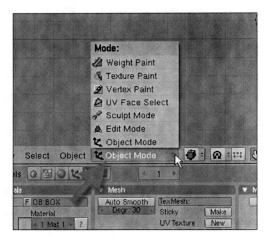

We have more modes, like the **Sculpt Mode** and **Pose Mode**, which activate sculpt modeling tools and character animation respectively. The most common Modes we will be using are the Object and Edit Modes. They are so important that we have a Keyboard shortcut to switch between them. If we press *TAB*, the active mode will switch between Object and Edit.

See when each mode should be used:

- **Object Mode:** This mode is used to manipulate and transform one or more objects. If you need to scale or move an object, use this mode. When we select an object in Object Mode, we won't be able to change it's shape, by altering it's vertices, edges, or faces.

- **Edit Mode:** In edit mode we will be able to select and edit the vertices, edges, and faces of an object. This way we can easily de-form and model an object. Use this mode only if you need to de-form and model an object.

Creating Objects

Now that we know how to manipulate our interface and deal with some basic aspects of Blender, let's learn how to create objects. To create anything in Blender we use a menu called Tool Box. This menu appears when we press the *Spacebar* on the keyboard, or use the *SHIFT+A* shortcut.

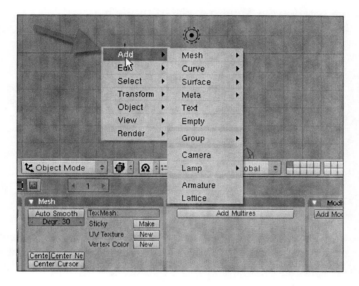

This menu has a lot of options, and one of them is the Add option. Here we can find all of the object types that can be created in Blender. In the modeling chapter we will deal with a lot of these options, such as curves and surfaces. To get started, let's see the most basic type of object which is the **Mesh** kind.

When we choose the Mesh type of object, some options such as Cube, Circle, Cylinder, and other basic shapes are available for us to choose. These are all shapes that can be deformed and divided into subforms to create more complex shapes.

To create an object, just place the 3D Cursor where you want the new object, and press the *spacebar*. Choose which kind of object you want and it will be created. After creating an object it is important to be aware of some common issues:

- After creating an object, Blender automatically switches to **Edit Mode.**
- All objects are created in a perpendicular view to the observer.

What these issues mean is that, every time we create an object, we must press the **Tab** key to switch back to **Object Mode,** unless we want to start editing the new object. This is very important since a lot of new users get this wrong, and create all objects in **edit mode.** If you do that, your objects will be created as a single block, and it will take some time to split it up later. So it's good practice to always switch back to object mode, of course, unless you want it all objects to be created together.

Another thing to remember is that all objects are created in a perpendicular view to the observer. This means that if you are creating an object in an orthographic view, as in the **top view**, everything will be fine. The object will be aligned in the orthographic view. But if we use the **perspective view**, this will cause the object to be created with some rotation , as shown in the example below.

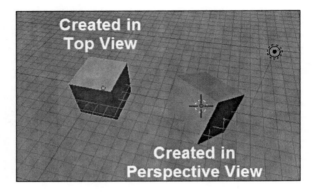

If you forget about this point and create an object in perspective view, just use the **Clear Rotation** command, and it will remove any rotation applied to the object. Just hit *ALT+R* to access this option.

Duplicating Objects

Creating copies of objects in Blender is very easy. Just select the object that will be copied and press the shortcut *SHIFT+D*. This is the simplest way of creating a copy for an object.

Transforming Objects

There are three basic transformations that we can apply to an object These are Translate, Rotate, and Scale. To apply these transformations to objects, we can use either keyboard shortcuts or a transformation **Widget**. The transform Widget is a simple icon that is displayed in the centre of all objects.

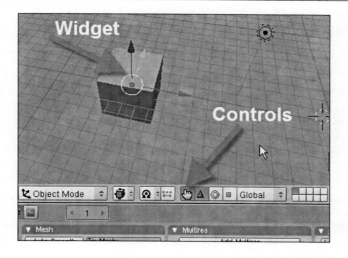

There are three kinds of Widgets for each transformation type. We can switch between them using the controls located in the Header of the 3D View. The symbols represent each transformation type:

- **Finger:** Turn on and turn off the Widget
- **Triangle:** Turn on the translation Widget
- **Circle:** Turn on the rotation Widget
- **Square:** Turn on the scale Widget

Each of these Widgets has individual controls for the individual axes. These controls are separated by colour: red for X, green for Y and blue for Z transformations. So, if we want to rotate an object just in the Y axis, we will use the green arc that represents this transformation in the rotation Widget. The same concept is applied to the other transformations. For a scale in the Z axis, we just grab the blue square in the scale Widget and drag it.

There is a shortcut to turn on and off the Widget, and select different types of transformations. We can use the *CTRL+Space Bar* to accesses a menu, which will let us enable or disable the Widget, and choose what type of transformation we want to use in the object. In the menu we will find a Widget called Combo, which shows all the transformation options at the same time.

The other way of making transformations to objects is using keyboard shortcuts. We can use these shortcuts to quickly transform any object. These are the shortcuts:

Key	Action
G	Grab (Move)
R	Rotate
S	Scale

In addition to these shortcuts, we can constrain the transformation to an axis with the use of more shortcuts. If just after pressing one of the shortcuts above, we can press X, Y, or Z keys to constrain the transformation to the respective axis. For example, if we press R key and then press Z, the selected object will rotate only in the Z-axis.

The coordinates used to make that transformation are the global coordinates, but we can use the local coordinates of an object. To do that, we must press the key corresponding to the axis twice. So if we select an object and press the G key, and press the X key twice, the transformation of the object will take place in the object's local coordinates.

Global coordinates are related to the scene coordinates, and they don't change. Because the local coordinates are related to the object, they change with the object. We can think of the global coordinates as the cardinal points, and the local coordinates as the front, back, left, and right sides of an object. No matter where you are, the cardinal points will be always at the same position. And the sides of an object will be relative to its orientation.

Cameras

Dealing with the camera in Blender is very important, because we can only render the camera view. Even with multiple cameras in a scene, we must always have an active camera, which will be used in the rendering process. The camera is a small pyramidal object that is placed in the default scene.

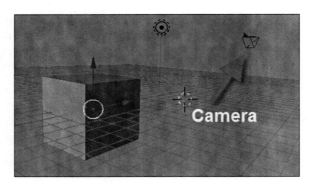

To see the scene or object from the camera's perspective, just press 0 on the numeric keypad, and we can see the camera view.

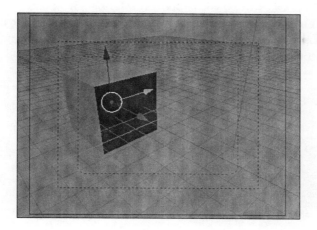

When we are in the camera view, select the camera by right-clicking on the camera frame, and press the transformation shortcuts to move or rotate the camera and change the view. In this way, we can adjust the framing and find a better fit for an object or scene.

Another way of adjusting the camera is to create a division in the 3D View and then, switch on the view to the camera view. Alternatively, we can just use the Widgets to find a good framing for the objects.

If we have more than one camera, it will be necessary to set one of them as the active camera. To do that, we must select the camera and press *CTRL+0*. The *0* must be from the numeric keypad. In Blender, every object can be turned into a camera. Just select the object and press *CTRL+0*, and it will become a camera. To de-activate the object from being a camera, just select this object, and press *ALT+0*. Now, the object is not a camera anymore.

Render Basics

Now that we know a lot of the basic aspects of Blender, it's possible to learn how to render scenes and make some small adjustments. All the set up for the render can be accessed in the **Scene Panel**, which is located in the Buttons window. To access this panel with a shortcut, press *F10*.

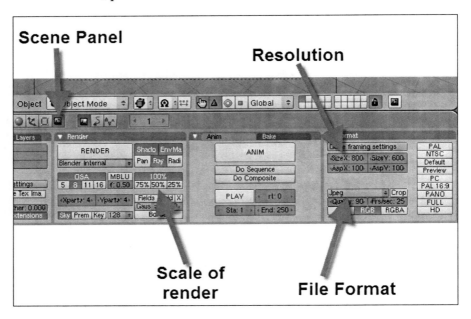

In this panel, there are two menus that hold the main options to set up the render. The first menu is called **Render,** and has the options to set the scale of the generated image. We can choose scales between 100% and 25% of the original size. The other menu is called **Format,** and here we can find options to set the resolution of the render, and a file format in which px to save our renders.

We can set up a render to be 640x480 in resolution and choose PNG, as the file format to save the image. If the scale is set to 100%, our image will have the full resolution. But we could run a test render at just 50% of the resolution. To do that, we must change the settings for the **Render** menu.

Changing the scale for the rendered image is a great way of producing small renders, just to test our settings for lights and materials. We will be using this feature a lot for exercises in this book.

When everything is ready, just press *F12* or click the Render button in the Render menu. A render window will appear. After the render is finished, just press *F3* to save the file.

 Make sure you have at least one light

If we don't has any light sources in Blender, the render won't show anything but a black screen. It's different from other applications that have a default light. So, if you press *F12* and all you see is a black screen, it's probably because a light source is missing.

Render Preview

Before starting a render, we can preview how it's going to look in the 3D View. There is a tool called **Render Preview**, which can be accessed with the shortcut *SHIFT+P*. When we do that, a small window will show up in the 3D View, as shown in the following example.

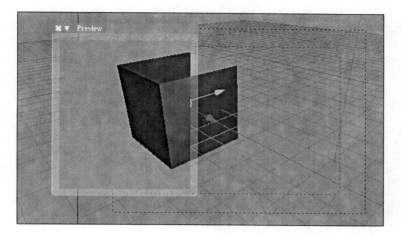

We can change the size of the preview, just click on the border of the menu, and drag your mouse. That's another great way of checking your settings, to make sure everything will be fine when we need to make a bigger rendering.

Summary

In this chapter, we had a glance at Blender and saw how to start using it. Even for a quick start, we saw a lot of new and interesting concepts about how to work with Blender. We just learned how to:

- Use the interface
- Set up the interface
- Select objects
- Work with modes
- Transform objects
- Create objects
- Copy objects
- Work with the camera
- Render a view

In the next chapter, we will start using more complex and advanced functionality related to modeling for architecture in Blender. Hence, this basic understanding of how Blender works is very important.

3
Modeling

Now that we know the basics of Blender, the next step is to start working with the modeling tools and techniques. This will give us a better bases to deal with specific aspects related to architectural and landscaping modeling.

Types of Objects

There are a lot of object types in Blender, which can be created via the Tool Box. This is a special menu, which we can use to create almost everything in Blender. To access the Tool Box, we must press the *Spacebar* key. The Tool Box will show the options to create Meshes, Curves, Surfaces, Text, and all other object types in Blender. Before we take any serious steps into modeling, we must understand the differences between these types, and when each one of them is best used.

Let's take a look at each object type:

- **Mesh:** This is by far the most important object type in Blender, and we will be using it a lot. Here, we have some primitive shapes such as cube, sphere, cylinder, and some others. We use these objects to create more geometric forms, which is exactly what we will be using to create architectural models for buildings. The objects here are composed of vertices, edges, and faces. Most architectural modeling tools use a different type of object to model, called solids. Solids are a heavy object type, which demand more computer resources. So, with meshes we have an advantage, and can work on more complex projects with less computer resources.

- **Curve:** The name says everything. These objects are curved lines that can be used to model and shape objects with perfectly curved edges. This kind of object will be very useful for building animation trajectories.

- **Surface:** The surface is a type of object that is not commonly used for modeling in Blender—at least not for the kind of models that we will be creating. But it can come in very handy when creating landscapes. It works with a surface that must be deformed to a specific shape, best using basic transformations. The technique required to create objects with such surfaces is very different from that of mesh modeling. This is because the surfaces and the curves, are based on NURBS curves, which are great for creating organic shapes.

- **Meta:** This type of object works like some kind of clay, in which we mold some primitives shapes such as spheres and cubes together, and create very organic shapes. The main use of Meta objects will be in landscaping terrains such as mountains.

These are the main object types in Blender. Of course, there are more, such as text and lamps, but for modeling, this is what we need. Although we won't be using all of them for modeling, there is one type that will require more attention, namely the Mesh object. We will be working with more geometric shapes, and Blender is designed to work better with a type of modeling called subdivision.

To work with subdivisions, we have to create primitive shapes and edit, transform, cut, split, and work on their vertices, edges, and faces. A lot of our modeling will be done using this method. If we think that a wall, floor, and other parts of building can be created with cubes and planes, it become very clear why subdivision modeling is best suited for us.

Before we head for subdivision of your primitive objects, let's see the main aspects of these objects, and how to create them. This is just the starting point. It may seem even boring, but it is an important step. When we understand and master the basics, we will be able to work more effectively on more complex aspects of architectural visualization with Blender.

Mesh Primitives

The first step in working with subdivision modeling is to learn what primitive shapes are available in Blender. Always, as our first step, we will create one of these shapes. To create Mesh objects, we press the *Spacebar* or press *SHIFT+A*. In the toolbox, we choose **Add | Mesh**.

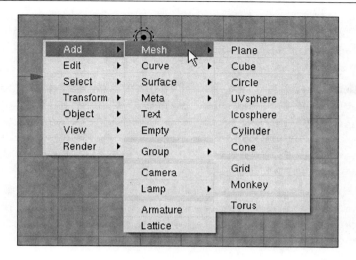

As we can see, there are a lot of primitive types to choose from. When we create some of these primitive types, some parameters, such as number of sides, and subdivisions, must be set. Let's see how it works:

- **Plane:** This option creates a simple plane with four vertices. There aren't any more parameters for this object. We can start almost any type of modeling with a plane—things like walls, roofs, floor, and a lot more.

- **Cube:** With this option, a simple cube is created, with eight vertices. Here also, there aren't any more parameters. Like the plane object, we can start almost any type of modeling with a cube.

- **Circle**: The name of this option could be Polygon, since this is what we can create here. When we choose Circle, we must specify two parameters: Vertices and Radius. The first one sets the number of sides for the circle, and the second sets the distance between the centre, and the border of the circle. If we need a square, we just create a circle with four vertices, or for a hexagon, with six vertices.

- **UVsphere:** Here, we can create a sphere with square faces. There are three parameters to be set: Segments, Rings, and Radius. Segments and Rings set the amount of subdivision for the sphere. Higher values results in more perfect spheres. But beware: higher values demand more from the computer, and could eventually crash it. Radius sets the distance between the centre of the sphere, and its border. The UVSphere has meridians and parallels, like the earth.

- **Icosphere:** Here too, we have a sphere. The only difference is that this sphere is made up of triangular faces, not squares as in the UVsphere. The setup here is simpler – we don't have the Segments and Rings options, just a Subdivision option.

- **Cylinder:** This option creates a cylinder, but like the circle option, we can also use it to create shapes such as a prism. We must set up three parameters here. In addition to Vertices and Radius (as in the circle), there are two more options, which are Depth, which determines the height of the object, and a button called Cap Ends. If this button is selected, the object will have two faces to cap its upper and lower extremities.

- **Cone:** Here, we can create a cone-like object, just like the Cylinder. If we define a lower number of sides, other types of objects can be created, such as pyramids. The options are almost the same as for the Cylinder, the only difference is the Cap End button, which will fill only the lower extremity of the object.

- **Grid:** This object works much like a plane, with the difference being that a Grid has more subdivisions than a plane does. To set up a Grid, we must provide the subdivision level for the X-axis and Y-axis, with the X res and Y res options.

- **Monkey:** Yes, we can create a monkey's head. If you are asking yourself: Why place a monkey head there? Well, this is Suzanne, who is the Blender mascot. We won't be using it to model anything, but since the head has some good geometry it turns out to be a great option to test materials and textures.

- **Torus:** Here, we have another object type, which will give us something like a donut. When we create a Torus, we must set four parameters. These are Major and Minus Radius, which set up the external and internal radii respectively of the Torus, and Major and Minor Segments, which determine the level of subdivision of the Torus.

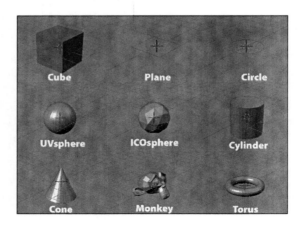

These are the Mesh type objects available to us in Blender. Which are the most important ones? We will be using a lot of the Plane, Cube, and the Circle to model. These are common shapes, and we can create other shapes easily from them. For example, a circle can become a cone with some editing and a plane can become a grid. It's just a matter of using the right tools.

How can a primitive shape become a more complex object, such as a wall or a window? This is the basis of the mesh and subdivision modeling, that are used by Blender. We can compare this modeling to some kind of sculpture, where we take something simple and cut, push, pull, and rotate it to create something complex. Let's learn how to apply these transformations.

Mesh Editing

To subdivide a Mesh object and create more complex shapes, we must apply some editing to these objects. For this, Blender has several Mesh Editing options to cut, slice, split, and manipulate the vertex and edges in a lot of different ways. Some of these tools are located in a menu called **Mesh Tools**, which is located in the **Editing Panel**.

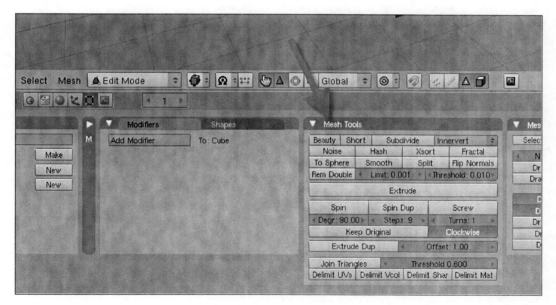

But these are not the only tools available. Some of them are placed in the Mesh menu, located in the Header of the 3D View window. This menu has options to edit vertex, edges, and faces.

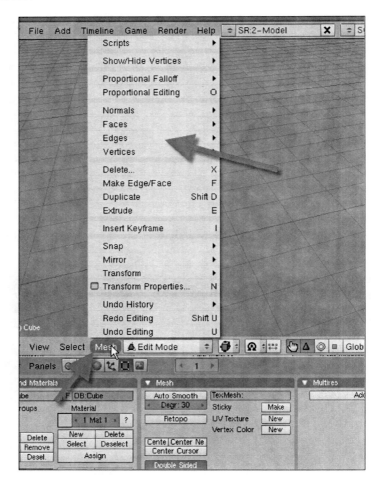

Let's see how to edit the Mesh objects using some of these tools. This will be important for us when we deal with more specific modeling for architecture and scenarios.

Since Mesh editing is important to architectural modeling, we will use a simple model of a building for most of our examples. This chapter is not aimed at architectural details or elements, but that doesn't mean that we can't contextualize our examples, to make things clearer.

Here is the model that we will be using in our examples.

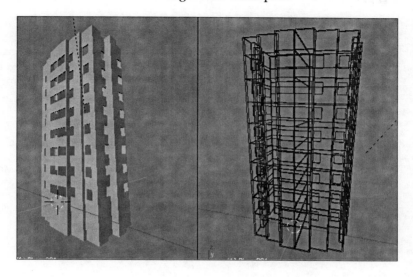

This is a simple building, but we can use it to demonstrate the mesh editing options. In the next chapters, we will be adding more details to this model, until we get to the final render!

Transformations

The first tool needed to edit Mesh objects is transformations. Although it is a simple tool, we can use it to create most deformations in meshes. If you don't remember the last chapter, we will remind you of the shortcuts to all transformations:

- G key: Grab or move
- R key: Rotate
- S key: Scale

These transformations can be applied to vertices, edges, or faces. We can also constrain the transformations by pressing with the X, Y, or Z key immediately after pressing the key corresponding to the transformation.

Transforming with Precision

To make transformations with precision, we can hold down the *CTRL* key to snap the transformation to the Grid lines. And to fine-tune the transformation, we can hold down the *SHIFT* key. This will cause the transformation to be increased by a very small amount, like 0.001

Loop Subdivide

When we create a cube or a plane, these objects come with no subdivisions, and very few vertices and edges. To create more complex forms, we will certainly need more edges to extrude and transform. There are two ways of performing a loop subdivide: we can use the Mesh menu, in the Header of the 3D View and choose Edge | Loop Subdivide, or use a keyboard shortcut, with the *CTRL+R* keys, which is a lot faster.

Before we use this option, we must select one Mesh object and enter Edit Mode, as Loop subdivides only work in this mode. If everything was done correctly, a pink line will appear around the object when we press *CTRL+R*, as shown in the example below:

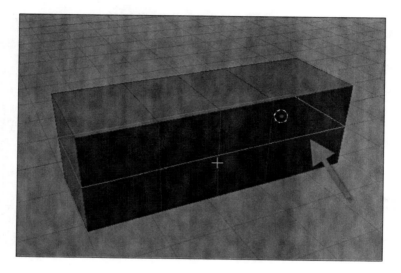

This line will position the loop on the model, and we can change the orientation of the cut by moving the cursor around the object. When we achieve the desired orientation for the cut, click once with the left mouse button to confirm. Then, a yellow line will appear for us to choose the correct place to make the cut. Just move the mouse cursor to position the cut where required, click with your left mouse button to finish, and a new edge loop will be added to the Mesh object.

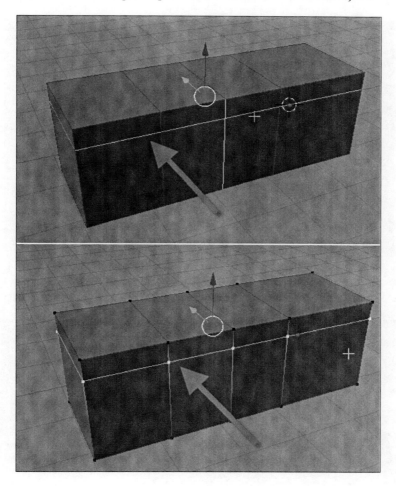

When we use this tool with more transformations, the possibilities for creating new shapes increase dramatically. Let's see an example:

1. With the Loop Subdivide, we can change the shape of a wall, and add different planes to it.

2. Suppose we have a model of a wall with an opening for a door.

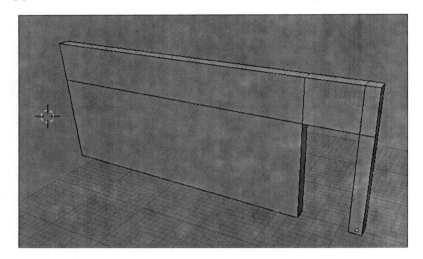

3. Let's change the geometry of the wall, using a loop subdivide. When we press the *CTRL+R* shortcut, a new loop subdivide will be added to the wall.

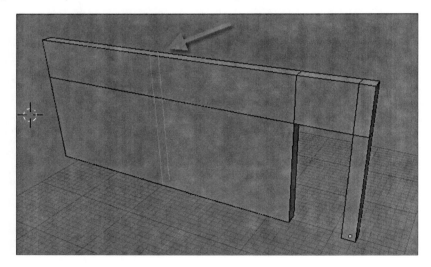

4. We can place the new loop just to the left of the door.

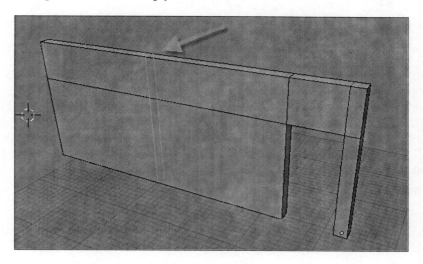

5. Now, we can select the vertices indicated in the image below, and move them in the Z-axis. This will make a slant plane.

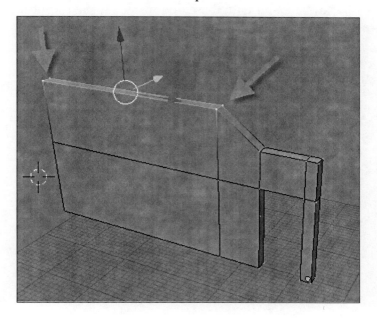

This new shape was possible through the use of a loop cut. Of course, there are other ways to create this kind of geometry, but this is a good example of what we can do with loop cuts.

Knife Tool

The loop cut is a great tool for creating regular subdivisions in Mesh objects, but we will sometimes need more irregular or non-orthographic cuts. For that, we have a Knife tool, which we can use to create cuts in a lot of different ways. To use this tool, a Mesh object must be selected, and the Edit Mode activated. Before we start, another important thing to understand about this tool is that the face or part of the object that will be sliced must be selected. So, if we are going to cut a specific face, this face must be selected before we start.

There are two ways to activate the Knife tool. The first is via the Mesh menu in the 3D View Header. If we choose Mesh | Edge | Knife Subdivide, the Knife tool will be activated. The other way is using a keyboard shortcut. By pressing *SHIFT+K,* we can activate the Knife as well. To create a cut, we must draw a cutting line, above the selected faces that we want to cut. Before we draw this line, there are some different types of cuts that we need to know about. We have three different types of options for using the Knife, and a menu with these options will always appear immediately after we activate the tool.

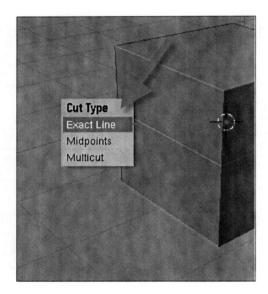

These options are:

- **Exact Line:** With this option, the cut will be created using the line that we draw over the Mesh.

- **Midpoints:** This option creates the cut using the midpoints of the selected face. The line that we draw will work as a guide, for the tool to choose which midpoints to use.

- **Multicut:** Here, we have the option to create multiple cuts for a face. After choosing this option, a menu will appear asking the number of cuts that we want to make to the face. If you choose three cuts, then your selected face will look like this:

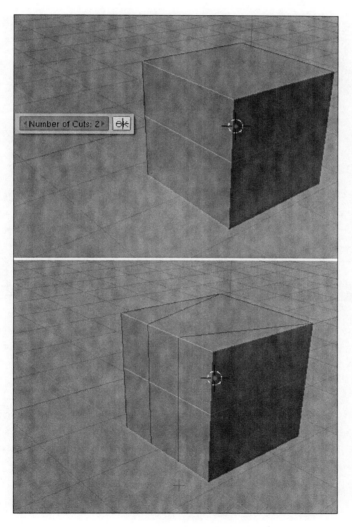

As we can see, this is more like an option to create cuts with non-orthographical lines, but it's a nice option for more geometrical modeling.

[

Loop/Cut Menu

There is a menu that has options to choose between the Loop Cut and the Knife Tools. When you are in Edit Mode, just press the *K* key, and a menu will appear with four options to enable quick access to these tools.

]

When we use the Knife tool, in some cases, we will have faces with three or four sides. Here is something very important to remember in Blender: avoid three-sided faces!, especially if you want to edit this object later!

Three-sided faces interfere with the edge loops, and will make the editing process harder. Let's see an example:

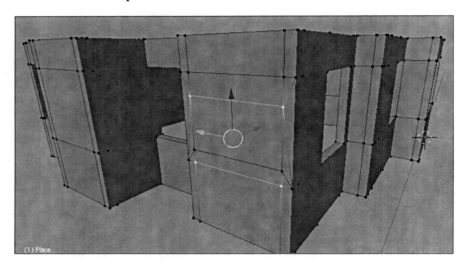

The image above shows the result of the Knife tool. The wall now has triangular faces that will be difficult to edit later.

Selecting Loops

We saw how to create some cuts for your Mesh objects, and added a lot of new vertices and edges to them. There will come a time when we will need to select these loops for editing, for example to move or scale a vertex loop. To help with these kinds of selections, we have a very useful shortcut in Blender.

Every time you need to select a loop, just press the *ALT* key on the keyboard, and click on one edge between the two vertices of that loop. This way, all other vertices will be selected. To use this shortcut, the selection mode must be set to Vertex.

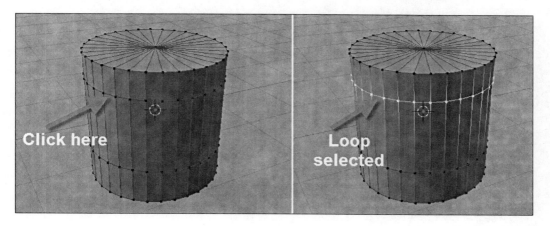

New Edges and Faces

Sometimes when we edit a Mesh object, we will have a hole, or some vertices that we will want to connect to a new face. For this kind of creation, Blender has a tool called Make Edge/Face. To use this tool, we must select two or more vertices that define a new face or edge. If we select only two vertices, then a new edge will be created. But, if we select three or four vertices, a new face is created.

Things can get messy not just when we have a hole in the mesh, but also when we have a geometric shape with a lot of triangular faces. The best option is to erase these faces and create new ones, using only four-sided faces.

Why only three or four vertices? Well, that's a limitation of Blender, which supports only faces with three or four sides. If we want to make more complex planes and faces, we will have to subdivide the shape into more than one face.

But don't worry, it's not a bad thing to only work with three or four vertices. Blender only shows us the internal subdivision of the faces, requiring a bit more of discipline in modeling, but giving us the same results. And the most important point is that there won't be any difference in rendering. So, if a lot of faces are co-planar, we won't see any differences.

After selecting the vertices or edges, always in Edit mode, we will activate the tool from the Mesh menu in the 3D View Header, with option Mesh | Edges | Make Edge/Face. There is also a way to activate it with a shortcut, which is the *F* key.

Let's see an example of how this works. The image below highlights a wall with a window opening. We want to create a new face, and close this opening.

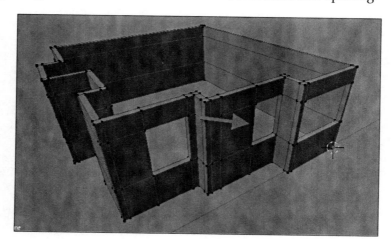

Select the four vertices that define this new face. We can press the *B* key in Edit mode and draw a box selection to make things easier. If you make any mistakes in the selection, press *A* to remove everything from the selection, and try again.

When the faces are selected, simply press *F* and a new face will be created. It works the same way as with two vertices, but a new edge will be created instead. If you want to try this, select two vertices and press *F*, and a new edge will connect those selected vertices.

This tool is very useful for making adjustments in models that have little holes or need heavy editing, such as window and door openings.

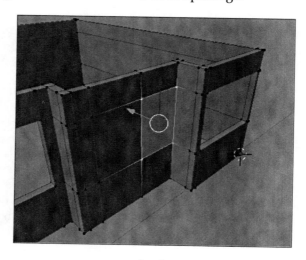

Merge

Another way of editing a Mesh object is to merge existing vertices into a single vertex. This can be achieved with the Merge tool, which is available in Edit mode. To use this tool, we can select any number of vertices from a Mesh, and then activate the Merge option. To do this, we have three different options, which are the Mesh menu in the 3D View Header, using the *ALT+M* keyboard shortcut, or pressing the *W* key and choosing Merge from the Specials menu.

After choosing one of these methods, we will have to choose a way to Merge. There are five different ways of performing a Merge. They are:

- **At first:** If we select the vertices one by one, choosing this option will make the Merge, and place the resulting vertex at the same place as the first selected vertex.
- **At last:** Here, we have the opposite of the previous option. The resulting vertex will be placed in the same place as the last selected vertex.
- **At center:** If we choose this option, the Merge will result in one vertex being placed at the middle point between all selected vertices.
- **At cursor:** With this option, the resulting point of the Merge will be placed at the position of the 3D cursor.
- **Collapse:** This option just collapses all selected vertices into one vertex.

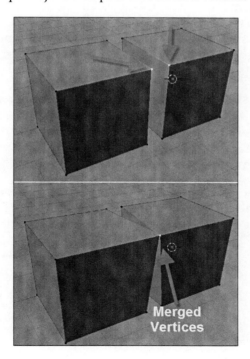

Merged Vertices

Every time a Merge operation is done, we will see a message in the 3D View, such as "Removed X vertices", where X is the number of vertices that are placed in the same position in space.

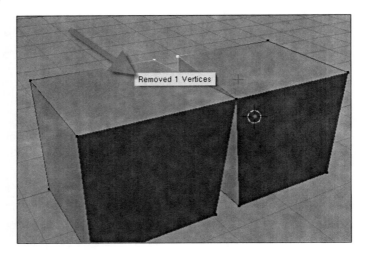

Removing Double Vertices

Having double vertices in a model is not a good thing, especially if we want to smoothen this model. This happens when two vertices share exactly the same point in space, and are not connected. This can confuse the editing process, since we will try to select and transform an edge or face, and it won't be transformed the way we want.

Some tools in Blender. such as the Merge tool, automatically remove double vertices when they find them, like the Merge tool that always remove double vertices. But sometimes, we will need to remove double vertices manually, because they can be the result of bad model editing or be caused by a wrong interpretation of an external file, such as when we import a 3D model from other formats inside Blender.

To remove these double vertices, just select any number of vertices in Edit Mode and press the *W* key, and then choose Remove Doubles from the Specials menu. If any of the selected vertices are doubled, this tool will merge them into one vertex.

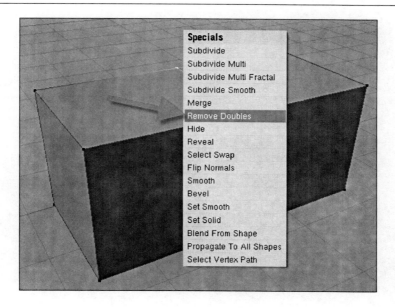

Besides the Specials menu, we can activate and change a parameter of the Remove Doubles option on the Mesh tools menu. This menu is located in the Editing panel, in Edit mode. If the Editing panel is not displayed, just press *F9* in Edit mode to open it. There is a button "Rem Double",which works exactly the same way as the Remove Doubles option in the Specials menu. And we also have an option called Limit, which defines the minimum distance that must exist between two vertices, for the Remove Doubles merges these vertices into one.

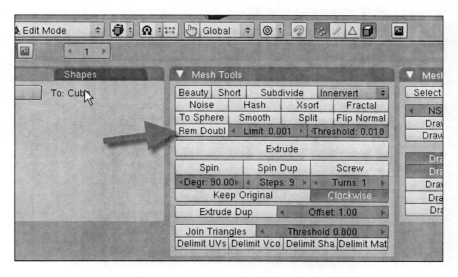

Extrude

One of the main tools we will be using for modeling is Extrude, which can make new geometry from selected vertices, edges, or faces. To create an extrude, the process is very simple. First, we must create some Mesh object and in Edit mode select a vertex, edge, or face of this object. When at least one object is selected, press *E* on the keyboard to make an extrusion.

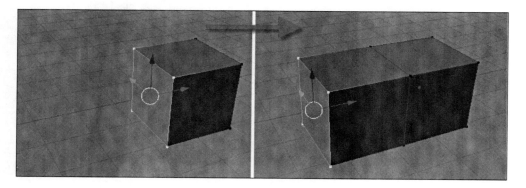

The extrude modeling doesn't work the same way for all kinds of objects. If we have a vertex, edge, or face selected, the result will be different. If you don't remember how to switch between selection modes, you just press *CTRL+TAB* in Edit mode.

Extrude with Vertex

When we have one or more vertices of an object selected, a small menu will appear every time the *E* key is pressed. This menu can have three options, depending on the number of vertices that are selected.

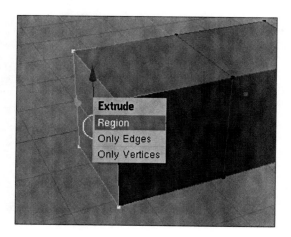

- **Only Vertex:** With this option, only the vertex will be extruded, and the result will be new vertices, and a line connecting these new vertices to the old ones. This option appears for any number of selected vertices.
- **Only Edges:** This option extrudes only the edges of a Mesh, creating new planes. This option is only available when we select two or more vertices.
- **Region:** Here, we will be able to create an entire face. This option is only available if we select a full face.

Extrude with Edges

The edge mode doesn't give us as many options as the vertex option. The only situation in which an option menu will be displayed is if we have edges that define a full face selected. As in vertex mode, an option called Region will appear in the menu. Otherwise, extrude will only create new planes from the selected edges.

Extrude with Faces

If we choose to work with faces, selecting a single face will enable us to create new geometry in a very quick way, because we will select a full face, and extrude it very quickly. The only situation in which an option menu will be displayed, when we are working with faces, is for an extrusion of more than one face. If we select two faces, there will be two options for the extrusion.

- **Region:** This is the default extrude, where all faces are extruded in the same direction.
- **Individual Faces:** With this option, the selected faces are extruded along their individual normals, just as if they were extruded individually.

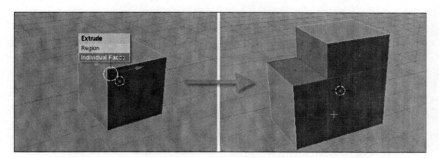

Extrude is a very powerful tool to create new geometry, but it won't do the job alone. Along with Extrude, we must use some other tools to edit Mesh objects, and create cuts and slices, and split the object. For this, there are some nice Mesh Editing tools in Blender.

Constraining the Extrude

If we want to constrain the extrusion along an axis, we can do that with a shortcut key. Use the shortcut key immediately after you call the Extrude:

- X, Y, or Z Key: If we press one of these keys, the extrude will be constrained to the global X-axis. Pressing it twice will constrain the extrusion to the local X-axis.

Here is an example of the same plane, constrained to the Z-axis.

Modeling Example

Now that we know how to work with meshes, let's take a look at how we can transform something simple, such as transforming plane into the walls of a building. This example will show how to start the modeling of the building that was presented at the beginning of this chapter.

The first step is to start with a primitive shape such as a plane. To work with measurements, there is an interesting option in the Editing panel: the menu called "Mesh Tools 1". On this menu, turn on the Draw Edge Length, to cause the length of all edges to be shown at the 3D View.

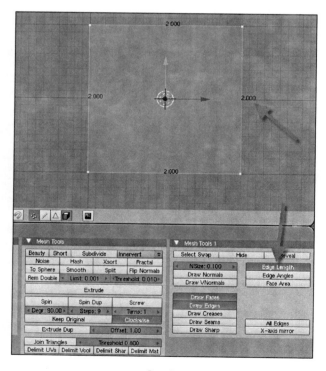

With the length of each edge visible, we can scale the plane until we get the right measurements. For instance, if the wall should have a width of 0.15 meters, the plane can be scaled down 0.15. To make the transformation more precise, remember to hold down the *CTRL*, or *SHIFT* key, or the combination of *CTRL+SHIFT* keys.

When the plane has 0.15 for each edge, we can start the modeling process. The process is basically a series of extrudes. To make the selection process easier, we can change the selection mode to Edge and select one of the edges.

Then start to extrude this edge. Always use the *CTRL* key to extrude these edges, and you will have the new faces snapped to the grid lines.

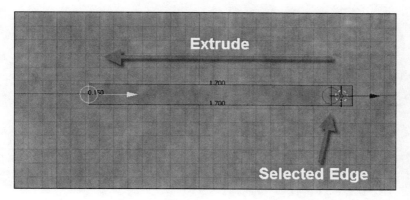

After a few extrusions, we will have the basis to create the walls. This was all done only with extrude.

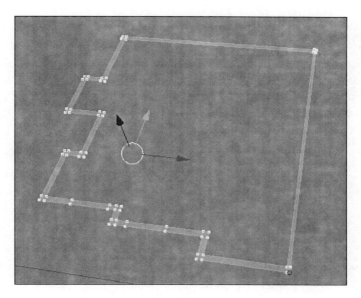

With all faces selected, we can make another extrusion constrained to the Z-axis. As with the extrude, we will have to edit a few more times, to get the shape of the wall. The whole process will be covered in the next chapter, but, most of the task involves use of extrude.

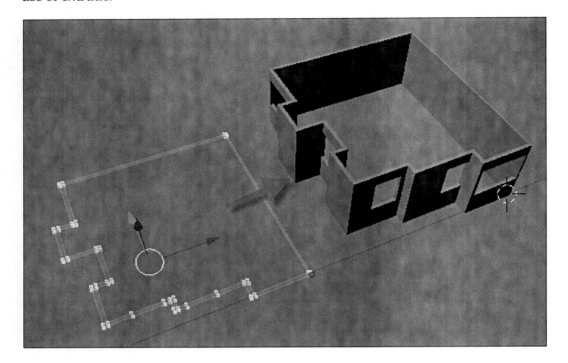

Modifiers

Besides the editing tools available on the Mesh menu, we have other tools called Modifiers, which are grouped on the Modifiers menu, in the Editing Panel. There are several different types of modifiers. Each one can help us with specific problems, but there are some that are very useful for architectural modeling. These are the Array, Subsurf, and Boolean modifiers.

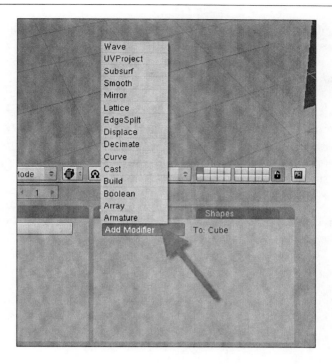

All of these modifiers give us a lot of flexibility in the modeling process, because we can make stacks of modifiers, to combine them. Because of this, the sequence of modifiers in the stack can change the way a model is affected by them. We can add a modifier to an object either in Edit or Object mode, but, some of the modifiers will only work properly when we are in a specific mode. To control and manage the modifiers, we can use these controls:

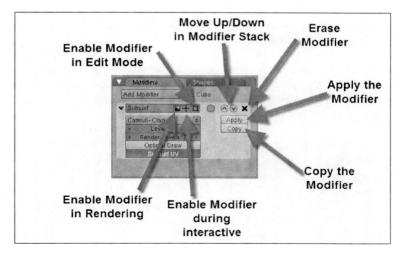

Let's take a look at three of these modifiers that will be very useful for us, in the modeling process for scenarios and architectural modeling.

Subsurf Modifier

The Subsurf Modifier subdivides the models to make them smoother. With more subdivisions, a model that initially looks crispy with hard edges between the faces can gain some soft edges between faces, and looks more organic. This is one of the oldest tools in Blender, and is heavily used in character modeling. For us, this tool will be more useful in furniture modeling and landscapes.

We can add this Modifier in either the Edit or Object mode in Blender. When the modifier is applied to a Mesh object, a few options to control how the subdivision works will appear in the Modifiers menu.

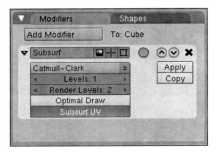

As we can see, there are two main controls that affect the level of subdivision a model has. The first one, called **Levels**, controls the subdivision of the model for the 3D View, and the other one, called Render Levels, controls the subdivision of the model for the rendering. This way, we can work in the 3D View with a low level of subdivision, just for editing. When the model is ready for rendering, a higher level of subdivision will create a smoother model.

There are two types of subdivision to choose from: Simple Subdivision and Catmull-Clark. When we choose the first type, the model face will be subdivided but not smoothed. The **Catmull-Clark** subdivision will give us subdivision and also smoothen the edges between the faces.

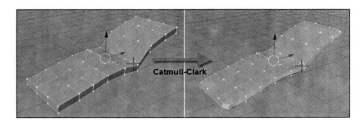

Catmull-Clark

If we want to control the level of subdivision and the way borders in different models work, we can use the Loop Cut tool with the subdivide. A new loop cut near the edge of a model, will make the radius of the smoothening smaller, giving us more control over the details. Let's see how it works:

1. If we apply the Subsurf Modifier to a Cylinder, it will turn it into something like a capsule.

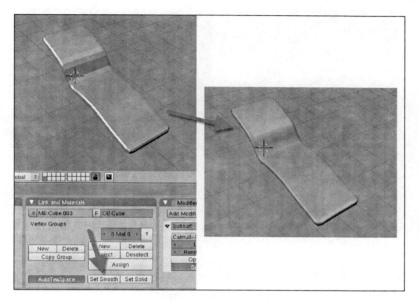

2. When we select this cylinder and make a new loop cut, we can see that the border near the cut becomes less smooth, and the radius of the border is smaller.

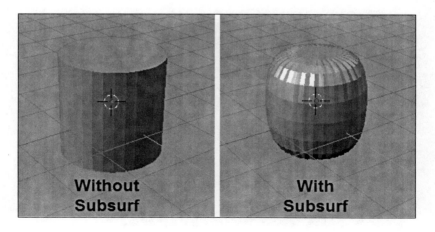

Smoothing Faces

Even for subdivided models, we will still see some small faces in objects. To make models look softer in the 3D View and render, we need to turn on a tool called Set Smooth. To do this, select the model and enter Edit Mode. Select all vertices, edges, or faces for this model. Then click the Set Smooth button, located on the Link and Materials menu in the Editing panel.

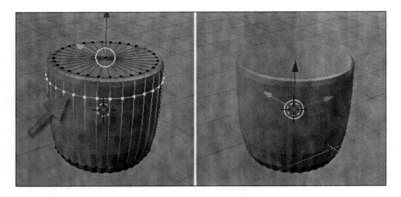

The models will look softer with this option, and won't show any faces, only a smooth surface. To return the surfaces to a faceted look, just click the Set Solid button.

Array Modifier

The Array Modifier is a great tool for creating copies of objects, and organizing them into lines and columns. With this modifier, we can easily place a chair in a room, or place any object over a surface in an organized way. To use the Array modifier, we must select one object first, and then choose the modifier either in Object, or Edit Mode.

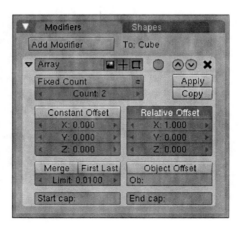

The first step in using this modifier is choosing between the three available methods of copying objects. Each of these methods distributes the objects in different ways.

- **Fit to Curve Length:** This option makes the copied objects follow a selected curve object. With this option, we can distribute trees or signs over a sidewalk. All we have to do is to draw a curve over the surface, and apply the modifier to the objects that we want to copy.

- **Fixed Length:** With this option, we will use a fixed length between the copied objects. Let's take the trees example. We can place copies of tree models in a straight line, and determine that between each copy, we will need a distance of 50 units. Then we will set up a total range for the array, such as 200 units. This way, in 200 units, we will have four tree models placed at 50 units intervals.

- **Fixed Count:** Here, we will make a fixed number copies of objects. What we have to specify here is the number of objects that we need, such as 10 objects, and the distance between each of them, such as 40 units. It doesn't matter if we will end up with a copy range of 400 units; the number of copies that we specify will be created.

To select each type of Array method, we use the combo box located at the top of the menu. When we choose each Array type, the text box below the option changes to reflect the parameters needed for each type of Array.

Array Example

Let's see how we can use the Array Modifier to make copies of our walls. We can select the wall model, created with the extrude option, and apply the modifier.

The Array tool can be set up to make the copies with a relative offset, and with one unit in the Z-axis. If we choose to make a **fixed count** of copies, and choose eight copies, it will result in eight copies of the wall, one above the other.

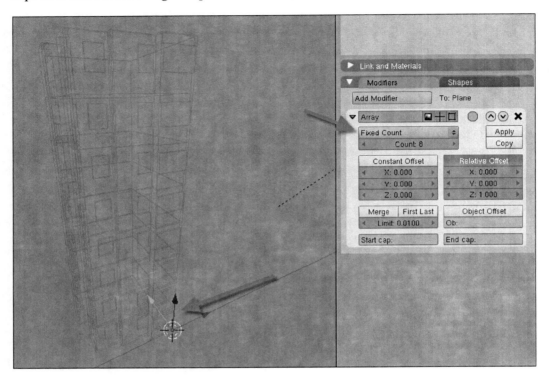

Boolean Modifier

This modifier gives us a few extra options for creating or editing complex meshes. If you have some experience with CAD software, you may be familiar with Boolean operations such as union, subtraction, and intersection. With these operations, we can model complex objects with only a few mouse-clicks, but at a price: in most cases they result in triangular faces, making any post-editing very difficult.

Let's see what we can do with each type of operation, and what they are called in Blender:

- Difference: With this option, we can subtract the shape of one object from another. For instance, we can open a hole in a wall, for a window. For this, we must create the wall model and another object with the corresponding shape of the hole. Then we apply the modifier to create a new object based on the subtraction of the two shapes.

- Union: Here, we can create a new object, based on the union of two different meshes.

- Intersection: This last type of operation creates a new object based on the area where two different shapes intersect.

Of these three operations, Difference is by far the most commonly-used for architectural modeling. Let's see an example of how it works. We will use the Boolean modifier to open a rounded hole in an object.

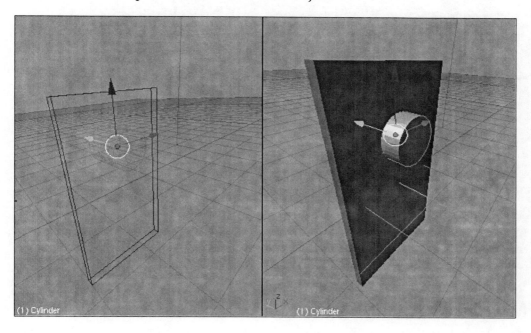

To create the hole, we have to make two simple objects, the shape of the first object, which can be a cube with a few scale transformations, and the cylinder for the hole.

Position both objects such that they share a common area. Select the rectangular object, and apply the modifier. Choose Difference, and type the name of the **cylinder object**. To finish this operation, click the **Apply button** to make a new object based on the difference.

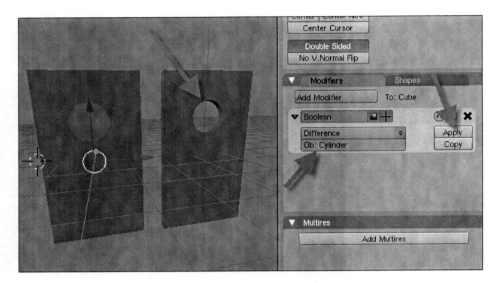

All other boolean operations works the same way. We must select one object, choose the operation, and type the name of the second object. Just remember to use this modifier only if you are sure that this object won't need any type of post-editing.

Mirror Modifier

Here, we have a time-saver modifier, which allow us to mirror one side of a model and make an inverted copy of the model. If your model has symmetry, it can use this modifier.

The modifier is pretty simple and easy to use. The only trick about it is that the center of the mirror must be set in the correct position. Otherwise, the mirror will generate the copy at the wrong position.

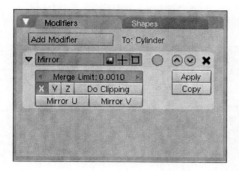

Let's see how it works with the same model to which we have applied the array modifier. The first thing to do is place the object center in the correct position. For this, we have to change the work mode to Edit, and then select one or two vertices and place them at the exact position where we want the object center to be.

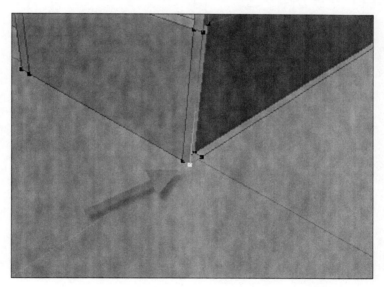

The center of the object will work as an axis for the mirror. After selecting the vertices, edges, or faces, press the *SHIFT+S* shortcut key, and choose Cursor | Selection. This will cause the 3D Cursor to be placed at the position of the selected object. If we select more than one object, the cursor will be placed at the median point of the selection.

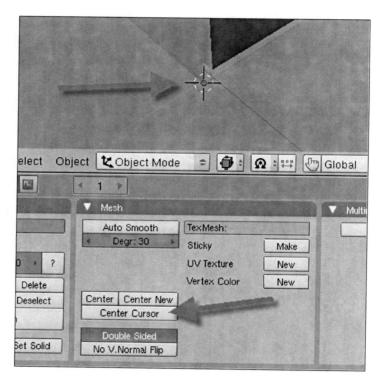

Change the work mode to Object, and in the Editing panel click the Center Cursor button. This will cause the center of the object to be placed exactly where the 3D cursor is.

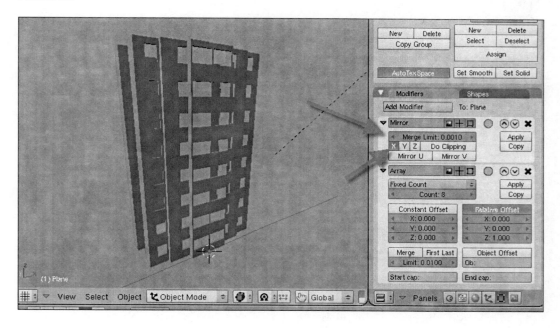

Now all we have to do is to apply the Mirror modifier and choose the axis of the mirror. Along with the axis, we can choose the proximity at which each vertex will be merged.

Groups

Groups aren't a modeling tool, but they help to organize complex models. As the name suggests, we can gather a lot of objects together using groups, and make them work as a single object. For instance, if we have a scene with a lot of chairs, instead of selecting each chair, we can group them for editing, and select the group with a single mouse-click.

We can use this example, with some chair models, to see how the grouping option works. There are two ways of dealing with groups. We have a keyboard shortcut, *CTRL+G*, and a menu in the Object panel. With the shortcut, we can do almost everything. But with the menu, we can manage all groups available in a scene.

How to Create a Group

To create a group, we must first select the objects that will be part of the group, and then press *CTRL+G*. Then a few options will be shown in the 3D-View.

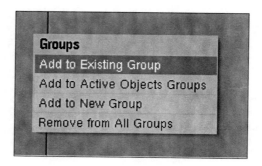

Here is what each option means:

- **Add to new group**: This option creates a new group with the selected objects.

- **Add to existing group**: Here, we can add the selected objects to a group that already exists. After we choose this option, another menu will allow us to choose in the group to which we want to add the objects.

- **Add to active object group**: If we select more than one object, the last selected object will always be the active one. If this last object is already in a group, we will be able to add all of the previously-selected objects to the same group.

- **Remove from all groups**: If the object is already in a group, this option removes the object from the group.

The first three options will add the objects to a group. Since our scene example doesn't have any groups yet, we can only choose the first one.

When a group is created, we can identify an object in the group by the green line that marks this object when we select it.

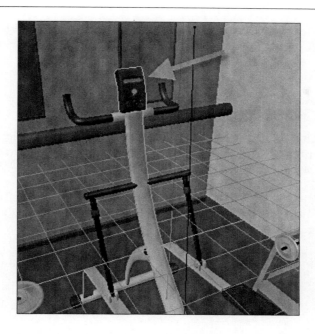

To view all groups available in a scene, go to the Object panel and choose the Object and Links menu. This will display all the groups available in the scene.

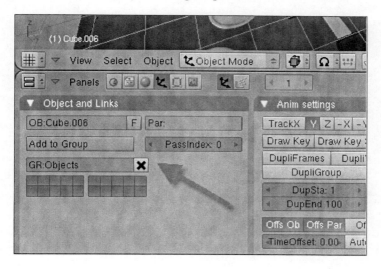

If you want to erase an existing group, just click the X button next to the group name in the Object panel. Erasing the group does not erase the objects, but just the group itself.

Proportional Editing

To conclude this chapter, we have a tool that is very important in landscape modeling. Proportional editing allows us to transform a vertex, and transfer part of the editing to the surrounding vertices.

Proportional editing can be turned on with the O keyboard shortcut, or through an option in the 3D-View Header. In the Header, we can find the selector for different proportional editing types.

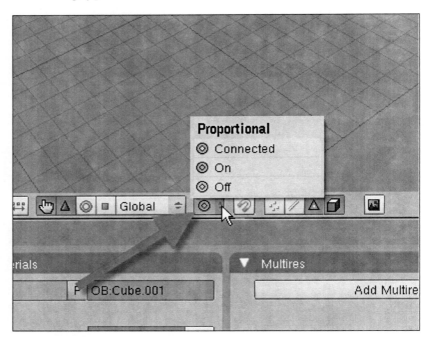

The tool works together with the transformation options. We must select one or more vertices, and press G, R, or S to begin. When the transformation is chosen, press the O key to turn proportional editing on. Along with the option to turn proportional editing on and off, we can choose from several types of proportional editing in the header.

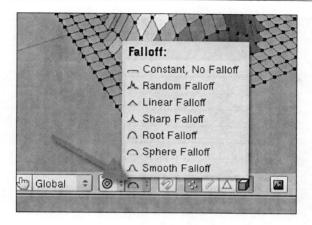

If we use the *O* key to turn on the proportional editing, and then press *G*, a small circle will appear, surrounding the selected vertex. This is the area of the effect of the transformation, and all vertices inside this circle will be transformed proportionally. Here is what happens if we proportionally transform this vertex in the Z-axis.

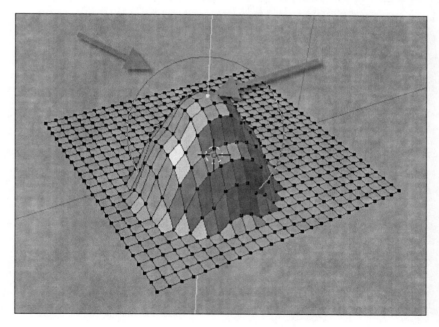

With the + and − keys on the numeric keyboard or by using the mouse wheel, we can change the size of the circle. Here is what we can do with proportional editing to create a landscape.

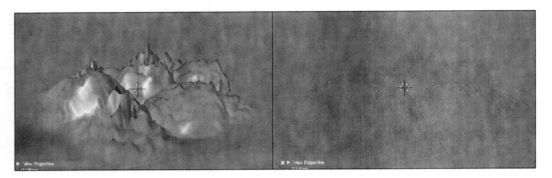

Summary

This chapter was about how Blender creates models. It was only the start of your experience with modeling, but we already have learned:

- How to create objects with Blender
- What meshes are and how they are edited
- The advantages of using meshes instead of solids
- How to transform the objects
- How to extrude vertices, edges, and faces
- How to work with modifiers
- How to work with groups
- How to model using proportional editing

In the next chapter, we will start to work with more options related to architectural modeling.

4

Modeling for Architecture

In the previous chapters we learned the Blender basics—how to create objects, how to model, and more. Now, we will put all of this knowledge together, to create models for architecture visualization. Let's look at some techniques for creating walls, floors, roofs, and other specific architectural elements. Some of these elements are pretty simple to create, while others require special tricks or adjustments in the modeling to
be created.

Architectural Modeling

Before we go any further in architectural modeling, let's see what are the differences and pecularities of this kind of modeling when compared to character and other types of modeling process. Here is a list of some of the characteristics of the models:

- The scales of models are usually big.
- All models are based on geometric forms; very few of them require organic shapes.
- The models are usually modular, with model parts that are repeated.
- The models must be created with the right proportions, to show the project in the best way.

These are the particularities of architectural modeling. Although it's not much, all those aspects must be very clear to us. The scales of architectural models are big, as they relate to buildings. (The only models that will require a smaller scale are the furniture.)

The shapes of the models are also important, since the construction processes which we use to build houses and buildings use mostly geometrical forms such as cubes. Our models will be strongly based on these shapes. This will make the process easier for some people, but don't forget that its geometrical forms require a lot of editing and tuning to represent architecture.

What about modular modeling? It's a common characteristic of architecture that, some projects are built with shapes that are repeated several times in a project. This makes the construction process easier and cheaper, and we can take advantage of this by using tools to copy models and accelerate the modeling process.

Another important thing is the precision of modeling, which is very important since all models must be an exact equivalent of a real object. But we don't have to stick to 'real-life' measurements, because if a wall must have four meters, and we don't create the wall with these dimensions, it's going to be difficult for anybody to measure the wall in a rendered image or video.

Does this mean that we don't have to use to real measures at all? Well, real measurements are important, but we can make changes, as long as the proportions of the models are kept the same. If we create the model with the right proportions, if not the right dimensions, it won't be a problem since the proportions are most important. These proportions will become more evident, when we add furniture, cars, or people to our models.

Modeling by Proportions

To understand how to model an object by its proportions, we can use a simple example. Suppose we had to model a table with the following dimensions:

- Height: 80 cm
- Width: 300 cm
- Depth: 100 cm

What if we wanted to change the dimensions of this table? As long as we kept the proportions, we should be fine. We could model the same table with half its original size, and keep the proportions the same:

- Height: 40 cm
- Width: 150 cm
- Depth: 50 cm

Or we could double the size too. It doesn't matter how we represent the measurements of this model, No one will be able to measure it with a ruler. Just be careful to keep the proportions the same and always check whether the model or object fits correctly in your scene.

This type of modeling is very useful for furniture modeling, where we have a picture of the furniture and we use this picture as reference to model the furniture. We can follow the picture reference to keep the proportions, and almost forget the dimensions. When the model is done, we can scale it to make the object fit at a specific scene.

Planning Is the Key to Success

I guess planning is important in all aspects of our lives. But in the computer graphics business, especially architectural visualization, good planning can save us a lot of time. And with the time saved, we will be able to create additional images and models. With more productivity, we will get more clients and can work with more projects. And with more projects we will gain more money. So here, time is money too.

Visualization projects can be divided into two types. The first is a project in which we are the authors, so every decision is up to us. I don't have to say that this is the easiest project to work, because we have the power to make all decisions and plan everything in the modeling process. But there is another type of project, which demands even more planning. It's the project that has somebody else as the author. This kind of project demands more planning because we won't be able to make changes to the project, if we find any problems in the modeling.

In any case, there are some rules that we must follow to make the modeling process easier. By following these rules, we can optimize our work.

- Model only those objects that are going to be visible in the rendering.
- Work with reusable objects.
- Copy as much you can.
- Take backups of all models.
- Use file versions with dates.
- Understand the lighting conditions of the environment.
- Know all materials and textures of surfaces.

If you are the author of the project, it's going to be easier to make most of these decisions. But if you are not, talk a lot with the author and try to clarify things, as much as you can.

The first rule says that we have to model only what's going to be visible. So before starting to model anything, think about how many renderings would be required for that project. When this is clear, the modeling process can start and we will be able to select only the visible parts of a project. For animations, we will have to make a small storyboard, or draw the camera path in the project as a reference.

Unless you have a reason to model all of the objects in a project, you shouldn't spend your time modeling things that won't show in the renderings. It's a very common mistake to model everything first, and then choose the camera view. With this kind of workflow, you will find yourself having a very detailed object, which takes hours or days to complete, but won't show in the rendering. This is extremely bad for your productivity, and can compromise the deadline and even the quality of the visualization, since you will have less time to work on lights and textures.

The second tip is to, use models from other projects that you may have worked on. A good library of models is very important in order to speed up modeling. There is an even greater market for those such objects with companies that only sell models of chairs, sofas, tables, and more. For every new project, keep all the small models that were used to compose the environments ready, and organize them into libraries.

The third tip is about copying as much as possible! Hey, don't misunderstand this! When we say copy as much as possible, we mean to say, make copies of our own models! Almost every model has a repetitive pattern of shapes, which allows us to create only a single piece of that shape, and then creates copies to build the rest of the model.

The fourth and the fifth tips are related, and they are about taking backups of our models. It's a very important task that can't be left aside, and most artists just don't find the required time to do this. A good habit is to create versions of our files, with some kind of identification for the dates or the subjects. This will help us identify the last time these files were updated, and create a new starting point if the project has to be changed. A very good file naming convention is to use "project_title_year_month_day" for all files, where project is the overall name for the project, and title may be a subtitle such as living room or kitchen.

Save your files

If you have any experience with architectural projects, you know how often a project can change while it is in development. These changes can make a mess of your models, if you are still working on them. If we don't have a backup of our files, from previous versions of the project, we may have to start from scratch, as the changes in the project won't allow us to adapt the existing geometry.

The sixth tip is about the lighting conditions for the environment where the project is placed. It is very important to have a reference for starting working on the simulation of that lighting. If we are the authors of the project, this is going to be easier. Otherwise, ask the author about it. Consider: Where is the north? What's the geographic location of the project? How does sunlight get into the rooms through openings?

And the last tip is about materials and textures, which are also important. A lot of projects go into visualization without a clear definition of what materials are going to be used, and the materials chosen can affect the modeling process. Having clearly defined what we will need, we can leave some details for the texture maps, and make the modeling faster.

I guess now it is very clear that planning the modeling is important, as it affects other parts of the process, such as lighting and texturing. Before a project begins, make a plan, and take note of every detail of the project. If you are not the author of the project, ask the author as much as you can about the project, and ask for feedback on your questions and suggestions on the visualization.

Precision Modeling

The first step to take, in order to get deep into architectural modeling in Blender is to learn how we can model with precision, to get the **dimensions** of our models into the right proportions. The easiest way to model with precision is to work with the Grid. You may have noticed that , there is a Grid in the **3D View**, which we can use to make our models more **orthogonal**. To use this grid, we have to hold down the *CTRL* key every time a transformation is applied to an object. There is an easy way to test this. Just select one object and press the *G* key to move the object. Before moving the mouse, just press the *CTRL* key and hold, and then move the mouse. The object will be moved, but now it won't slide across the **3D View**. It will make small jumps because it's using the gird lines as a guide. Use the status bar, to track the distance moved.

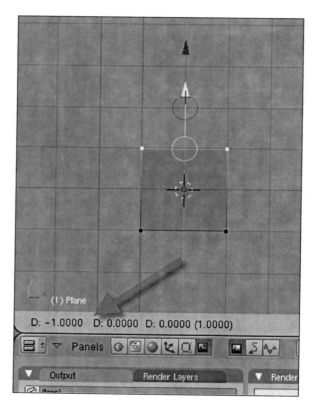

We can use the grid lines to move, rotate, and scale objects. And it works not only with the entire object, but with **vertices**, **edges**, and **faces** too. If we select a face, and press *R*, the face rotation will use the **grid lines** as guide, and the rotation will become more regular.

The default grid lines are suitable for almost any kind of model. But we can customize their appearance to suite our needs. The distance between these lines are one unit, which could represent one meter, one centimetre or one inch. It will be up to the artist to choose a scale unit to work, but if we need a smaller or larger distance, there is a way to change it.

Use the **View menu**, located in the **3D View Header** and choose **View Properties**. This will reveal a menu, with some options to change the appearance of the grid.

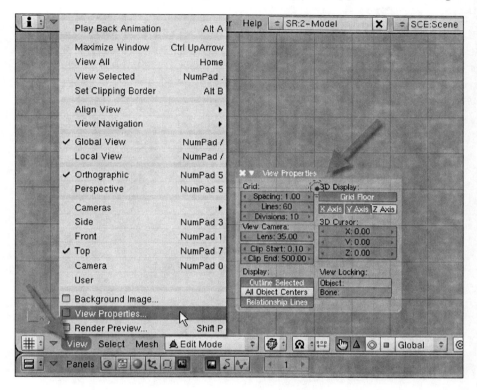

Let's see what we can do with these options:

- **Spacing:** With this option, we can set up the distance between the major grid lines. The default is 1.00, but we can change to any value that best suits our modeling.

- **Lines:** This option controls the number of lines that are displayed in the 3D View. By displaying a limited number of lines at the same time, we can save computer resources.

- **Divisions:** Between the major grid lines, we have some division lines to make a more precise use of the grid. We can set up the number of division lines with this option.

- **Grid Floor:** This button turns the visualization for the **Grid on** and **off**. Even though the Grid is a very helpful tool, we can turn the **Grid off** with this button, and make the **3D View** more clear.

Edge Length

Another way to keep control over our model dimensions is by visualizing them while we create and transform the models. To do this, we have to select an object and enter Edit Mode. There is a menu called **Mesh Tools 1**, which has an option called **Edge Length**. If we turn this option on, every time we select an edge, it's length will be displayed.

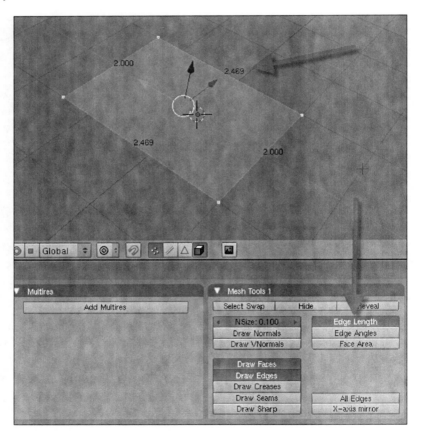

This is a great way to check the distance between two vertices very quickly. If you want to keep track of all the distances while modeling, just leave this option turned on.

Transforming with Precision

Another way of working with precision in Blender is by applying transformations using numeric values. We use this very often in CAD drawing, when we need to move an object, say, just four units on the X axis. To do this kind of operation in Blender, we must use the **Transform Properties** menu, which allows us to give numeric values for all transformations. This menu can be opened with the *N* key or from the **Object Menu**, in the **3D View Header**.

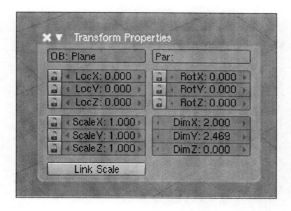

A good thing about this menu is that it can be opened from almost any Blender window. If the window allows us to draw or manipulate anything, it has a **Transform properties** menu. Let's see how it works. Just select one object, and press the *N* key. Immediately after the menu appears, just type the new value for the transformations in the text boxes.

- **Loc X/Y/Z**: This option controls the position of an object. We can set up a transformation using a numeric value here. If we type 3 in the Loc Y field, the object will move 3 units in the Y axis.

- **Rot X/Y/Z**: Here, we have the rotation controls. Similar to the Loc option, if we type -30 in the Rot Z field, the object will rotate -30 degrees over the Z axis.

- **Scale X/Y/Z**: This works much like the previous options, but here, we can control the scale of the objects.

- **Dim X/Y/Z**: This looks a lot like the Scale option, but the difference here is that the model bounding box is changed.

If we know that an object won't have any changes in a particular transformation, there is a way to lock all transformations for that object. This menu has small locks, next to all transformation options. If we turn the lock on, we won't be able to apply any kind of transformation for the selected axis. If you know that your object is done, and placed at the right position, it would be a good idea to lock it.

Layers

Almost all **modeling packages** have some kind of layer system to let artists organize their environments. In Blender, it's no different. We have a layer system which let us control when an object should be visible. The layer control buttons are located in the **3D View Header**.

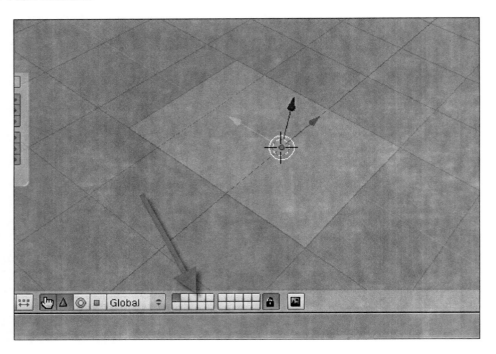

There are twenty layers on which you can place objects, and the use of the layer buttons are very simple. To put an object into a different layer, just select the object, and press the *M* key. A small menu will appear, where we have to choose a layer to which to send the object.

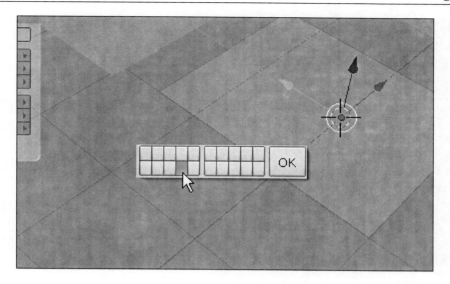

If we want to turn on or of multiple layers, we must hold the *SHIFT* key while clicking on the layer buttons.

Another way of dealing with layers involves the use of render layers, which are very useful for complex scenes. We set up the objects that should be rendered. Even if they are visible in the **3D View**, it is not necessary that they will be rendered. We will explore this in more detail when we deal with post-production.

Layers for backup

We can use Layers to take backups of models inside a scene. If we have to make a very complex editing into a model. It's a good practice to make a copy of this object, and put it into another Layer. If the editing doesn't work, or the project changes, we will have a backup to return to.

Modeling in Practice

Now, let's get our hands dirty! It's time to make some architectural models. To make things easier, we will split the **modeling process** into different parts. In the first part, let's learn how to deal with walls.

Walls

What's the best way to create walls? Well, there isn't one best way. What we have are some techniques that can be used to create this kind of object. Since each project has different needs, we have to analyse the project, and choose the best way to model.

In most cases, starting with a simple shape such as a plane can produce very good results. If we start with a plane, there will be a limited number of vertices for us to edit and manipulate. This way, our modeling will be easier and less troublesome. With this plane, we will build a base for our walls, and when all the base is created, it's just a matter of extruding the faces to create the rest of the walls. To see how it can be done, let's model these walls.

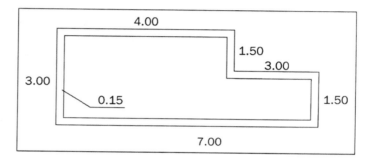

Since we will be using planes to model, it's a good practice to split all parts of a plan into rectangular parts. This way, it will become clear as to which are the faces to be created. If you don't have much experience, don't worry! You can do this even on a piece of paper if you don't want to use the computer. It's going to be a sketch of the model, with the divisions.

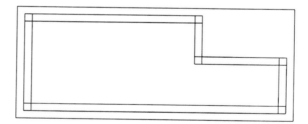

Note that this top view, doesn't have the openings marked. So, we won't be concerned with them yet. The first step is to create a plane that will have the dimensions of a corner of the room. According to the plan, the wall should have a width of 0.15. So, we have to create a plane with 0.15 on both sides.

To make things easier, change the work mode to **Edit** and turn the **Edge Length** option on. With the scale transformation, resize the plane until it has a width of 0.15. Hold the *CTRL* key to use the grid lines if you need to.

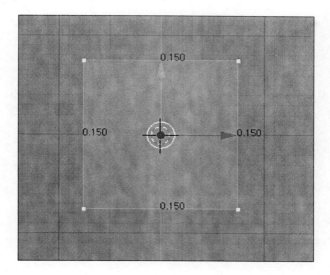

With the right dimensions for the plane, we can start to extrude an edge to create the other parts of the walls. While in Edit mode, change the selection mode to **Edge** by using the shortcut *CTRL+TAB*, and select one edge of the plane.

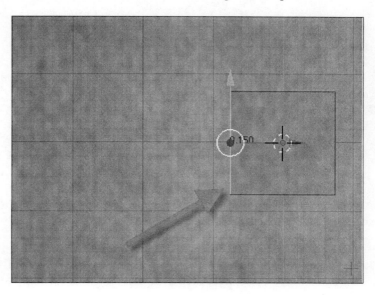

Now press *E* and **extrude the edge** to create new planes. To help this process, just hold the *CTRL* key and use the **grid lines**. Now, the new faces will be created in the correct alignment.

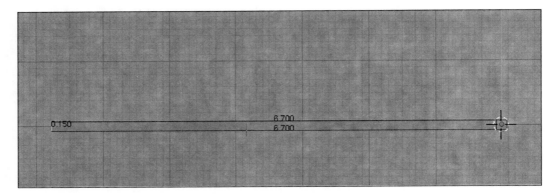

When we reach the correct dimension for the plane, create another small plane, and follow the **sketch for all the planes**. At the end, we should have something like this:

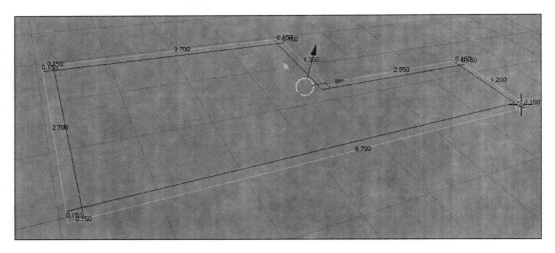

Once we have all the required planes, it's time to start removing any **duplicated vertex**. Press the *A* key to select all objects. Then, press the *W* key and choose **Remove Doubles** to remove all **duplicated vertices**.

Now, it's time to extrude the faces to actually create the walls. With the faces still selected, press the *E* key to extrude. Hold the *CTRL* key to use the **grid lines**, and place the upper faces in the correct position. Let's say that these walls have to be 2.70 units tall.

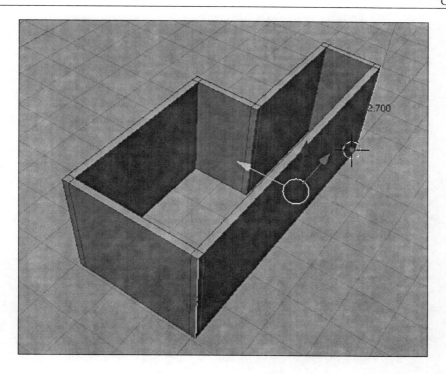

That's it! Now, we have our walls and the project in 3D! This may have been easy, but things are going to become more difficult. Walls without openings are very easy to create. But when we start to work with openings, we have to plan even more to get the work done.

Top View
Make sure to create your models in the top view. Just press the 7 key, on the numeric keypad.

Rounded Corners

How we can create a wall with a rounded corner? Well, to create such a wall, we must use a tool in Blender called Spin, which can create extrusions of an edge based on a rotation. The first thing we have to know, before doing anything, is the radius of the rounded corner. Otherwise, it will be very difficult to create the arc required for this wall.

Let's say we have a wall with a rounded corner and a radius of 2.

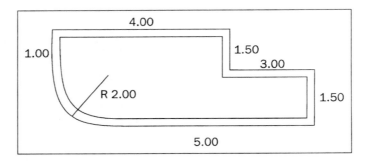

To create a wall like this, there is a little trick with **Snap and Spin tools**. First, create the planes, until we get to the beginning of the **rounded corner**.

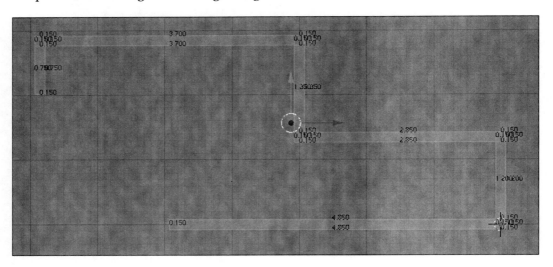

The trick to drawing the arc is to use the Spin tool, which takes an object and rotates it around a point. This point is determined by the 3D cursor. So, we have to find a way to place the 3D cursor at the center of the arc. This can be done with the **Snap tool**. But before we use the **Snap**, there is one thing that we must do.

If the selection mode is not at a vertex, then change it to select just the vertex identified in the example below.

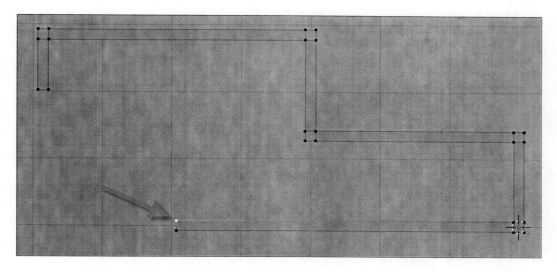

When this vertex is selected, press the *E* key to extrude only this vertex. Hold down the *CTRL* key down, and place the new vertex at the center point for the arc. To do that, use the radius distance to move the vertex.

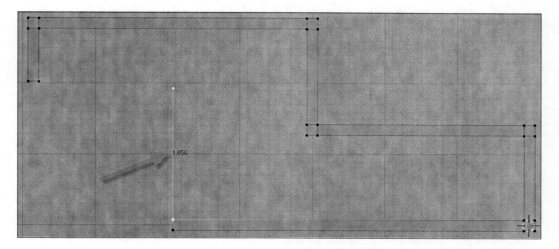

With the new vertex still selected, press *SHIFT+S* to activate the Snap, and choose **Cursor | Selection**. This will make the **3D cursor** jump to the position of this vertex. Now that it's placed where we want it, let's make the Spin. The new **vertex and edge** that we had created to place the **3D cursor**, won't be necessary now. Change the selection mode to Edge, select this edge and press the *X* key, and choose Edge to erase it.

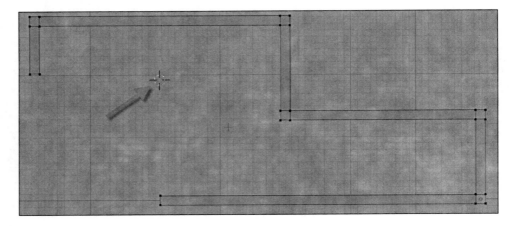

The Spin tool works with a selected object, which may be a **vertex, edge,** or **face**. When this object is selected, we can set up the **Spin**, which is located in the **Mesh tools menu** in the **Editing Panel**.

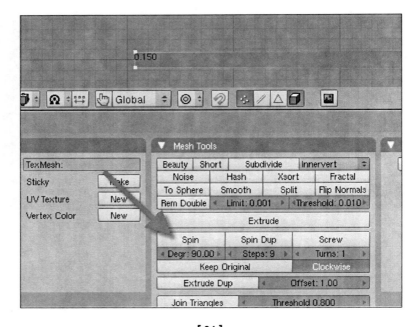

There are two parameters that we must set up, which are **Degrees and Steps**. The first one determines the **rotation angle** for the Spin; for us it will be a 90 degree rotation. In addition, we can specify how many steps our rounded corner will have, in the Steps parameter. If we specify a high number, a more perfect corner will be created. Try to use values above 12, and if this is not enough, raise it until you are satisfied. But remember that this will make the model heavier, with a lot more vertices. At the bottom of this menu, we have a button labelled **Clockwise**, which determines the direction of the **Spin rotation**. If this button is not clicked, then we will have a **counter-clockwise rotation**.

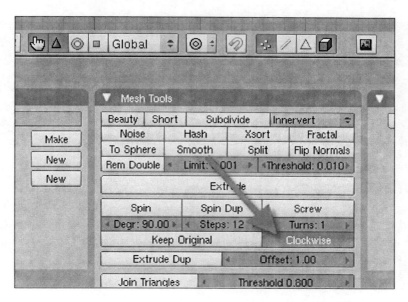

Make sure that you are in the **Top View**, because, with the Spin, all faces are created at a perpendicular plane to the **Viewer position**. Therefore, it's very important to be in the Top View. Otherwise, the new planes won't be created in the correct position.

Now, press the **Spin button** and the rounded corner will be created. Remember, if the arc isn't as rounded as the project demands, increase the Steps value and it will be more rounded, but with more geometry.

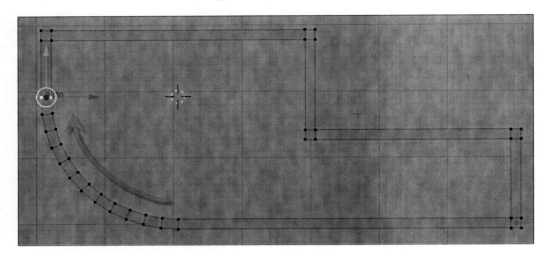

Symmetry

Very often, architectural projects have symmetrical parts where a section of a project is **mirrored** to create another part. It's a very good project practice, that makes the visualization process faster, because we need to model only half the project, and apply a mirror modifier to create the rest.

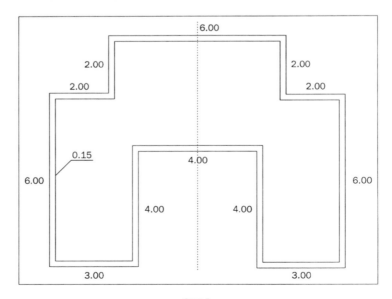

If we have a project similar like the one shown in the image below, ensure that, the right side of this project is symmetrical to the left side. So, if we model only one of them, the other side can be mirrored. Let's see how it works. We have to first model one side of the project. In the example below, we have the left side of the project, with all of the walls created.

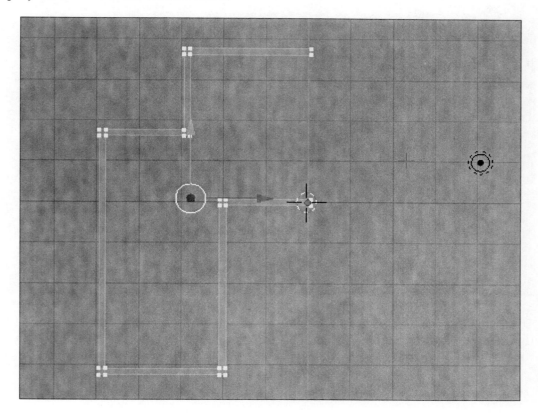

The trick is to use the **Mirror modifier** to place the center of the objects in the correct position. As the **modifier** uses the center as the basis for the rotation, we need to sure that the center is at the **middle axis** of the **pre-project**.

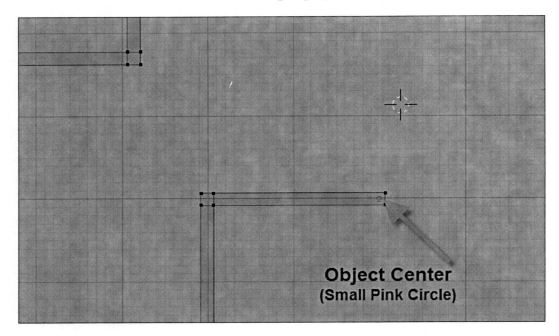

To change the position of the center point, we have an option in the **Mesh menu** that manipulates the center of objects. If you haven't noticed, the center of objects is represented by a small pink circle.

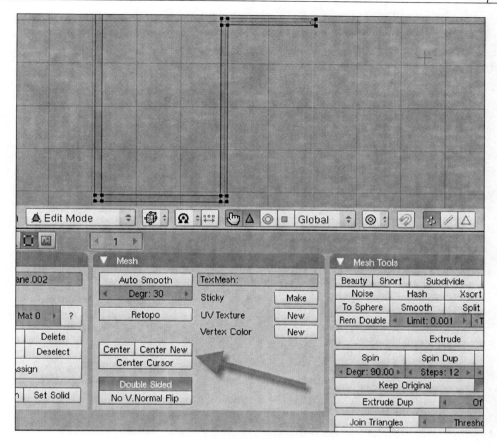

In this menu, we can move the center point in three ways, which are:

- **Center**: Here, we can place the object geometrical center at the object center position.
- **Center New**: Here, we can place the object center at the object geometrical center position.
- **Center Cursor**: Here, the object center will be placed at the position of the 3D cursor.

The option that will be most suitable for what we need to do is the last one, which can place the center at the location of the 3D cursor. Here is what we need to do: select an edge or two vertices that define an edge, press the *SHIFT+S* shortcut to call up the **Snap men**u, and then **choose Cursor | Selection**.

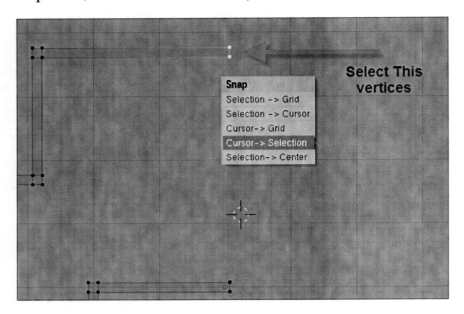

This will make the 3D cursor, jump to the center of our selected edge. When the cursor is correctly positioned, select the **Center Cursor option**. Make sure that the work mode is set to Object, since this option works only in **Object Mode**.

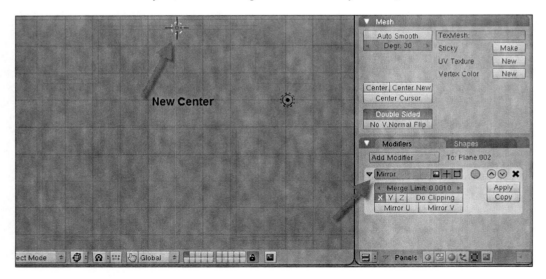

Now all we have to do is to apply the **Mirror modifier**, and choose an axis for the **mirrored object**. If the project needs another mirror, just apply more modifiers and change the mirror axis, so that more symmetrical parts are created.

Openings

It's hard to imagine any project without openings. So get used to creating a lot of openings in walls. The best way to deal with openings is to know exactly where they are placed, before we start creating them. If we do that, we won't have to create new loops in walls, and use a lot of Boolean operations to create holes. The trick is to create the walls, already with the space for windows and doors.

If we look at the following plan, we can see some openings. All these openings should be marked before we start to model.

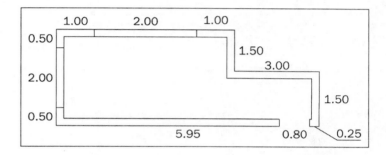

The technique is to start modeling the walls, and just leave a plane for every opening. This will mark the place for the posterior extrude. When all of the planes have been created, select the planes, and remove any plane that represents a door. Then make a first extrude up until the wall reaches the level of the bottom of the lowest windows.

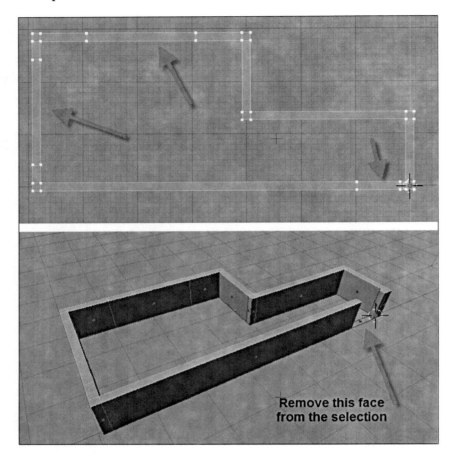

Then, remove the faces that mark the windows. After removing the faces, make another extrude until we reach the level of the top of the windows and doors. And to finalize, make the last extrude until the top of the wall.

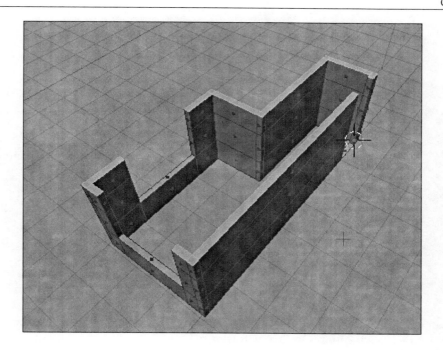

Well, now we have our walls with some big holes. To close these holes, we have two options. The first one involves some keyboard shortcuts, and the other one is very simple, and makes use of a scripted tool called **Bridge Faces/Edge-Loops**. Let's start with the easiest. To use the script, just change the selection mode to faces, and select two faces that must be connected.

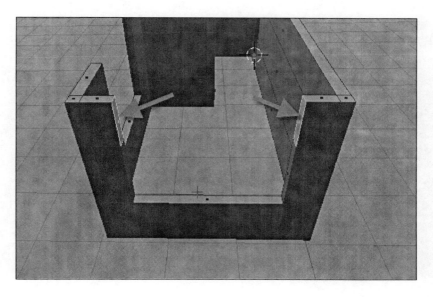

When the faces are selected, use the menu **Mesh | Scripts | Bridge Faces/ Edge-Loops**. This will create new faces to connect the previously selected faces. For this script to work, the faces must be exact parallels.

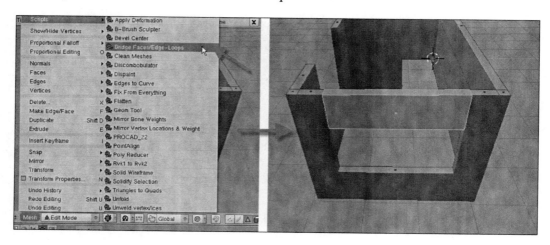

The other method works like this. We have to extrude both faces and then scale them until they touch each other. Do this as follows:

1. Select the faces that must be connected. When the faces are connected, press the *E* key to extrude them, and immediately after pressing the *E* key, just press *ESC* to cancel the extrusion. Here, it's important not to move or click with the mouse.

2. Then, press the *S* key to scale them down. Immediately after pressing the *S* key, press the key corresponding to the axis that is perpendicular to the planes. In my case, it's the X-axis, so here we will press the X key.

3. To finish, press the 0 key on the alphanumeric keypad to change the scale to zero. This will connect the faces.

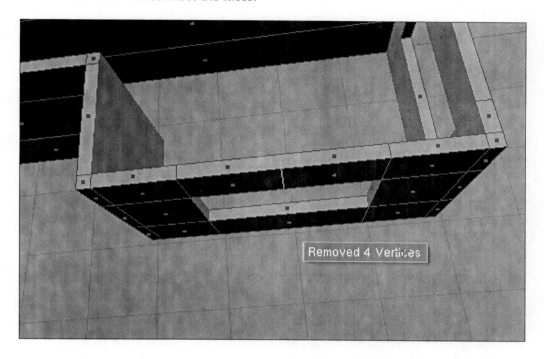

4. Press the W key, and choose remove doubles to erase any duplicated vertices.

As we can see, the first method is a lot easier. Try to use it where possible, and if the script doesn't work, try the second technique.

Floors and Lining

To create floors and sealings, we can work with new geometry or use the plane to start the model as a single piece. It works like this: we create a base plane, and with this plane, the edges are extruded to make the basis for the walls. What's the best way? Again, there isn't a best way. You have to try both methods, and choose the best one for each project.

Modeling Using the Walls

A good way to start is to try to make the floor and lining from a single piece. Let's take one of the projects we have worked on, like the following one:

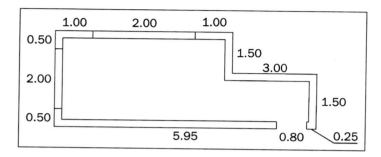

Select one entire edge from the side identified in the image below, and press the *E* key to extrude. Hold the *CTRL* key to use the grid lines, and create a more regular plane.

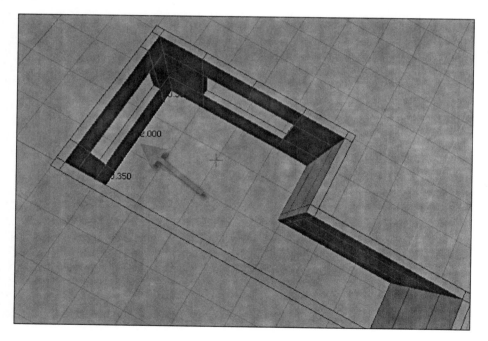

Keep making extrusions until the entire floor plane is filled. As we must fill the floor using square faces, a small sketch of how these faces will be distributed can help. If you are not comfortable with picturing this, just grab a piece of paper and make a sketch.

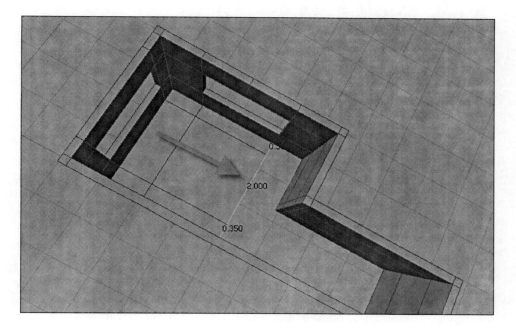

We can do the same thing for the lining. Just select one edge, and extrude it until the entire plane is filled. When you have finished, remember to select all objects and remove any duplicated vertices.

Use this method for simple projects or for interactive animation, as it will be easier to manage and manipulate the planes. If you are going to use complex textures, it may be a little hard to set up **UV Mapping**.

Modeling with Separated Objects

If you want to make a separated object, just create the plane to start the modeling. With this method, we will have to use a small trick to align the plane with the wall, using the Snap tool. The trick is to place the object center at a corner of the plane, and put the 3D cursor at the other corner to use the **Snap Selection | Cursor**.

Let's see how it works. First, create the plane or the cube. Then select a vertex in a corner that will be placed near the wall.

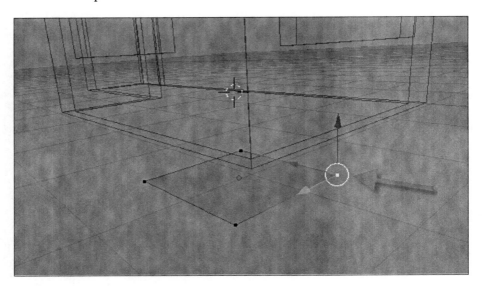

Press *SHIFT+S* to call up the Snap menu, and choose **Cursor | Selection** to make the 3D cursor go to the same position on the selected vertex. When the 3D cursor is in the required position, go to Object mode, and in the Editing panel, click the Center Cursor button. This will place the object center at the position of the 3D cursor.

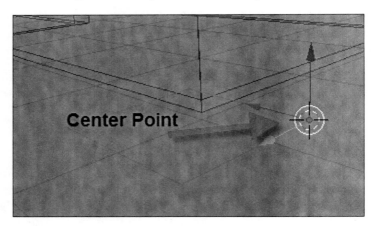

Now, we have to select a wall vertex, which will work as a reference for us. Immediately after selecting this vertex, press *SHIFT+S* and choose **Cursor | Selection** from the **Snap menu**. This will cause the **3D cursor** to jump to the vertex position.

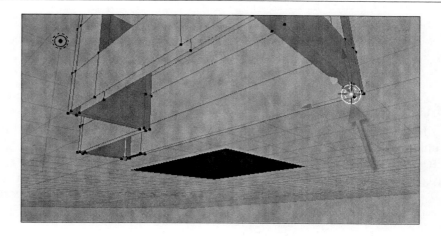

To finish this operation, select the plane that will be our floor or lining, in Object mode. Press *SHIFT+S* and choose **Selection | Cursor**, and you will see that our plane is placed in the correct position, aligned perfectly with the wall. This may be a hard technique, with a lot of keyboard shortcuts, but it's the best way to align objects in Blender using the default tools.

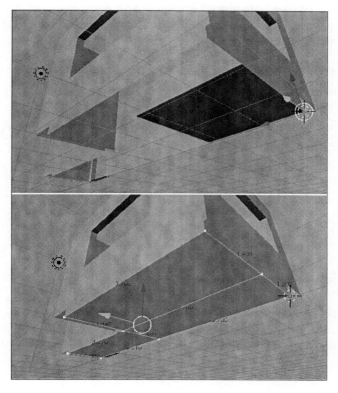

This method works best for complex models, where we may want to hide the walls and work only with the floor or lining. It makes the process of texturing easier too, allowing us to work only with the floor or lining planes.

Starting From a CAD Drawing

We have to learn how to deal with CAD files, because a lot of projects that come from architects are in DXF or DWG formats. Let me tell you that Blender cannot read DWG files. So if you get any such files, ask your clients to provide the same file in DXF, or you may have to convert it yourself. Almost any CAD software can save files in the DXF file format. It makes Blender compatible with most of these software.

Preparing the DXF Files

Before we import a DXF, there are a few things we can do to make the DXF file cleaner and smaller. When we make a technical drawing using CAD software, it is full of symbols and other objects that won't be very useful for 3D modeling, such as text, architectural symbols, and hatches.

If we remove some of these objects, the file size and complexity of the DXF will decrease, and make everything easier. Here is a list of things we can do to prepare the DXF file in your CAD software:

- Erase everything that you won't need. Just leave the lines of the drawings.
- Erase layers and other CAD related stuff. Remove any line types, hatches and other CAD related stuff.
- Try to save your DXF in the format of AutoCAD 12. It's more compatible with Blender.
- If your project is too complex, try to split the drawings into more than one file.

These are simple tasks, but can really improve the compatibility of your technical drawings and Blender.

Importing DXF files

Working with CAD files is sometimes better if the project has complex shapes, because, we won't have to measure edges to get the right dimensions. The CAD file will already in the right dimensions, and then we can focus on the geometry only. To get the file into Blender, just access the File menu and then select Import | DXF.

After we have the CAD file inside Blender, we will have to do some editing, because these kinds of files come with the edges separated. We can see that in the following image:

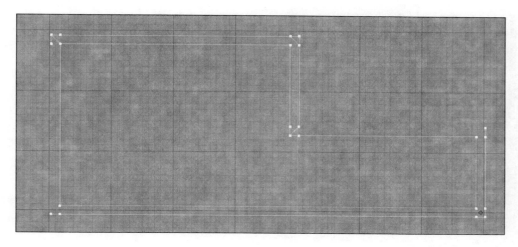

If your CAD file doesn't come in with just the lines that define walls, and openings, it will be necessary to do some heavy cleaning by erasing the extra data such as text and symbols.

What we have to do here, is select the vertices that should be together and perform a merge. Just select them and press the *W* key, choose **Merge,** and select method. Usuall,y the best method is At Center. When all vertices have been merged, we will have to build the faces. For this, we will have to select four vertices of a face, and press the *F* key. This way, we will create a new face, which will be required for a posterior extrude.

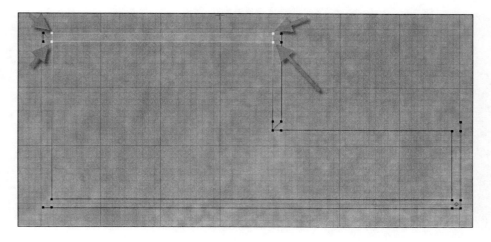

A bad thing about DXF files is that they don't support curves. If our drawing has some splines, we will have to turn them into polygons. To make things easier, we can use the Spin tool.

As we can see, using CAD files requires a lot of editing work. There are no major advantages to using these files except that we won't have to worry about dimensions and proportions, as the file already has the right measurements.

Summary

We have learned a lot now! Some of the most important elements of architectural visualization, which we can model in Blender , have been explained. Here are the main topics that we discussed:

- Planning the modeling
- Modeling with precision
- Organizing our scenes in layers
- Creating walls
- Creating openings
- Creating floors and linings
- Starting a model from a CAD file

In the next chapter, we will go deep into the details on modeling, to make our models more complex.

5
Modeling Details

The next step for us is to learn how to add more details, such as windows, doors, and stairs to our models. In the previous chapter, we saw how to model walls, and import DXF files into Blender. Let's use the objects that we had modeled previously, and give them a more realistic look, by adding details.

A great level of realism is achieved in architectural visualization by adding details such as window frames and more to models. If you want to give the images a good level of realism, a big part of this is related to details. So let's see how we can model these parts and make our scenes more real.

Level of Detail

Before we start, it's important to discuss about something called level of detail. This is a common term in game development, but we can use it in architectural modeling as well. Level of detail deals with how much detail a model must have to be seen by the camera. It would be pointless to produce a highly detailed model if the object is to be placed far away from the camera.

That's why I say, make sure where every camera is placed in your scene before you start modeling anything. Otherwise, there is great chance that most of the time taken in modeling will be wasted.

Windows

In the previous chapter, we modeled the walls and prepared the geometry with a hole for the window. But besides the opening, we must prepare a window frame to receive the glass, and other common elements for windows. There are a lot of window types such as:

- Double-hung sash window
- Single-hung sash window

- Horizontal Sliding window
- Skylight
- Roof window
- Fixed window

One of the most common window types, at least in the countries that speak English, is the **Double-hung sash window**. Besides the type, we have to know the material the window is made of and it's dimensions, to start a model.

The dimensions of the window will be important for determining the amount of sunlight that will enter the scene. This will be important when we deal with lighting. To make a window model, we will use the same technique we used to make the walls. All this starts with a **primitive mesh** such as a cube, and then we extrude this cube to build the geometry needed for the window frame. Let's use this **Double-hung sash window** as an example:

Remember, what we have to do here is create a visual representation of this window. We don't have to follow all visual aspects of the frame. But to do things properly, we have to know the measurements for all the parts of the frame. If we don't follow these measurements, our window model won't look real.

Another thing to remember is that we will use subdivision **modeling**, which means that the first step is to choose a **primitive shape**. In this case, we'll choose a cube and deform it until the shape of a window is achieved.

1. If you don't have a cube in your scene, press the Spacebar and create one with **Add | Mesh | Cube**.

2. If you already have a cube, change the work mode to Edit. Otherwise, after adding a new cube, the work mode will change automatically to **Edit**. Now, press the *A* key to select all the objects. Then, change the **selection mode** to Faces, to make the selection process easier.

3. Select the **Edge Length button**. This will make the editing process easier, if we want to keep track of the measurements.

4. With all objects selected, press the *S* key, and scale down the cube until it reaches about 0.10 for all edges. Use the *CTRL* or *ALT* keys while you move the **mouse cursor** to have more **precision** for the scale.

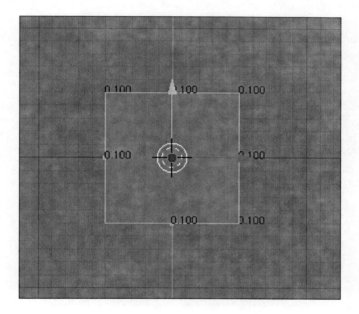

5. Since our window will have all of its parts based on this small cube, let's create a copy of it, before we start to subdivide. Change the work mode to **Object** and press **SHIFT+D** twice, to create two copies of the cube. Just place the copies somewhere near the **original cube**. We will use these copies later.

6. Now, we need to select the face of the cube, and right-click on it.

7. When the face is selected, press the E key to extrude this face, and move your mouse until the new face reaches 2.00.

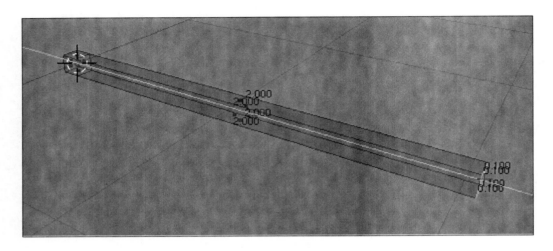

8. With the face still selected, press *E* again, and make another **extrude** until it reaches 0.10.

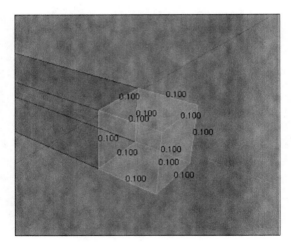

9. Remove any **face selected,** and then select the **small top faces** on the left and right sides.

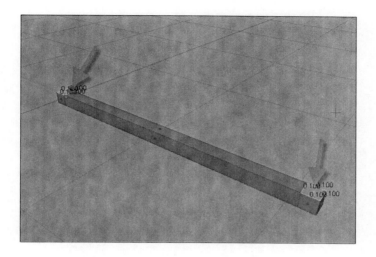

10. Extrude this faces until it reaches about 1.00 unit.

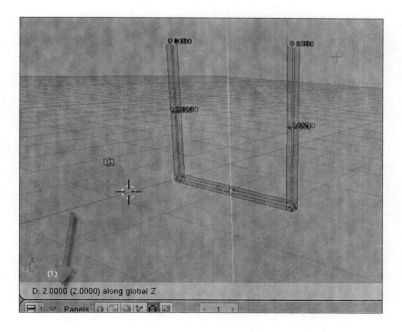

11. Repeat this **extrusion seven times**, and give each part the following measurements: 0.10, 1.00, 0.10, 1.00, 0.10, 1.00, and 0.10 units.

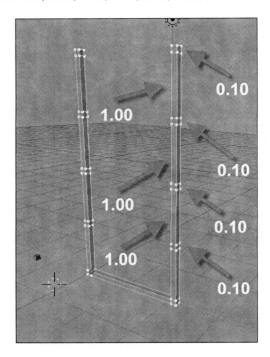

12. Now, we will make a connection between the middle faces, with the **Bridge Faces/Edge-Loops Script**. Select the two faces identified in the following image:

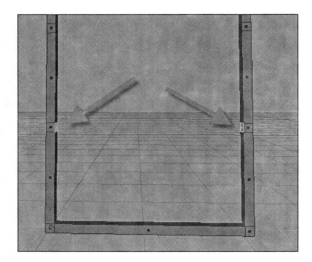

13. When the faces are selected, use the **Mesh menu** and access **Scripts | Bridge Faces/Edge-Loops**. The script will connect both the faces.

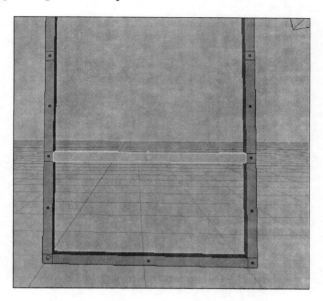

14. Repeat the same process with all the other **smaller faces** until we have a **model** like the one shown in the following image:

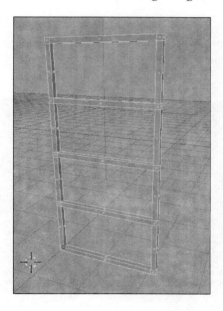

15. Remember the copied cube, which we had created in the beginning? Let's apply the same modifications that we just did. Repeat all the previous steps until we have a model like the one shown in the following image. Just use a smaller distance between the two main vertical parts; for this model, a distance of 1.00 unit works fine.

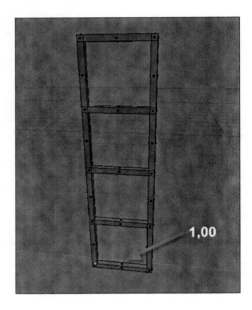

16. Now, we will have to align both models. Select the edge pointed in the image, and then press *SHIFT+S* to call the **Snap menu**. Choose **Cursor -| Selection** to make the **3D cursor** jump to the middle point of the edge.

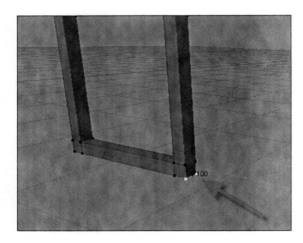

17. When the cursor is in the correct position, change the work mode to **Object** and, at the **Editing Panel**, press the **Center Cursor button**. This will make the object center jump to the place where the **3D cursor** is.

18. With the center of the first object placed in the correct position, we have to do the same thing for the second one. Select the edge identified in the following image:

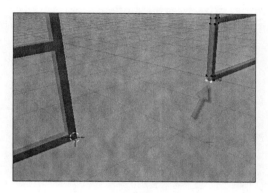

19. When the edge is selected, press *SHIFT+S*, and choose **Cursor | Selection** again.

20. Finally, we have the objects with the required conditions for alignment, so change the work mode to Object and select the object which had the center point edited first. When this object is selected, press *SHIFT+S* and choose **Selection | Cursor**.

21. This will make the object jump to the correct position. Using the center point and the 3D cursor is the most efficient method to align objects with **precision** in Blender. You may be asking yourself: Why not make both objects as one? Creating two objects will make our life easier if we want to add some animation to the scene. But, it's completely normal to build the models as just one piece.

22. We have the **model** now, so what's the next step? Before we move forward to make the other parts, let's build the upper part of the **window frame**. Select the other cube which we copied in step number five. Move it until it reaches the top of the window, at the right side, just as shown in the following image:

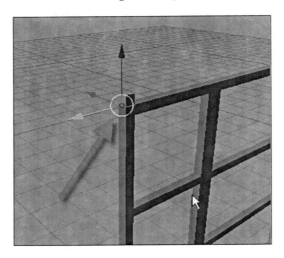

23. Enter Edit mode, select the correct face for this cube, and **extrude** it four times with the measurements: 1.60, 0.10, 1.55, and 0.05 units .

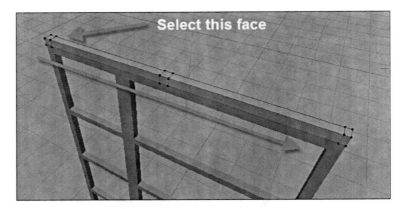

24. Now, we have to extrude the three small faces, identified in the following image. Extrude them until they reach 1.00 unit high.

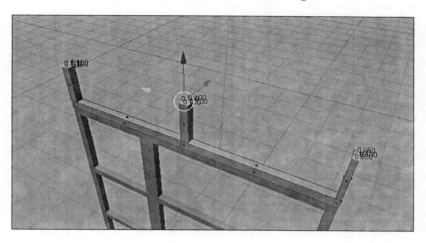

25. With the faces still selected, make another extrude of 0.10 unit.

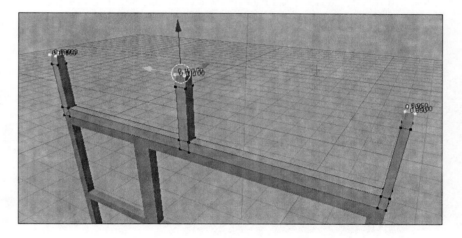

26. To connect the interior faces, just select two of them, and in the **Mesh menu,** access **Scripts | Bridge Faces/Edge-Loops**. Repeat the process two more times until the models looks like the following image:

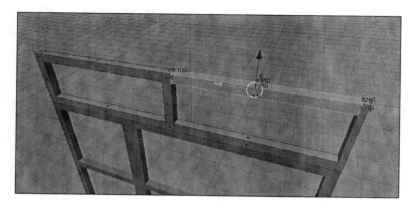

27. With most of the frame created, we can create the objects that will represent the glass. Select the edge at the bottom of the frame, identified in the following image. When the edge is selected, use the **Snap** option to align the **3D cursor** with this edge, and choose **Cursor | Selection**.

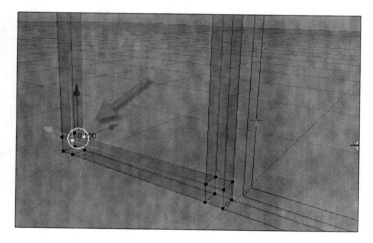

28. Change the view to **Front**. Depending on your model, it could be the 1 or 3 keys on the numeric keypad. Make sure you are in **Object mode** and create a cube.

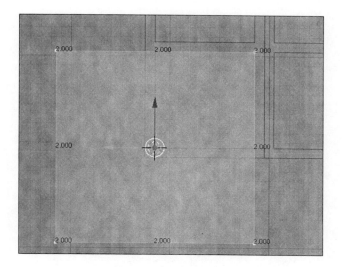

29. With the **Box** selection and the **Grab transformation**, move the vertices to adjust the size of this cube until it fits in the correct place in the frame.

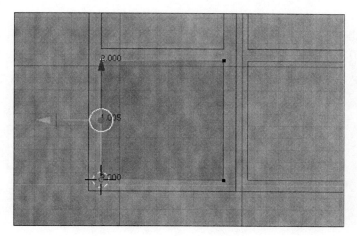

30. Change your view to **Top** and with all vertices selected, press the *S* key to scale down the model. After pressing the *S* key, press the key corresponding to the X-axis, to perform the scale only along this axis. Scale it until it reaches 0.03 units.

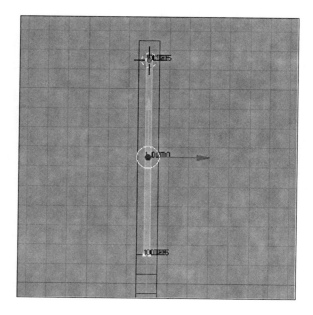

31. With the cube still selected, press *SHIFT+D* to create a copy, and move the copy to the next **hole**.

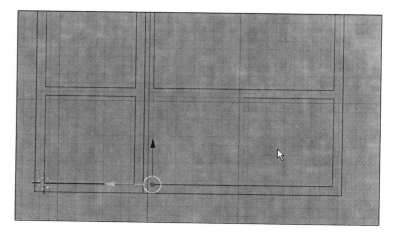

32. In edit mode, select the vertices for this new cube, and adjust it's size to fit in the frame.

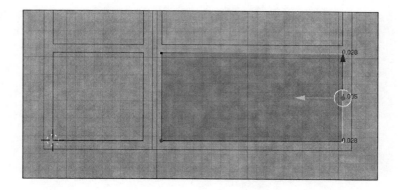

33. Now, let's distribute the cubes into the other holes in the frame. To do this, we will use the **Array modifier** and make four copies, which will use a **relative offset** of 1.10 units. Apply the modifier to each cube.

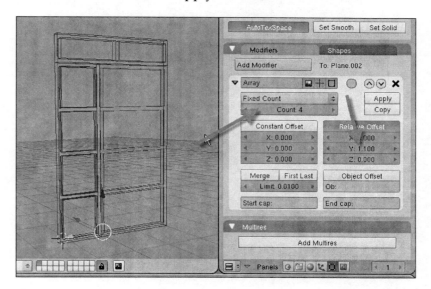

34. Use the same technique to make the cubes for the upper part. If you want, you can duplicate the cubes used previously, and remove the **array modifier**. Adjust their size to fit the frame.

35. To apply a **Mirror modifier** and complete the model, we must set the objects, centre to be at the position identified in the image below. Remember that you won't have to set up the position of the **3D cursor** for every object. Just place it once, and then select one object and press the **Center Cursor** button, in the **Editing Panel**.

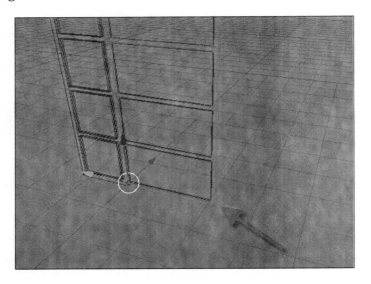

36. When the centre is set up, just apply a **Mirror modifier** to all the objects, and the window will be ready.

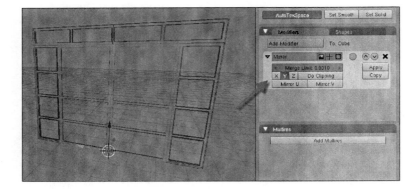

Level of detail

The camera view will determine how detailed the window must be. If the camera is near the window, we have to add more detail. In most cases, it won't be necessary, but it's good to know the **camera view** before starting to model anything. It can save a lot of time, especially if the camera is placed far away from the model.

Doors

Modeling doors is a lot easier than windows, because most doors don't have the amount of detail that do windows. But depending on the type of door, we can have pieces of glass or ornamental details; it will depend on your project.

As we did with windows, let's use the door shown in the image below to see how we can create a door model using a frame.

As you can see, the model is simple. But depending on the **camera view**, we may need to add more details to the model. Let's get started. The first thing to do is to create a plane. Don't worry about the measurement yet. At the end of the **modeling** process, we will apply a scale to the model.

1. While you still are in **Edit mode**, select the right edge of the plane and drag it to the left. Drag it until we get a distance of 0.3 units for the upper and lower edges.

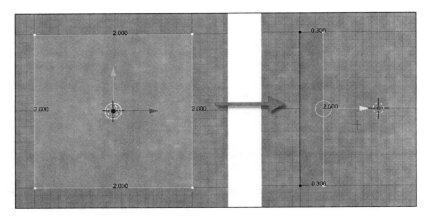

2. Change the **selection mode** to Edge; this will make your work easier. Select the **upper edge**, and then extrude it to 0.10 units. Repeat the same editing for the lower edge. Now we have to select the small edges on the left, and extrude those edges to 0.10 units. Remember to hold the *CTRL* key to help place these **extruded edges** at their correct positions.

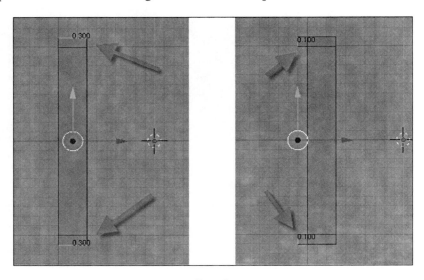

3. With the **face loop cut**, let's add two new edges to the plane. Just press *CTRL+R* to activate the tool, drag your cursor to the point identified in the following image. Click twice to mark the cutting position. Repeat the same process to add another edge.

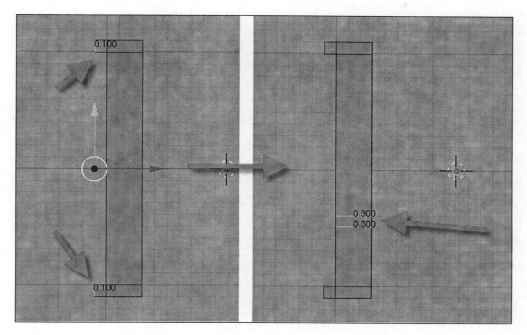

4. Select the small edge between the two new edges added with the face loop cut. When the edge is selected, extrude it to 0.10 units. Now we have the base plane to create the door frame. The next step is to select all edges and extrude them.

5. Before you extrude it, orbit the model to have more **visual control** over the extrusion. When all the edges are selected, extrude them until we get a measure of 2.00 units.

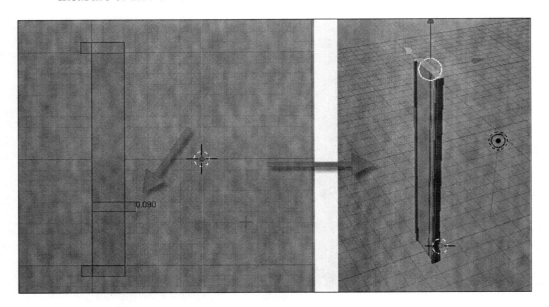

6. Change the selection mode to Face, and select all faces on the top of the model. When all faces are selected, extrude them by 0.10 units. With the faces still selected, extrude them once more, but now for 0.30 units. Now, we have to select only the small faces at each side of the top plane. With these faces selected, **extrude** them for a distance of 0.10 units.

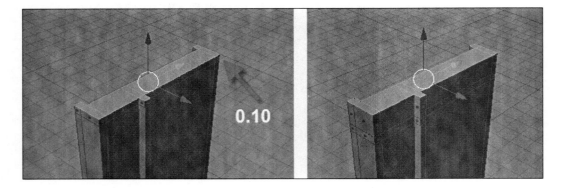

7. Select the two faces identified in the following image, and press the *X* key or *Delete* to erase those faces. We have to erase these, or they will be overlapping with the extrusion that we will use next. Select the faces identified in the lower image and extrude them, until they measure 0.10 units.

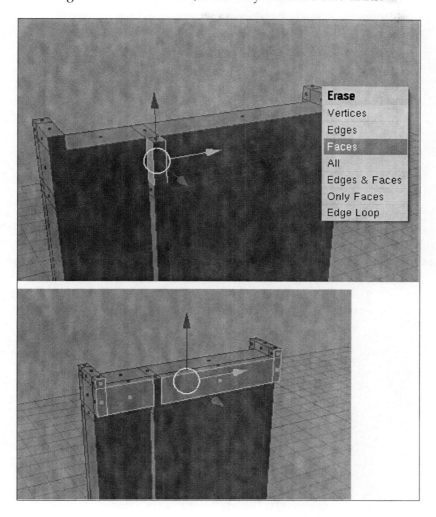

8. When the extrusion is done, select all faces. Now, extrude them until they get for a measurement of 4.00 units.

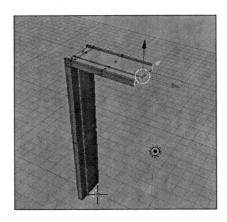

9. We have half the model ready. To create the other half, we can use a **mirror modifier**. To use the mirror, let's set the center of this model to the right of the mirror. With the faces still selected, press *SHIFT+S* to activate the **Snap menu. Choose Cursor | Selection** to make the **3D cursor** jump to the center of the selected faces. Change the work mode to Object and in the **Editing panel**, click the **Center Cursor** button to place the object center at the position of the **3D cursor**.

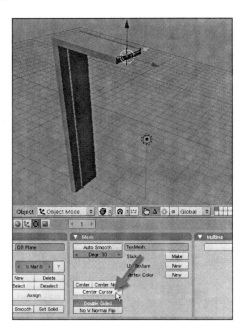

10. Now, we can add a **Mirror modifier**. There aren't any special parameters to define here, just select the right axis to make a copy. In this case, the axis is X. But depending on our **model orientation**, it could be Y instead, so it is a good idea to perform a test first. If the X axis doesn't give the result shown in the following image, try Y.

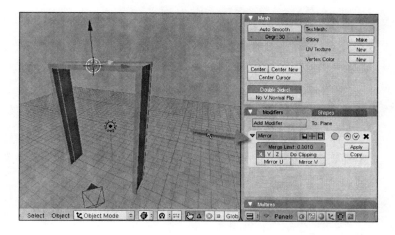

11. Now that we have the door frame, it's time to make the door. Change your view to Top, and create a cube. Remember to create the cube in **Object mode**. Use the S key to change the **scale of the cube**, to make it fit the frame.

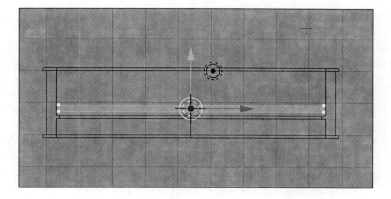

12. Change the view to Front, and adjust the cube again with the *S* key. Make it fit the **door frame**. Use the *CTRL* or *SHIFT* keys to adjust it with more precision.

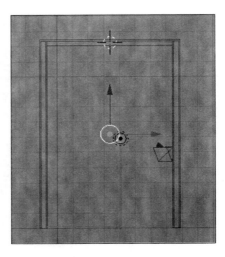

13. Now that our model is the required size, we can rotate the **cube** just a bit to make the door look as though it is being opened. If we just select the cube and rotate it, the rotation will take place at it's center, and won't give the effect that we want. To make it rotate at the correct pivot point, place the **3D cursor** at the point that should be used as the **rotation center**, and change the **Rotation/Scale Pivot** to **3D cursor**, as shown in the following image.

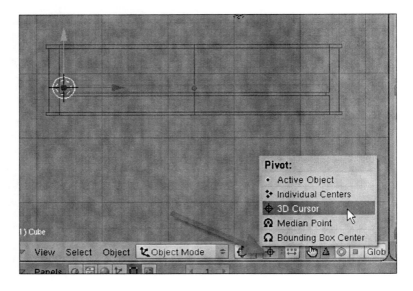

14. With the **pivot point** in the correct position, just press *R* to rotate the model. Don't rotate too much - just enough to give the impression that the door is half opened.

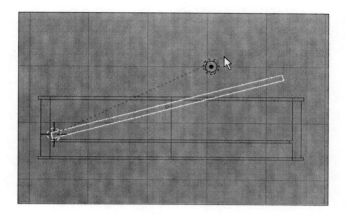

> **Removing doubles**
>
> Since we erased some faces in this model, it's a good practice at the end to select all objects, and with the **Specials menu**, remove all duplicated vertices.

And with that, our door model is ready. Again, depending on the requirements of the project, we could add more detail to the frame and the door. The tools and techniques for this will be exactly the same as the ones we have used to create this model. Just focus on this kind of modeling, which is called **edge modeling** and is based on extrusions of edges, to build your models.

Summary

In this chapter we have learned how to use the tools and techniques of Blender to create some more details for our models such as windows and doors. Although this is a complex subject, because of the many types of doors and windows used in architectural projects, we saw how to apply subdivision tools to create these models.

Some of the concepts learned in this chapter are:

- Rotation/Scale pivots
- Arrays to create multiple copies
- Applying mirror modifier to create symmetrical models
- Level of detail for models

6
Modeling Furniture

The next step for our scenes is to add some furniture, to further increase the realism. As furniture is a key element, every item of furniture that we add to the scene increases the level of detail, and the sense of realism. We can classify furniture into two : internal and external furniture.

With the first type, we have all the objects that populate our interior scenes such as sofas, beds, and chairs. The second type refers to items of urban furniture such as cars, fountains, and fences.

This kind of modeling deals with smaller scales, and because of this, sometimes, we have to work at a more detailed level than we are used to. This can cause the modeling process to take a bit longer than usual, but only if we need to create a good level of detail for our models. In this type of modeling, we will use the concept of level of detail again. We discussed this at the beginning of Chapter 5.

As we mentioned in Chapter 5, to use the concept of level of detail effectively, we must begin our projects with good planning. Otherwise, it will be useless to do any kind of optimization without knowing, for example, where the cameras will be.

Another interesting thing about furniture is that we can keep the models that we create to build a good library. With a good 3D models library, we can easily add previously created furniture into new projects, decreasing the time needed to fill up the scene with furniture.

We even can download or buy models on the Internet. The only thing that we will have to do in this case is import the model into our scene.

Create Models or Use a Library?

There are two possibilities when working with furniture. We can create new furniture, or use pre-made models from a library. The question is: when must we use each type? Some people say that using a pre-made model is not very professional thing but what they forget to say is that most projects have a tight deadline, and we need a quick modeling process to be ready on time. So, what's most important for professionals? Getting things done, or telling the client that all the models were created just for his project?

Of course, the deadline is the most important, and your clients normally won't mind if you use pre-made models. Probably they won't even notice. So don't be ashamed to use pre-made models they won't make your projects any less professional. It's even recommended to use these models to speed-up the process, and allow you to spend more time on lighting or texturing.

Is there any situation that demands the creation of a furniture model from scratch? Well, there are some. First, if you can't find the model in any library that you know, then it's going to be necessary to create it from scratch.

If you are working with an architect who designs the spaces and furniture as well, you will probably have to model the furniture too, since it won't be available at any public library. Any project that deals with customized furniture will require that we work on the modeling for the furniture.

Create your own library

A good practice for anyone doing architectural visualization is to collect a lot of 3D models from public libraries for use in future projects. Keep these models for later, but don't forget to check if the author has released the models with no restrictions for commercial use. Otherwise, you must get their permission to use them. If you want to create your library, with no restrictions, why not create your own models? This could be a good exercise: take a few examples, and start creating some furniture. With time, you will have a good number of models.

How to Get Started?

In most cases, we have to get used to all that furniture modeling. We will have to start from scratch, with no blueprints available. The only references that we will have would be the photos, either provided by our clients, or provided from some web resources.

If you have the time, visit a real store, and take some pictures and measures on your own. Sometimes, these stores will give you fliers and brochures, especially if you work with architecture. With time, you will get a lot of good reference material, and some of them come with measurements.

But, if you don't know where to get started, let me point out some great web resources:

- http://www.e-interiors.net
- http://resources.blogoscopia.com
- http://blender-archi.tuxfamily.org/Models
- http://www.katorlegaz.com/
- http://sketchup.google.com/3dwarehouse

The first link has a lot of reference images classified by furniture type and designer. And sometimes, they even provide free 3D models. Most models there are saved in DXF, or 3DS file formats.

Appending Models

Before we start to model, let's see how we can import a model form an external library into Blender. The process is very simple, and what we have to do is to use the **File** menu, and access the **Append or Link** option. There is a shortcut for that too - just press *SHIFT+F1* to call the same function.

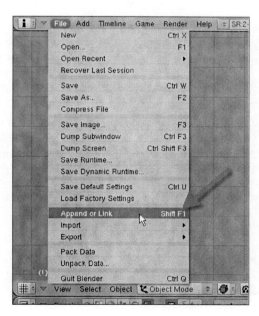

With this option, we have to select file that is already in the **Blender file format.** This option won't import files in other formats. When we select a file, a list of elements available in that particular file will be displayed, for us to select what we want to import. In most cases, the models will be stored under **Object.**

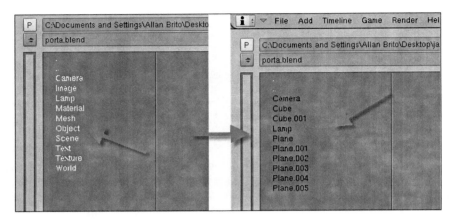

When we click the Object option, all of the objects available in the file will be listed. If you know the name of the object that you want to import, just select the name, and click **Load Library.** The object will be loaded into our scene.

Here, we have two options to handle this object: **Append or Link:**

- **Append**: If we choose this option, the object will be merged into our current scene.

- **Link:** With this option, an external link to the object file will be created. Any modifications to the original file will be reflected in our current scene.

What is the best method to use? It will depend on whether we are willing to track all modifications applied to our furniture models. Using the Link method is a great way of keeping the furniture updated, because every modification at the original file is reflected immediately in the scene in which this model is placed. However, we will have to take the original file with the scene file every time we need to put our scene on another computer. They always have to go together.

But if you choose to use the Append option, things will be a bit simpler, because the object will be incorporated into the scene file. We won't have to be worried about moving the furniture file along with the scene.

Always use the **Append** option when you want to use furniture, or any other model, saved in another Blender file. To use a furniture model saved in another file, with a type other than "**.blend**", we have to use the Import option.

Importing Models

To import a model, the process is very simple. We must use the **File** menu and select, **Import.** Then we have to select the proper file type from the list. The best file type, and the most common for furniture blocks, is the 3Ds file format, which belongs to the old 3D Studio application. There are some other good formats that work well with Blender, such as OBJ and LWO.

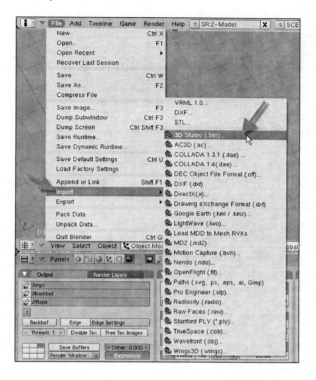

The 3Ds file format can store lights, and it works well with Blender. The only thing we have to take extra care about is that most models imported come with triangular faces, which are a bit harder to edit. But, if you don't need to make any modifications to the model, this won't be a problem.

Append or Import?

Just to make things clearer, if you download a furniture model from a web site, and it's saved in the Blender native file format **(.blend)**, you should append the model. If you download or get a furniture model on any file format other than **".blend"**, you will have to import it. Since most models aren't saved in the Blender native file format, we can safely say that almost all furniture models that you find will require an **import** action to be placed in your scenes.

Modeling a Chair

Let's start with something simple, such as a chair. Even for a simple model, it will help us deal with smaller dimensions and details. Here is an image of the model:

What's the main objective of this modeling? We have to create this chair, with the minimum use of faces and vertices. A good amount of detail can be left for textures, and it's always a good choice to use a lower number of vertices and faces in a model. If you consider one model, it won't matter much. But with a large number of chairs, such as in a theater room, it can make a difference in render time.

Let's get started with a simple cube. Select this cube, and change the **work mode** to **Edit.** Select all vertices and press the *W* key. This will open the **Specials** menu. Choose subdivide, just once, from this menu. This will create new vertices and edges. Once these new vertices have been created, as shown in the image to the left, below, press the *A* key to remove all of the objects from the selection.

Now, select the vertices to the right, using the *B* key. Remember to change the **view mode** to Wireframe before using the *B* key, otherwise, we won't be able to select the vertices behind the visible faces. When these vertices are selected, press the *X* key and choose **Vertices** to erase only the selected vertices.

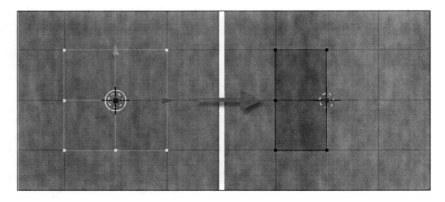

Using the *CTRL+R* key, add a new edge loop to the model, as shown in the following image:

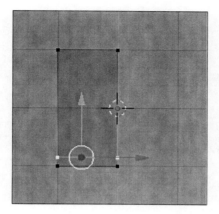

The next step is to change the scale of our model. Rotate the view to see the model in perspective view. Select all objects and press the *S* key, immediately after pressing the *Z* key. This will make the scale work only in the *Z* axis.

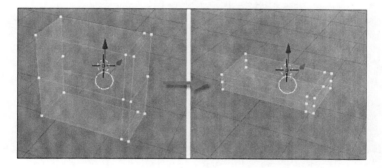

Now, select the vertices identified in the following image and erase them using the *X* key.

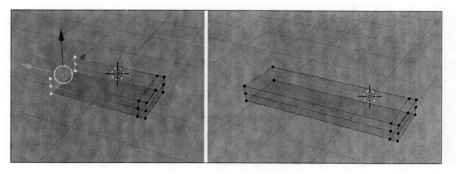

Change the **selection mode to Edges,** and select the edges identified in the following image. With the edges selected, press the *E* key to extrude them.

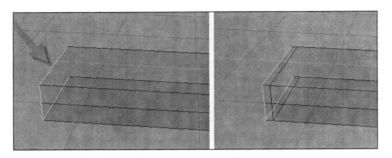

With the new faces created, we can now add some detail to the model. Select only the top edge of the previously created faces. Move this edge down just a bit. This will add a small declivity to the seat.

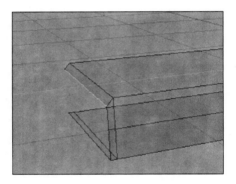

Now, we can move on to the next extrude, which must be from the selected edges identified in the following image. I'm not using any kind of measure for this example, but if you like to work only with real measurements, remember to hold the *CTRL* key every time a new extrude or edge is moved. This way, all transformations will use the grid lines. For this model, I'm not using vertex snap.

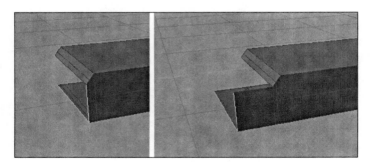

With the new faces created, select just the two edges identified in the following image. Extrude these edges until they reach the other side of the base model. Hold the *CTRL* key, while you extrude them, to help with the precision. If you already want to remove duplicated vertices, select all objects, and press the *W* key. Choose **Remove doubles** to erase any duplicated vertices.

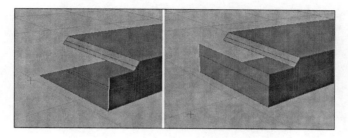

Select the edges identified in the image to keep adding more parts to the chair.

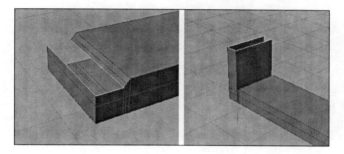

Extrude the edges three times until you have the same structure showed here.

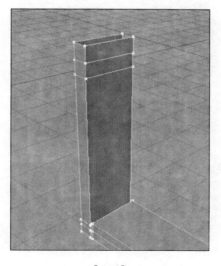

Now, we have to close the top with a face. To do that, we must select all four vertices on the top. When the vertices are selected, press the *F* key to create a new face.

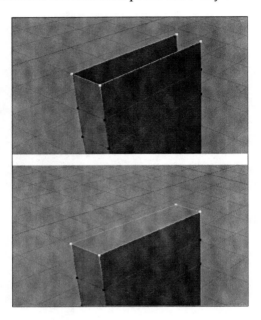

The next step is to select the small side edges to create some detail. Select just one edge, beginning from bottom to top, and move it just a bit. Repeat this operation with the other edges until we get the edges positioned as in the following image.

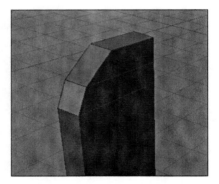

The basic shape of our chair has now been created. Now, we can make some adjustments for improving the overall proportions. Select all edges or vertices on the left side, and move them a bit to the left. This will make the model wider.

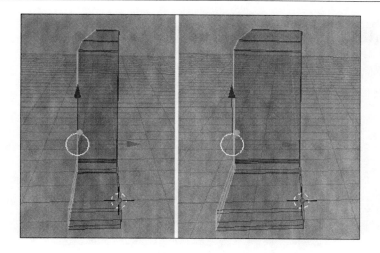

Did you notice that we have modeled only half a chair? Now we can make the other half, using the **Mirror modifier.** Add the modifier, and choose the right axis to make a perfect copy. If the **center point** for the model has been moved, you might need to edit the model to create a perfect mirrored match. Don't worry if you have moved the model by accident - this can happen sometimes. Along with the **Mirror modifier,** add a **Subsurf** modifier, too.

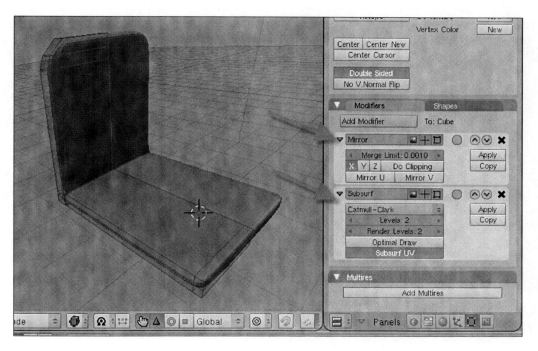

With the **Subsurf modifier,** we realize that this model needs a new edge loop on the left side. Just press *CTRL+R,* and add a new loop, as in the following image.

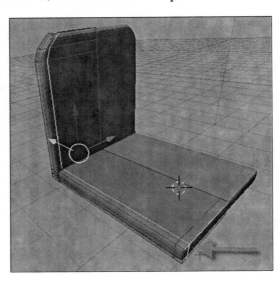

We can make the chair a bit curved at the back of the seat. Just select the vertices identified in the following image. Select them, and move them just a bit to the back. With the **Subsurf modifier,** we will be able to create a curved surface. Along with this curve, we can make some adjustments such as **downsizing** the seat.

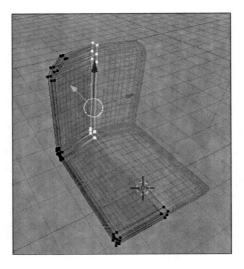

To finalize the model, we must add the support. Just add a cube and size it down until it looks like the following image .

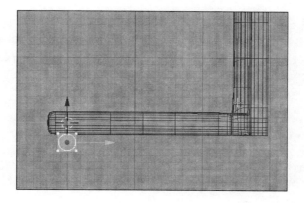

To change your view to one of the side views, just press the **3 key** on the numeric keypad. Select the vertices at the bottom of the cube, and move them down. When you place the vertices at the bottom, press the *S* key to scale them down. Create a copy of this cube, and place it at the back of the chair. With this copy, select the bottom vertices and move them to the right.

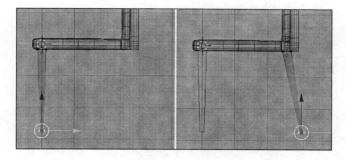

And now we have a chair model! I know it's simple, but we use the same principles for modeling more complex objects. All we have to do is use the tools wisely.

Modeling a Sofa

It is very simple to create certain kinds of models, as we saw in the last example. Almost every object can be modeled from a cube with some extrudes. And with a few adjustments, complex shapes can also be generated. But it only *looks* complex. In our next example, we will create a sofa from three cubes.

The first step in creating the sofa is to add a cube, if you don't have any objects in the **3D** view. Change your **view** to see the model from the **front view.** After selecting the cube, change the work mode to Edit, and select all the vertices of this cube. In this example, every transformation will be created holding the *CTRL* key down. This way, we will have more control over the proportions of the model.

When all vertices have been selected, move the cube a bit to the left. You can see in the image below that the **3D cursor** is placed to the right of the model. It means that the **object center** is placed there too.

Remove all vertices from the selection. Then select just the top **vertices**, and move them half way down. Hold down the *CTRL* key to make it easier. To finish this part, select only the vertices on the left side.

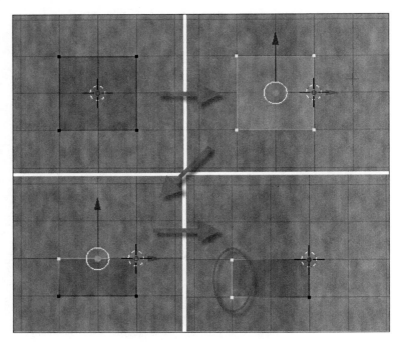

With the extrude tool, we create a structure like the one shown in the following image. The first thing to do is move the vertices a bit to the left, and then extrude the faces by using the *E* key. If you notice, all the new faces and edges are now perfectly aligned with the grid lines. This is because we are using the *CTRL* key.

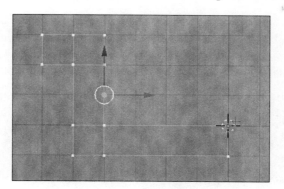

Now rotate your view, and select the faces on the back of the object. When the faces are selected, just move them to make our model a bit bigger.

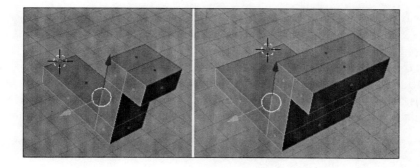

We must now rotate our view, to select the faces identified in the following image. These faces will be extruded.

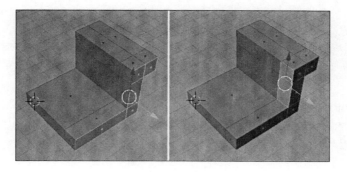

Press the *E* key to extrude the faces, again holding down the *CTRL* key. At the end of this process, select all faces and press the *W* key, and choose **Remove doubles.** We have to remove any duplicated vertices to clean up the model, since we created overlapping faces. But don't worry, with some editing, it won't have much effect on the final model.

Another thing to do before we go ahead is to select the faces identified in the image in the right. We have to erase the faces, since a **Mirror modifier** will be applied to the model. Once the faces are selected, just press the *X* key and choose **Faces**.

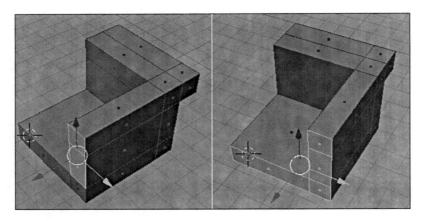

Now that the larger part of the sofa has been created, let's add some more details. Change your **view** to see the model by the **front.** Then, create a cube, and change the size of this cube to fit the place for the seat, as shown in the image on the right, below You can also change the view to adjust the model from the top, if you prefer.

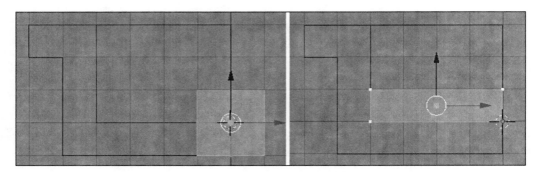

Create a copy of the cube, and adjust it's size to make it fit the back seat. A good thing to do here is to add more **edge loops,** using the *CTRL+R* key. This is necessary because we will apply a **Subsurf modifier**.

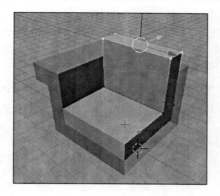

Using the *CTRL+R* key, add six new loops to the cube. Repeat the same process for the other cube. We have to add these new loops close to the existing edges, to control the curvature created by the **Subsurf,** later.

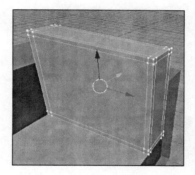

Select all vertices from the larger part of this sofa and press *W*. Choose the **Subdivide Multi** option. As a factor of the **subdivision**, choose 2, and we will have the following image as the result.

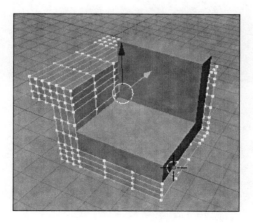

To complete this phase, add a **Subsurf modifier** to all objects. Since we've added a lot of new **edges loops,** there won't be any major problems with the resulting object. But if you think there is something that needs to be adjusted, feel free to add more details.

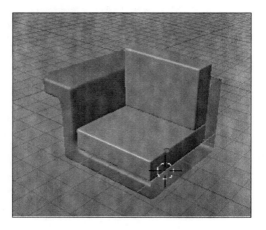

With a **Mirror modifier** added to each object, we will see the final result of this modeling. A simple sofa can become more detailed with a good set of textures or lighting.

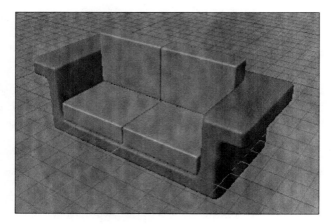

Building a library

You don't have to model all the furniture in the scene of a complex model. For instance, for the scene of a dining room, the walls can be modeled in one scene, while the tables and chairs can be modeled in others. To gather all these together in one single scene, we will use the **Append** option. You can follow this simple action: model single objects as individual files, and append them to the main scene. After a few projects, you will have built a significant number of individual furniture files, which will turn into your own furniture library.

Summary

We learned in this chapter how important it is to use furniture in our models and scenes to give the environment more details and realism. Here are some other things that we have learned:

- We can model our furniture and use a pre-made library too.
- Sometimes it is better to use a pre-made model.
- How to build your own furniture library for reuse in future projects.
- How to model a chair.
- How to model a sofa.

7
Materials

After passing through all the modeling processes, now we can work on some materials for our objects and overall scene. But what are materials? And what they can do for us? With materials, we can set up an object or surface, and determine how it interacts with light. This is the main concept: materials set up how a surface reflects or does not reflect the light. And of course, some other things such as textures and details.

If we get to think about it, this concept makes a lot of sense. The main difference of a stone surface and a wood surface is how they reflect visible light. Of course, I'm not talking about physical properties! Actually, the colors of all objects that we see are the colors of the reflected light, from the object's surface. This is how we see an object in the real world, and in the 3D world.

It is very important to understand this, because a lot of the parameters of the materials are based on how the material will react to light.

On account of this interaction with light, some artists usually set up the environment lighting, before setting up the materials. This will make the adjustments a lot easier in some cases. But for the overall process, you can start to work on the materials before lighting. Don't take it as a rule. Try setting up materials before and after, and see what works best for you. There is nothing like trying it yourself!

Now that we know more about materials and how important they are for improving the realism of your scenes, let's start working with them.

Creating and Organizing Materials

Before we start to use materials, let's see how to create and organize them. To apply a material to an object, we have to first select this object, and choose the material from the **shading panel**.

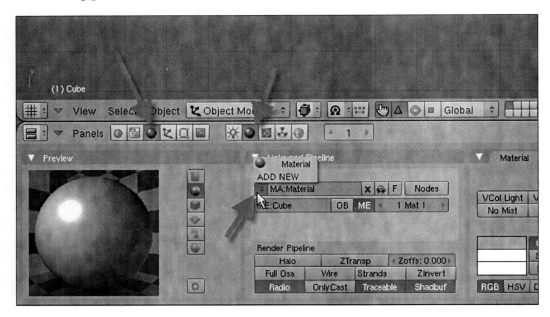

To select a material, we use the **combo box** point at **the image.** If we don't find any material that matches the properties of this particular object, we can always create a new one with the **ADD NEW** option. Sometimes, it can seem more practical to create a new material for every object, but avoid this kind of behavior. Try to use existing materials as much as possible, to optimize the resources for a scene. If you already have a glass material created, there is no point in creating a new material for another object, if they have the same configurations. Unless they have different properties, try to use the same material.

[**Shading Panel**
To open the **shading panel**, we can use the hotkey *F5*.]

Besides creating these materials, another good practice is to set unique names for all the materials. If we take a closer look, Blender always gives materials an auto-generated name, such as Material.001 or Material.002.

If a material has a name that represents the properties of some surface, it will make the process of searching for a specific material a lot easier. For instance, a material called **"Window_Glass"**, means a lot more than something called **"Material.005"**.

Changing the name of a material is very easy. Just select the material, and type this new name at the text box, as indicated in the following image.

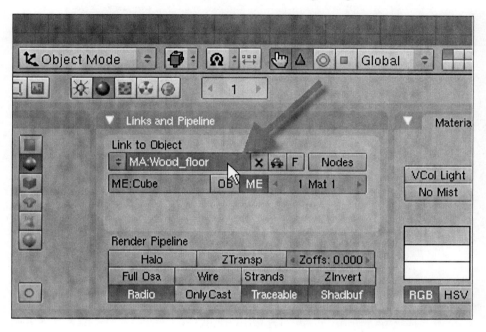

By the end of a big project, we will have a lot of materials organized and classified with semantic names. The best part of organizing the materials is that we will be able to use them again with future projects. Yes, we can import materials from other files with the **Append or Link** option in Blender.

To use this, we have to use the **Fle** menu and choose **Append or Link**. The same option can be called by the hotkey *SHIFT+F1*.

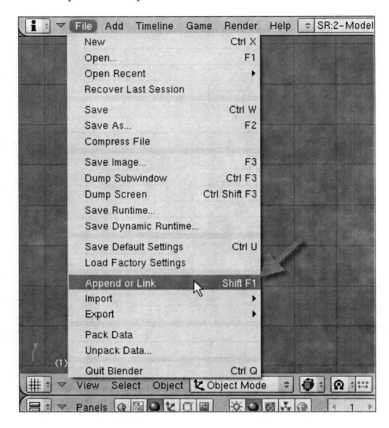

When we choose this option, a new window will appear. Then, we have to find the file that contains the materials that we want to import. Select the file, and browse through its contents. Of course, we have to select **materials** to see the list of materials available to import.

This list shows the names of all materials available with that file. See how important it is to give materials a good name? In this kind of situation, if you don't remember what kind of surface the material represents, a good name can be very helpful.

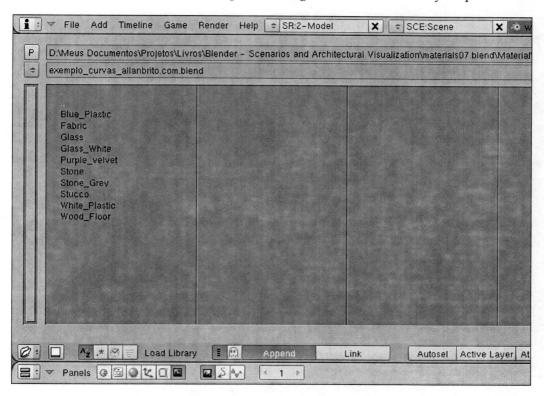

When you finish selecting the material, press the **Load Library** button.

If we have a material for a particular object, can this material be reused with changes in a few the properties? Well, consider that you have a scene where two objects that must be represented by glass have almost the same properties. We can create one material, and make a copy of this glass material, and paste its properties into another material's slot. Then all we have to do is make the necessary adjustments.

To create these copies, we have to use two small buttons. The button on the left is for copying the material properties, and the button on the right is for pasting the information into another slot.

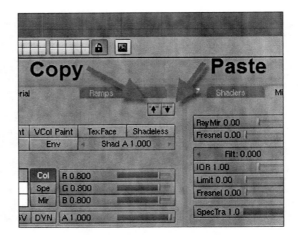

Material Color

Now that we know how to set up names and import materials from other scenes, let's start to work with the look and feel of materials. The first and the most basic aspect of any material is its colors. To give a material a particular color, we have two options: a solid color, or a gradient color. The first one is the simplest, and we choose it with the **colour picker.**

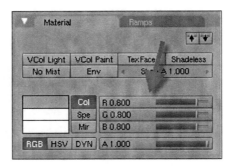

Just click over the small rectangle, and choose the desired color. If you find it more useful, we can use a mixer to choose the color by blending different indexes of RGB, HSV, and DYN. Looking from an artist's point of view, the **color picker** is the best choice, but feel free to choose the color anyway you like it.

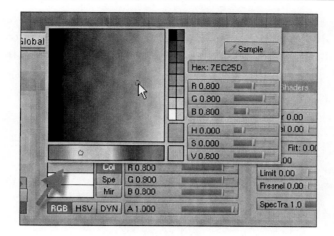

If we take a closer look, there are three color pickers, which can set up the color in three different aspects of the material.

- Diffuse Color
- Specular Color
- Mirror Color

Gradient Colors

Besides the solid colors, we can choose **gradient ramps** for our materials. To use this kind of color, choose the **Ramps** tab.

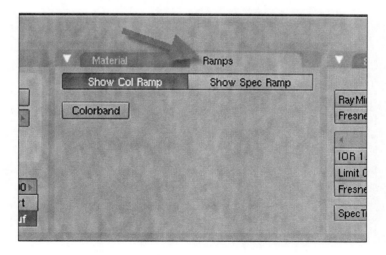

In this menu, we can turn on the use of color ramps for materials. There are two options: choose **Show Col Ramp** or **Show Spec Ram**. When we turn any of these options on, and press the **Colorband** button, the **ramps** menu will show all the options available to set up these colors.

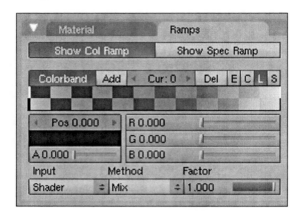

To work with these menus, we have to understand how they manage colors. First, there is a horizontal bar, which represents the gradient. All gradients are created by a collection of color indexes, which are represented by numbers. At the beginning, only two indexes are created. The position of an index is represented by a vertical white line. We can easily move this line by clicking on it, and dragging the mouse.

When the line is moved, the color position and the gradient changes.

Let's see a few more important commands for these gradients:

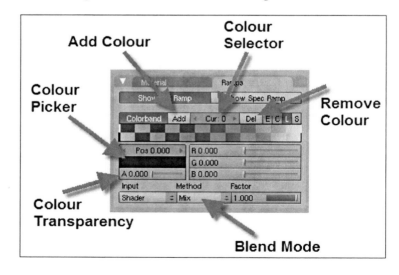

- **Color selector**: With this option, we can select the active index.

- **Add Color**: Here, we can add a new color index, if we need more than two indexes.

- **Remove Color**: If you want to remove an index, use this option. Before hitting this button, select the index that must be removed as the active index.

- **Color transparency**: Here, we can set up how transparent the color will be. If we have a very transparent color, the background of the material will be visible at the rendering.

- **Blending mode**: This option determines how the ramp will blend with the material color and background.

- **Color picker**: Here, we have a color picker to choose a different color in a more visual way.

With these options, we can set up a good color gradient for our materials, and give them a very organic look. Here are some objects and surfaces which can easily be represented by ramps:

- Vegetation
- Velvet
- Skin
- Fabrics

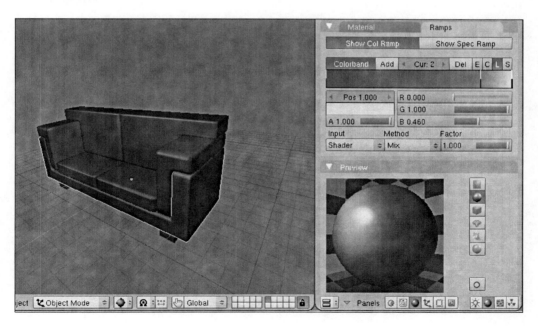

Shaders

The shaders determine how a material reacts with visible lights. On the materials panel, we can choose two types of **shaders**: **diffuse and specular shaders**.

Diffuse

A diffuse shader determines how much light is reflected by the surface. Let's make things clear here. It doesn't mean that the object will generate illumination. If we set up a high reflection value for the diffuse shader, it will mean that the object will be brighter.

We have five different kinds of shaders at the **Blender materials panel**.

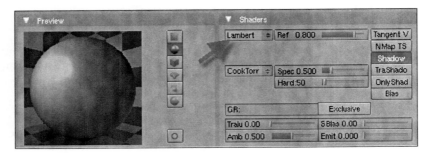

All these **shaders** share common parameters, like the **Ref**. This option sets how much light is reflected. So if we set up a high value, the material will look very bright, and lower values will make the material darker.

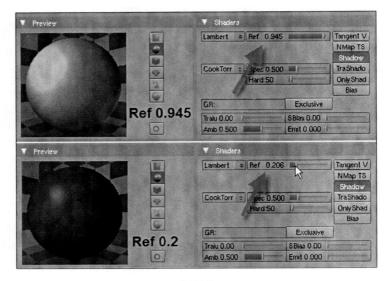

What is the best setup? It will depend on the type of surface that you want to simulate. The key to set up a good diffuse shader is the **Ref**.

Specular

The specular shader controls a kind of reflection of light, which depends on the point of view and the angle at which the light hits the surface. This **shader** is very important to set up materials such as glass, metals, and other reflective surfaces. All those surfaces have a particular way of behaving with reflections.

Just like **diffuse**, we have five different **shaders** here. All those **shaders** share common parameters. The most important are **Spec and Hard**.

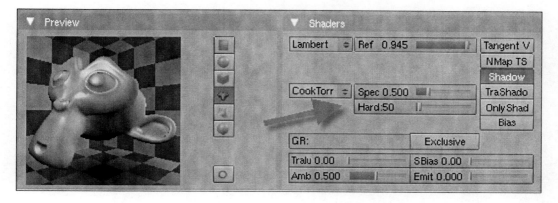

- **Spec:** This option will set up how hard the **specular reflection** is. High values will make the reflection stronger.

- **Hard:** With this option, we can make a soft or hard border for **specular** reflections.

With these two options, we can simulate a lot of materials. For instance, surfaces formed by glass objects have a high **Spec** and **Hard** values. Surfaces such as concrete have a medium **Spec value**, and a very low **Hard value**.

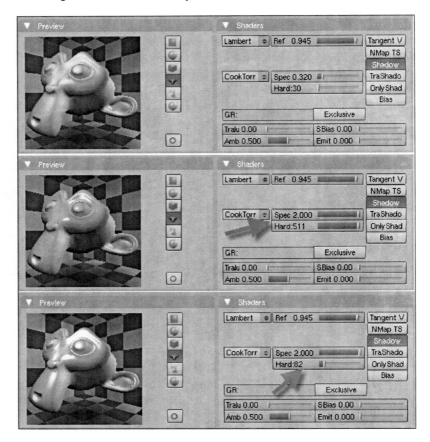

Ray Tracing

Materials that use ray tracing parameters can have an extra level of realism, because they can show reflections and transparency based on more sophisticated calculations. With these options, we can make more realistic materials such as glass and mirrors.

To use these options, we must set up the **MirrTransp** menu. This menu holds all the options to set up ray tracing materials.

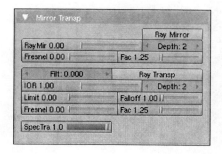

Creating Glass

To create a good glass or transparent material, we have to turn on the **Ray Trans** button. When this button is turned on, all materials will have better transparency. Along with this option, we have to use the Alpha value to make the material transparent.

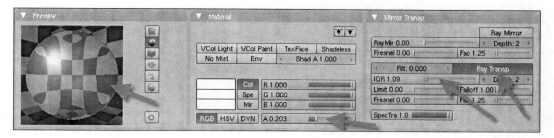

If the **Ray Transp** is turned on, and the alpha is set to any value below one, the material will be transparent. Another aspect of transparency that we can set up is the IOR, which determines how the object changes the **light rays'** trajectories.

The base value for some kinds of materials can be preconfigured, according to these values:

- Glass: 1.5
- Water: 1.33
- Diamond: 2.4
- Plastic: 1.46

If you want to render a material with this configuration, just make sure that the **Ray** button is turned on in the **rendering options**.

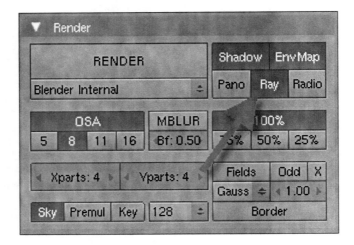

Together, these options can produce almost any kind of transparent material; we just have to find the best options for a particular case.

 Turn off Ray for test renderings

If you want to speed up the rendering for test purposes, always turn off the **Ray** Button. When you do that, all properties that uses ray tracing will be off. So, the render time will drop. When you feel that the rendering is fine, turn it on again.

Simple Glass

If the objective is to produce a simple glass, just decrease the **Alpha value** and turn on the **ZTransp** button. This button is right below the text area where we can set up a name for the material.

ZTransp is different from the **Ray Mirror** option in that, with **ZTransp,** we can see through an object, based on its **alpha value**. There are no calculations for color, or anything else. It's simpler and faster, but not very realistic.

Mirrors and Reflections

The other option for ray traced materials is reflections, which allows us to create mirrors and materials with reflections. To use reflections, we must turn on the **Ray Mirror** button, and set up the **RayMir slider**. Higher values will produce a stronger reflection, and make the material look like a mirror.

To control the amount of reflection, we can use the **Fresnel slider**. It controls how reflective an object is, based on the angle from which we view the surface. With a **Fresnel** value of 0, we have a perfect mirror. But with higher values, the reflection will decrease based on the angle from which we view the surface. For instance, if we have a varnished wood floor, even though it's reflective, it's not a perfect reflection. Depending on the view angle, it's more or less reflective.

The **Fresnel** setting can be used for reflections and transparency as well, with the same objective, that is, to control the amount of ray trace by the viewing angle. Right next to **Fresnel** is the **Fac** option, which controls the blending amount for the **Fresnel effect**.

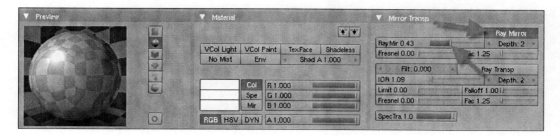

Almost all materials have some level of reflection, especially materials such as glass, water, stones, and some kinds of wood. If you have a scene where these types of materials are used, applying some kind of reflection will increase the realism.

Again, the best level of reflection will depend a lot on the various other factors in your scene. So, don't be afraid to test and play a bit with this slider.

If you want to create mirrors, don't forget to change the material color to something closer to black.

Reflections and transparency

Remember that while all these options can make our scenes look more real, they make the rendering process longer. Use these options, but remember not to use them everywhere, unless you have very strong computer hardware.

Ray-traced Shadows

If we work with transparent materials such as glass or plastic, we may want these objects to cast shadows based on their respective colors. For instance, suppose we have a window with a glass that is green. In the real world, all the shadows cast by this glass won't be a hundred percent black and will turn their color to green. We can achieve the same thing in Blender.

To use it, we must turn on the **TraShadow** parameter in the **Shaders menu**. This option must be turned on for the material that has to receive the shadow, and not the one that will cast it.

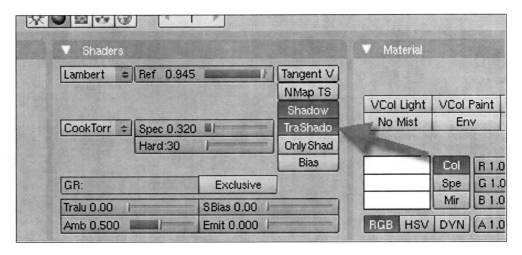

For instance, a glass object is casting a shadow, and this shadow will be projected on the floor. The floor material must have the **TraShadow** turned on to receive a shadow based on the material color and transparency level.

Wireframe Materials

With an option called **Wire,** we can determine that some materials should be rendered only with the wire frame. If you want to show a more structured view of a 3D model, this can be a very interesting option. Just select the material, and turn on the **Wire option**.

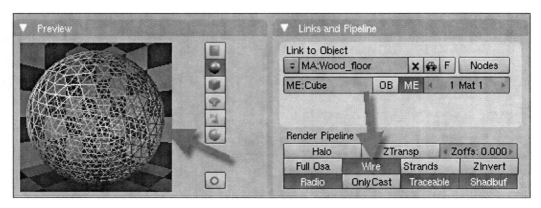

Self-illumination

There is a very interesting option available in the materials setup, which allows us to set up a material to emit light. But it won't generate any kind of illumination for the scene; it will only make the material brighter.

To use it, we can set up the **Emit parameter** in the **Shaders menu**. Make the adjustments to get the desired look, but remember that higher values will make the material color look very saturated.

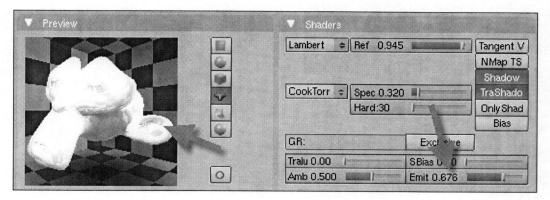

Why can't this option generate light? The Blender internal renderer can't do global illumination. With Blender, light energy can be cast only by light objects such as lamps. There is nothing wrong with it, and that's the way most 3D packages work. If you want to do global illumination, which is another way to work with 3D materials and lights, Blender has some nice external **renderers** that can do **Global Illumination** such asYafRay and Indigo.

In Chapter 12, we will take a detailed look on how YafRay works and use Global Illumination in our scenes.

Summary

In this chapter, we have learned what materials are, and how they can give more realism to our scenes. Let's see what we have learned:

- How to create materials
- How to organize materials
- How to import materials between scenes
- How to set up a material color
- How to determine how the material reacts to light
- How to use ray-tracing materials
- How to create transparent materials
- How to create materials with reflections

With materials, we can create more realistic scenes. What we have to do now is practice and apply these materials to a real scene. The next chapter will push materials to the next level with textures.

8
Textures

In the last chapter, we talked about materials and how they can increase the level of realism in our scenes. Well, with textures we can take this realism to a higher level. With textures, the "magic" really happens!

Before we start to dig into textures, let me say that the biggest problem of working with them is actually finding or creating a good texture. That's why, its highly recommended that you start as soon as possible to create your own texture library. Textures are mostly image files, which represent certain kinds of surfaces such as wood or stone. They work like wallpaper, which we can place on a surface or object. For instance, if we place an image of wood on a plane, it will give the impression that the plane is made of wood. That's the main principle of using textures. We will make an object look like something in the real world using a texture. For some projects, we may need a special kind of texture, which won't be found in a common library. So we will have to take a picture ourselves, or buy an image from someone.

But don't worry, because often we deal with common surfaces that have common textures too.

Procedural Textures vs. Bitmap Textures

Blender has basically two types of textures, which are procedural textures and bitmap textures. Each one has both positive and negative points. Which one is the best will depend on your project needs.

- **Procedural**: This kind of texture is generated by the software at rendering time, just like vector lines. This means that it won't depend on any type of image file. The best thing about this type of texture is that it is resolution independent, so we can set the texture to be rendered with high resolutions with minimum loss of quality. The negative point about this kind of texture is that it's harder to get realistic textures with it.

- **Bitmap**: To use this kind of texture, we will need an image file, such as a JPEG, PNG, or TGA file. The good thing about these textures is that we can achieve very realistic materials with it quickly. On the other hand, we must find the texture file before using it. And there is more. If you are creating a high resolution render, the texture file must be big.

Texture Library

Do you remember the way we organized materials? We can do exactly the same thing about textures. Besides setting names and storing the Blender files to import and use again later, collecting bitmap textures is another important point. Even if you don't start right away, it's important to know where to look for textures. So here is a small list of websites that provides free texture download.

- http://www.blender-textures.org
- http://www.cgtextures.com
- http://blender-archi.tuxfamily.org/textures

Applying Textures

To use a texture, we must apply a material to an object, and then use the **texture** with this material. We always use the texture inside a material. For instance, to make a plane that simulates a marble floor, we have to use a texture and set up how the surface will react to **light and texture**, which can give the surface a proper look of marble using any **texture.** To do that, we must use the **texture panel**, which is located right next to the materials button. We can use a keyboard shortcut to open this panel: just hit *F6*.

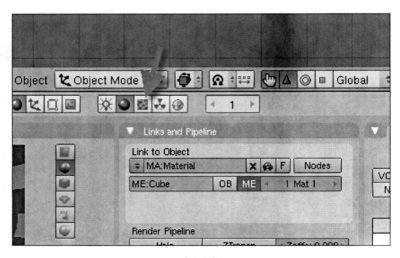

There is a way to add a texture in the **material panel** as well, with a menu called **Texture**.

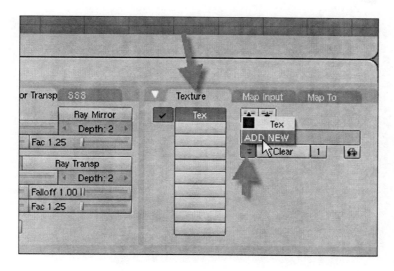

The best way to get all the options is to add the texture on the **texture panel**. On this panel, we will be able to see a lot of buttons, which represent the **texture channels**. Each one of these channels can hold a texture. The final texture will be a mix of all the channels. If we have a texture at channel 1 and another texture at channel 2, these textures will be blended and represented in the material.

Before adding a new texture, we must select a channel by clicking over one of them. Usually the first channel is selected, but if you want to use another one, just click on the channel. When the channel is selected, just click the **Add New** button to add a new texture.

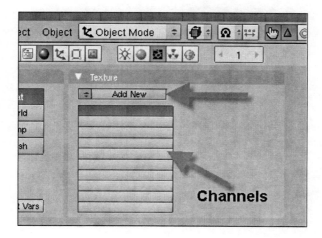

The **texture controls** are very similar to the **material controls**. We can set a name for the **texture** at the top, or erase it if we don't want it anymore. With the **selector**, we can choose a previously created texture too—just click and select.

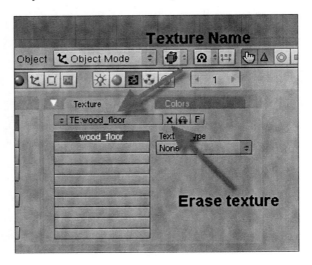

Now comes the fun part. Having added a texture, we have to choose a **texture** type. To do that, we click on the **texture type combo box**.

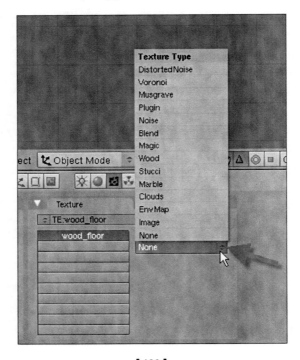

There are a lot of textures, but most of them are **procedural textures** and we won't use them much. The only texture type that isn't procedural is the image type.

We can use textures like **Clouds** and **Wood** to create some effects and give surfaces a more complex look, or even create a **grass texture** with some dirt on it. But most times, the **texture type** that we will be using will be the **Image** type.

Each texture has its own set of parameters to determine how it will look in the object. If we add a **Wood texture**, it will show the **configuration parameters** at the right.

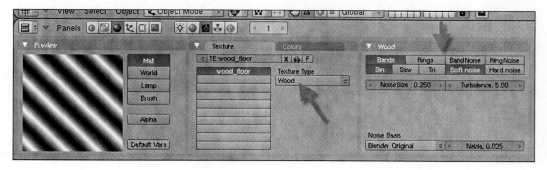

If we choose as texture type **Clouds**, the parameters showed at the right will be completely different.

With the image texture type it's not different, this kind of texture has its own type of setup. This is the **control panel**:

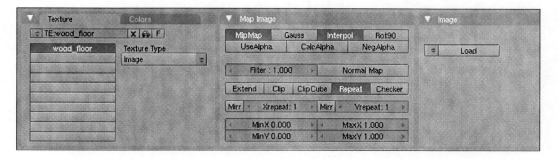

To show how to set up a texture, let's use an image file that represents a **wood floor** and a plane. We can apply the texture to this plane and set up how it's going to look, testing all the parameters.

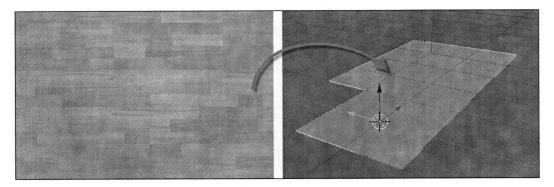

The first thing to do is assign a material to the plane, and add a texture to this material. We choose as texture type the **Image** option. It will show the **configuration options** for this kind of texture.

To apply the image as a texture to the plane, just click on the **Load button**, situated on the **Image menu**. When we hit this button, we will be able to select the **image file.**

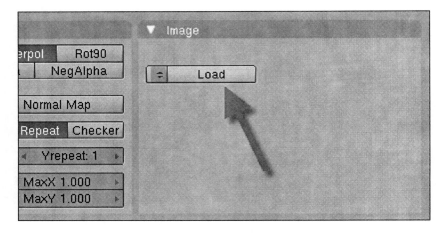

Locate the **image file** and the **texture** will be applied. If we want to have more control over how this texture is organized and placed on the plane, we need to learn how the controls work. Every time you make any changes to the setup of a texture, these changes will be shown in the **preview window**; use it a lot to make good changes.

Here is a list of what some of the buttons can do for the texture:

- **UseAlpha**: If the **texture** has an **alpha channel**, we have to press this button for Blender calculate the channel. An image has an alpha channel when some kind of transparency is stored in the image. For instance, a .png file with **transparent background** has an **alpha channel**. We can use this to create a texture with a **logo**, for a bottle, or to add an image of a tree or person to a plane.

- **Rot90**: With this option we can rotate the texture by 90 degrees.

- **Repeat**: Every texture must be distributed on the **object surface**, and repeating the **texture** in **lines** and **columns** is the default way to do that.

- **Extended**: If this button is pressed, the texture will be adjusted to fit all the **object surface area**.

- **Clip**: With this option, the texture will be cropped and we will be able to show only a part of it. To adjust which parts of the texture will be displayed, use the **Min/Max X/Y options**.

- **Xrepeat / Yrepeat**: This option determines how many times a texture is repeated, with the repeat option turned on.

- **Normal Map**: If the texture will be used to create **Normal Maps**, press this button. These are textures used to change the face normals of an object.

- **Still**: With this button selected, we can determine that the image used as texture is a still image. This option is marked by default.

- **Movie**: If you have to use a movie file as texture, press this button. This is very useful if we need to make something like a **theatre projection screen** or a **tv screen**.

- **Sequence**: We can use a sequence of images as texture too; just press this button. It works the same ways as with a **movie file**.

There are a few more parameters, like the **Reload button**. If your texture file suffers any kind of change, we must press this button for the changes get accepted by Blender. The **X button** can erase this texture; use it if you need to select another image file.

When we add a texture to any material, an external link is created with this file. This link can be absolute or relative. When we add a texture called "wood.png", which is located at the root of your main hard disk, like C:, a link to this texture will be created like this: "c:\wood.png", so every time you open this file, the software will look for that file at that exact place. This is an absolute link, but we can use a relative link as well. For instance, when we add a texture located in the same folder as our scene, a relative link will be created.

Every time we use an **absolute link** and we have to move the ".blend" file to another computer, the texture file must go with it. To imbue the **image file** with the **.blend**, just press the icon of **gift package**.

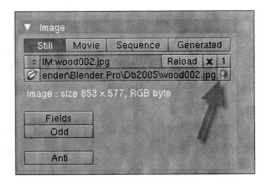

To save all the textures used in a scene, just access the file menu and use the **Pack Data option**. It will make all the texture files embedded with the **source blend file**.

Mapping

Every time we add a texture to any object, we must choose a mapping type to set up how the texture will be applied to the object. For instance, if we have a wall and apply a **wood texture**, it must be placed like wallpaper. But for **cylindrical** or **spherical objects**, or even walls, we have to set up in a way that makes the texture adaptable to the topology of the surface, to avoid effects such as a stretched texture.

To set this up, we use the **mapping options**, which are located on the **Map Input menu**.

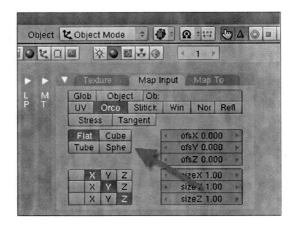

On this menu, we can choose between four basic **mapping types** which are **Cube, Sphere, Flat, and Tube**. If you have a wall, choose the option that matches the topology type with the model. In this case, the best choice is the **Cube**.

Another important option here is the **UV button**, which allows us to use another very powerful type of texturing, based on **UV Mapping**.

Normal Map

This is a special and useful type of texture, that can change the normals of surfaces. If we have a **floor and a texture of ceramic tiles**, the surface can be represented with smaller details of that tiling, using this kind of a map. It's almost like modeling the tiles. But everything is created using just a **normal map**.

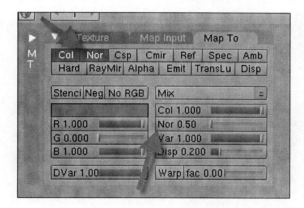

To use this kind of texture, we must turn on the **Nor** button on the **Map To** menu. When this button is turned on, we can set up the **Nor slider** to determine the intensity of the normal displacement.

It works based on the pixel color of the texture. With **white pixels**, the normals are not affected, and with **black pixels**, the normals are fully translated. If you want to optimize the **normal mapping**, using a special texture is much recommended. Some texture libraries even have this type of normal maps ready for use. They can be called **bump maps** too.

Here is an example of how we can use them. We take a stone texture and a **tiled texture** with a **white background and black lines**.

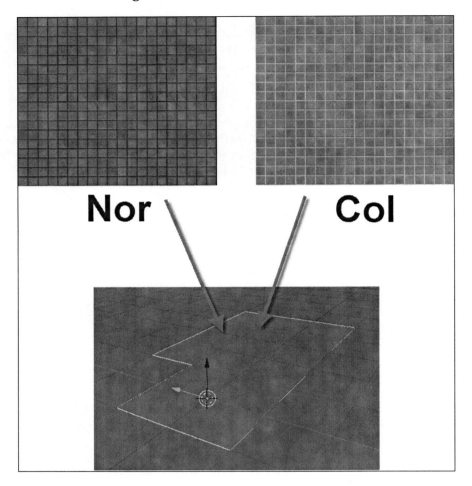

The stone texture is applied to the floor, and the **tiled texture** is used to create a tiling for the floor. The setup for that is really simple. Just apply the texture at a **lower channel**, and turn off the **Col button** for this channel. Turn on the **Nor button**, and this texture will affect only the normals and not the material color. Any image can be used as a normal map, but we will always get better results with a greyscale image prepared to be used as a normal map. Now, just set up the **Nor intensity** with the **slider**, and see the **render**.

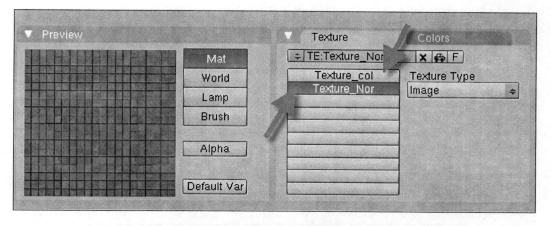

[

Turn on positive and turn on negative

Some of the buttons on the **Map To menu** can be turned on with positive
and negative values. For instance, the **Nor option** can be turned on with
one click. If we click on it again, the **Nor text** will turn yellow. This means
that the Nor is inverted with negative values. Some other buttons may
present the same option.

]

UV Mapping

For some models, just placing an image at a surface is not enough. We have to take
more control over all textures, and even create a more **personalized texture** for a
model. With **UV Mapping**, we can create a **texture image** that fits exactly with all
the surfaces of a model, with the possibility to add details, such as dirt and small
imperfections to the texture image. Some of the painting of a texture can be done in
Blender. We will take a look at that in the next chapter.

This kind of editing has to be done outside Blender, with painting software such as Gimp or Photoshop. Once this editing is created, we have to just apply the new texture again to the model.

What do we have to do to create a texture like this? The process for using this kind of texture is simple, although the task can demand a bit of editing. We must mark the model with some cutting lines called **seams**.

Let's see how it works with a wall. The first step is to select the model and change the work mode to **UV Image Editing**.

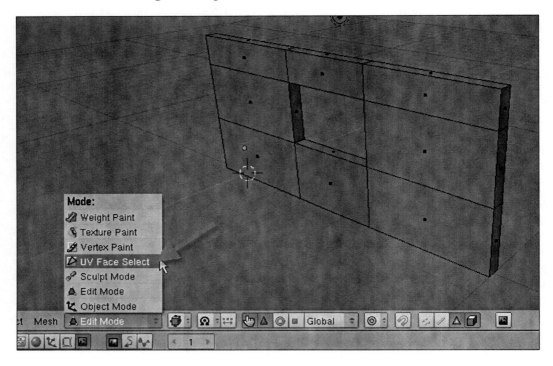

Change the selection **mode** to **edge,** and select a few edges. Press the *CTRL+E* shortcut, and choose the **Add Seam option**. With this, we will mark the cutting for the model. What's the best **edge to mark**? Well here, we will have to use a bit of imagination.

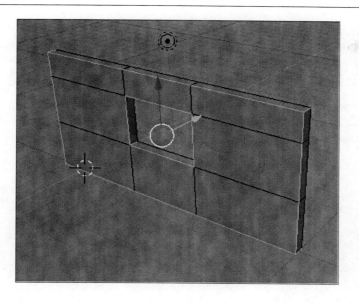

To choose the best edges, we must imagine the best places to mark and unfold the model. When the seams are marked, open a new window, and change the **window type** to **UV/Image Editing**.

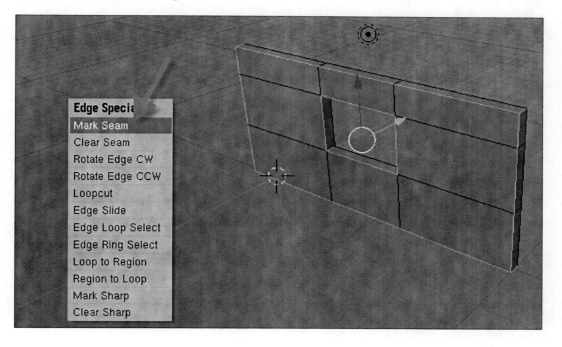

When this new window is opened, press the *U* button. It will call the **unwrap function** and create a flat layout with the **unfolded model**. Sometimes this operation requires a lot of testing and adjustment to produce a good result. But with the right seams, it will produce a nice and good flat image with all surfaces.

Now, we have to export this layout as an image. To do that, we use a very good script called "Save **UV Face Layout...**". Just access the UV menu in the **UV/Image Editing window** and choose **Scripts | Save UV Face Layout...**.

It will call a small menu, with the options for this script.

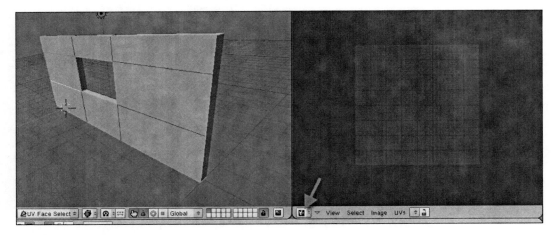

To set up the layout, we must change the following parameters:

- **Size**: Here, we can set up the size of the image. Always use a big value to create high-resolution textures. Use 1024, 2048, or bigger.
- **Wire**: The layout will be saved with the wires from all faces. This option will determine the width of these wires.
- **Object**: With this button turned on, the object name will be used for the file name.
- **All Faces**: This button sets up the script to export all faces, and not just the selected ones.
- **Edit**: With this button turned on, an image editing software is opened right after the layout is exported.

After editing the layout, we can apply the layout as a texture. But we must turn on the **UV button** at the **Map Input menu**. It will make the material look for a **UV Mapping** image to be shown.

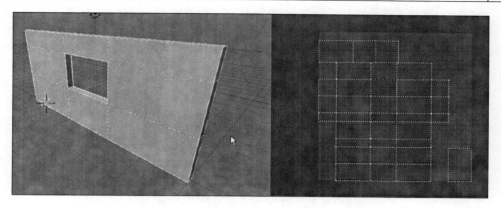

Now, all we have to do is press *F12* to render the image, and the texture will be applied to the object.

Unwrapping Scripts

The operation of creating a UV Mapping can be very annoying for some people, because we have to imagine the unfolded model to mark the seams. To help us in this task, there are a few Scripts to automatically create the seams and unfold the model. One of them is projected especially for architectural models.

The name of this script is **ArchiMap UV Projection Unwrapper**, and it's very easy to use. Just open a new window and choose a **UV/Image Editor** as the window type. Then, with the **UV menu**, choose the **Scripts option** and call the **script**.

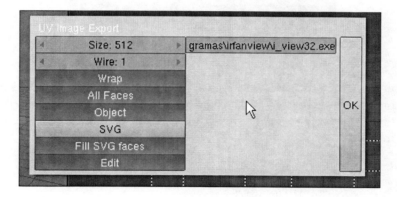

The **Angle Limit** will determine how the faces will be unfolded. Bigger angles will generate layouts with grouped **faces**, and smaller angles will create layouts with more islands. The selected **faces** button makes the script unfold only the **selected faces** or all faces.

The **Stretch to Boun** button, makes the layout fit the **UV layout**. The **Bleed Margin** determines a limit for the **UV layout** to grow outside the limits of the window. And with **Fill Quality**, we can set up the overall quality of the filling for the faces, if the **Fill Holes** button is pressed.

See how it works for this model:

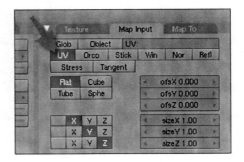

Selecting the model and calling the script will result in the following layout.

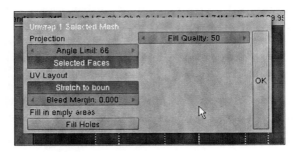

Summary

In this chapter, we have learned how to use textures to give our materials more realism. There are basically two types of textures, which are procedural and bitmap. For us, the bitmap textures will be the most useful, for the creation of scenes with more realism.

Besides that, we also learned how to:

- Choose and organize textures
- Apply and set up a bitmap texture
- Map a texture around a model
- Use normal maps
- Create UV Layouts to create more complex textures

9
UV Mapping

If you try to use textures on any kind of 3D model, you probably know that one of the biggest problems of textures, besides making them, is the adjustment process required to apply the image over the surfaces. Most people simply tile the textures, using a small image to fill up a big surface. It may appear faster, but the end result is very artificial and poor.

This is because the viewer will be able to see a lot of the repetitive patterns normally associated with computers and artificiality, which gives away the fact the image was produced with a computer.

How do we solve the problem? Avoiding the use of tiled textures is the first step. But if we avoid them, we still have to fill up the surface of your models with the textures. This is where UV Mapping enters, letting us customize and have full control over the textures, without the use of tiles.

What is UV Mapping?

With UV Mapping, we can tell the software to place textures at an exact location. The U and V are transformed coordinates used to place texture on a 3D surface. When we create a UV map, the computer has all instructions to place the textures that the artist wants on a face.

The process of UV mapping is very simple. We mark the edges of a model and break it into several parts to unfold the 3D model, as if it were made out of paper. These cuts have to be made at the key edges of the model, otherwise it won't unfold correctly. After that, we have to generate an image that contains all the faces of the model. With this image, we go to an image editing software such as Gimp or Photoshop to add and edit the texture map.

When the **texture** is placed, we save the image and take it back to Blender, where the same image can be aligned with the faces. Then, we will have all the **textures** placed and adjusted correctly.

Why UV Mapping?

Are you asking yourself right now if this is the best way to texture a model? Well, it's certainly not the easiest way, but a the tool that gives us more control over textures and helps us avoid the use of tiling. Work on the textures can be the key reason for the success or the failure of a project involving Architectural Visualization. Even if you manage to create an incredible illumination for the model, giving it a realistic look, a poorly textured wall or floor can give it away.

Use the UV Mapping technique only when you need full control over textures, or for the Interactive Animations created with the Blender Game Engine. Depending on the type of surface or project, a tiled texture will sometimes be the best choice.

Marking the Model

The first step, that we have to accomplish to use UV Mapping is the slicing of the model. Here, we won't use tools such as the knife or the Loop Cut, but a different tool, which will allow us to mark a seam on the model. To do that, we use a short cut —just press *CTRL+E*, and a menu that groups all edge operations will appear.

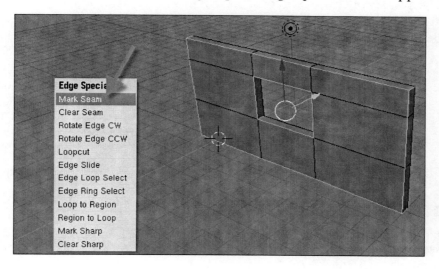

When we press this shortcut, a menu will appear giving us a lot of options. One of these options is the **Mark Seam**, which we will use to actually mark the edges of our model. These marks will be used to unfold the faces of the model.

In order to use this option, we have to select an edge either by selecting two vertices, or selecting the actual edge. Once you select it and activate **Mark Seam**, an orange line will mark the edge, making it easy to identify where the seams are.

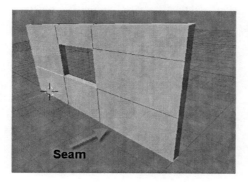

To remove a **Seam**, use the same shortcut and choose **Clear Seam**. As you may be wondering, making only one **Seam** won't help us much. Sometimes a model, depending on the complexity, may require a lot of **Seams** to be unfolded. Before you start marking them, take some time to plan which edges will require **Seams** for your model.

It won't be a waste of time, if we consider that this process can actually save the time spent on revision and rework. So, take a few minutes before you start to visualize where the seams will be required to unfold your model.

Don't change the model!

If you decide to use UV Mapping, it's very important to use only the final version of your models. Any kind of change in the topology of the model will require all work on the UV Mapping to be restarted. So, don't start to mark seams if you know that your model may have some changes. And if your client, or you project requires some changes in the topology of the model, be ready to start all over again.

What Makes a Good Seam?

Creating the seams is only a part of the task, whereas creating the seams in a way that makes your job easier is the real challenge. But what makes a good seam? Where are the best places to mark?

If you want to make your job easier while **texturing**, try to leave all faces that get the same type of texture together. For instance, all the faces of walls should be left together. This way, it will be easier to adjust a **brick texture**, which should then be applied to all of them.

The best way to organize these faces is with islands of faces. Before you organize the faces, try to identify the faces that should be placed together as islands. Grouping them by type is a good start, such as putting faces for walls, floors, and ceilings as islands.

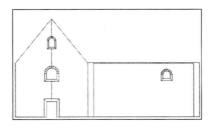

With that in mind, we can plan the best places to mark the seams that will result in those islands.

Unfold the Model

When all the seams are marked, the next step is to **unfold** the model. Before we unfold the model, there is a special window type that will help us in the process of **UV Mapping**. To see it we create a new division in the Blender interface and in the new window choose the **UV/Image Editor window**.

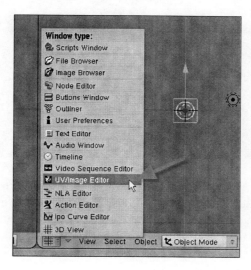

With this window, we will be able to see the **unfolded model** and handle all types of images for texturing. There is even a small editor and paint tool, which allows us to edit and paint the texture without the aid of an external image editor.

With this window open and all seams marked, we have to press the *U* key in the **3D View** to activate the UV tools.

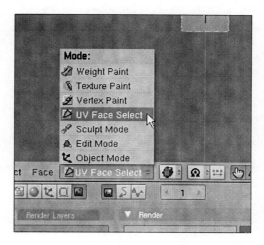

After all that, all we have to do to unfold the model is to choose the **Unwrap** option. It will then unfold the model, and show the resulting image in the **UV/Image Editor** window.

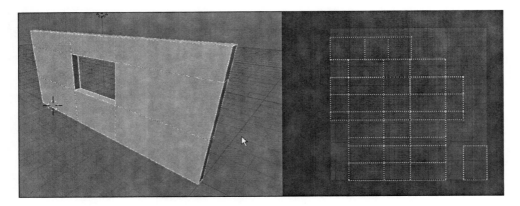

Don't worry if things are not the way you wanted at the first result. Make a small analysis of the faces, and try to identify areas that require more seams. Very often, 3D artists find themselves working on this kind of task over and over again until they feel satisfied with the result.

Editing the Unfolded Model

Even with a lot of planning and work on the right edges to mark as **seams**, a few adjustments are required to make the **unfolded mesh** look the way we wanted. All we have to do here is use the basic editing commands of Blender, just as if we were modeling something.

In the **UV/Image Editor Window**, we can use the following shortcuts to select and adjust the **unfolded mesh**:

- *B* key: Box select the vertices
- *G* Key: Move the selected vertices
- *S* Key: Scale the selected vertices
- *R* key: Rotate the selected vertices
- *A* key: Select all/deselect all vertices

As you can see, most of the standard shortcuts for modeling work for the **UV/Image Editor** as well.

Along with this command, we can use a few more options to make it easier. A very useful option is the **Pin**, which allows us to fix a vertex at a selected point. For instance, if you know that a few vertices are at their right positions, just select them and press the *P* key to pin them. Now, if we try to move or edit them, they won't go anywhere.

Always use the **Pin** to avoid any undesired changes on the **unfolded mesh**. To release them, use the *Alt+P* shortcut to unpin the vertices.

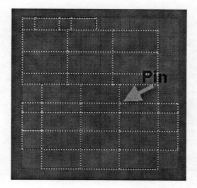

Besides the **pin** option, pressing the *W* key will make a menu appear with a few more options. There, we will find these options:

- **Weld**: If two or more vertices are selected with this option, we can weld them to look like only one vertex.
- **Align X/Align Y**: Use these options to align a group of vertices on the X or Y axis.

Export the Unfolded Mesh

When the **unfolded mesh** is just the way you want it, it's time to export it as an image. To do that, we use a very good script called "**Save UV Face Layout...**". Just access the UV menu in the **UV/Image Editing window**, and choose **Scripts | Save UV Face Layout...**.

It will call a small menu, with options for this script.

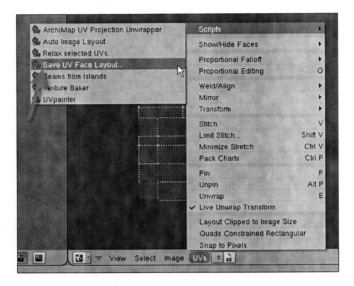

To set the layout up, we must change the following parameters:

- Size: Here, we can set up the size of the image. Always use a big value, to create high resolution textures. Use 1024, 2048, or bigger values.

- Wire: The layout will be saved with the wires from all faces. This option will determine the width of these wires.

- Object: With this button turned on, the object name will be used for the file name.

- All Faces: This button sets up the script to export all faces, and not just the selected ones.

- Edit: With this button turned on, right after exporting the layout, an image editing software is opened.

After saving the image, we have to open it in an image editor to add the textures. Try to organize everything in such a way that all the guidelines, created by the wireframe of the mesh object, are overlapped by the texture. Otherwise, we will see these lines on the model.

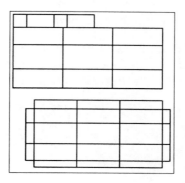

If we go back to Blender, we can apply the texture to the object and turn on the **UV button**, in the **Map Input menu**.

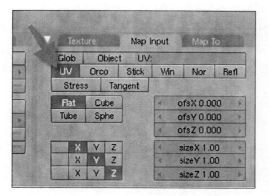

Unwrapping Scripts

The operation to create **UV Mapping** can be very annoying for some people, because we have to imagine the unfolded model to mark the seams. To help us in this task, there are a few scripts to automatically create the seams and unfold the model. One of them is projected especially for architectural models.

The name of this script is **ArchiMap UV Projection Unwrapper**, and it's very easy to use. Just open a new window and choose a **UV/Image Editor** as the window type. Then, with the **UV menu**, choose the **Scripts option** and call the script.

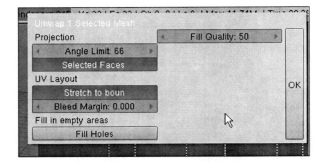

The **Angle Limit** will determine how the faces will be unfolded. Bigger angles will generate layouts with grouped faces, and small angles will create layouts with more islands. Clicking the **selected faces** button will make the script unfold only the selected faces or **all faces**.

Stretch to boun, makes the layout fit the **UV layout**. The **bleed margin** determines a limit for the **UV layout** to grow outside the limits of the window. With the **Fill Quality** we can set up the overall quality of the filling for the faces, if the **Fill Holes** button is pressed.

See how it works, for this model:

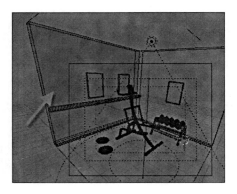

Selecting the model and calling the script will result in the following layout.

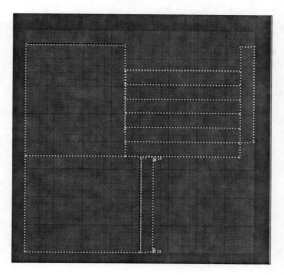

Summary

This chapter showed us how to use UV mapping to have more control over textures. We can create special images with this, which can be adjusted to fit a face of any model. With that, we can avoid the use of tiled textures, and create more realistic textures.

Here is a list of what we have learned:

- What UV Mapping is
- Why we should use UV Mapping
- What tools are required to created an unfolded mesh
- How to export the unfolded mesh as an image
- How to use scripts to create unfolded meshes faster

10
Light Basics

This is the last thing we have to learn to make our scenes look real. Dealing with lights can really make the difference, when we have a virtual scenario or architectural model. If you have ever worked with architecture, you must know that a big part and the key for a good project is the behavior of light in the environments.

A scene with a poor light setup can be unpleasant in both the real and virtual worlds. Or it can be even worse. In a project that requires good lighting, say a living room, a set up that make the scene looks dark can jeopardize the chances of the project getting sold.

Though being aware that a good light setup is the key to success with Architectural Visualization, why do we still see a lot of images with poor lighting? The problem with light is that every project requires an almost unique setup. This is the reason why most people think that light setup is very hard.

If you have some natural skills for painting or photography, setting up light may be a lot easier. What about the people who do not have this skill? Don't worry, even without this skill it's still possible to create incredible lighting.

To make that possible, we have to focus on three things. The first is to understand how light works with Blender or any 3D suite. And the second is to be patient, especially when we have to work on some complex scenes or worse, a scene with no information on how the light should be placed. This kind of situation requires a lot of testing and prototyping for lights.

The third thing, and maybe the point that can really save a project, is planning the light. As part of the project, you must know where all the lights will be placed and how these lights work. For instance, a daylight lamp can generate a unique kind of light. If we know that all lamps for our scene are daylight lamps, our job will be a little easier.

But unfortunately, it's very hard to find a project that requires visualization and has so many details. Most of this setup part is up to the visualization artist to decide where and how light should be setup for that particular scene.

This chapter is about how light works in Blender, the different requirements, and the types of setup available.

Lamps

Blender has five different types of light, with each type having a particular effect on the scene lighting. Before anythingelse, we must know all those light types and understand the consequences of each one of them on our scenes.

The light sources in Blender are called **lamps**. To create a **lamp**, just press the space bar, and choose the **Lamp** option. Then, choose the desired **lamp type** in the menu.

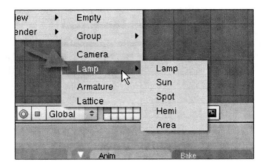

All lamps share some common parameters, such as intensity, influence, color, and more. These parameters are shown in the **Light panel**, placed right next to the materials panel. If you already have a light created, just select this **lamp** to access this panel.

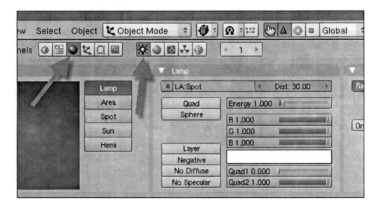

With the big buttons placed to the right of the **preview window**, we can easily switch between light types. For instance, if you have created a sun lamp, but realize later that what your scene needs is a spot lamp, just select the **lamp** and press the **spot button**.

Energy

Let's see how the common parameters work for each type of lamp. The first parameter is the energy. This **slider** determines how strong a light is. A good value here depends on the **scene scale**. For instance, for big environments, a value of five or more may be the best fit.

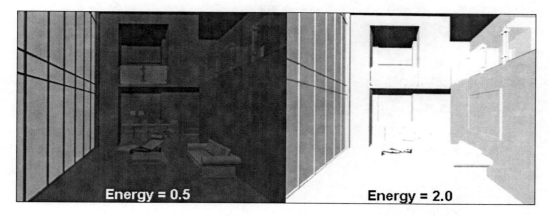

For small scenes, we may have to set up the **energy** under 0.5 or close to zero! Remember, this is the value that we have to fine tune when we deal with distribution of light.

Distance

Using the parameter called **Dist**, we can determine how far the light energy can go. The use of distance can have a direct impact on the **energy parameter**. For instance, a lamp with a small energy value and a big influence distance will be very weak,. because a low light energy is spread over a long distance. A big distance will spread more light energy, and with small distances, the energy will be concentrated. It means that, even with a small energy setup, lowering the distance value will make the light appear brighter.

Color

All lamps, from the simplest to the most complex, have a color. This color can be set up with the **color picker**. Picking the right color can give the light a warm or cold sensation. If you don't know which color to pick, choose **white**. Most lamps emit light with a white color, so the chance of getting the right feeling will increase.

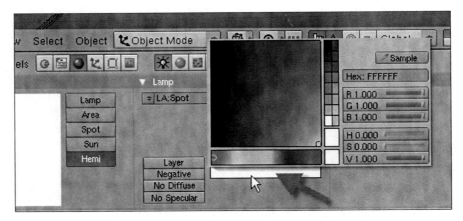

Kelvin chart
If you don't have any idea of the color of the lights, try to use a good reference to pick the right colors. There is a chart called a Kelvin chart, which presents a scale of colors with a representation for each light and environment type. For instance, choosing the color for Cool White Flourescent or Halogen lamps is easier with this chart.

Controlling Light

Besides these options, we can also choose which objects get illuminated by our lights, and some more options, using the buttons placed in the lower left down corner. Let's see what we can do with them:

- **Layer**: If this button is turned on, the lamp will illuminate only objects that are in the same layer. It can be useful to create lamps that only generate light for a particular piece of furniture or a set of walls. Just place all of them in the same layer, and press this button.

- **Negative**: Using this option, we can make a lamp cast negative energy. This means that we can remove light energy from the scene. It's great for generating contact shadows, or balancing a very strong spot of light.

- **No Diffuse**: This button makes the light affect only the Specular shader of materials.

- **No Specular**: And here, we have the opposite, with the light affecting only the diffuse shader.

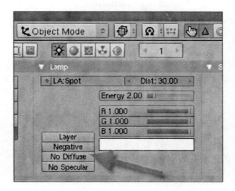

 Naming lights
Similar to materials and other objects, we can give unique names to lamps. Always set a name before adjusting the lamp. It will make things easier when you need to find or search for a particular lamp.

Hemi

The Hemi lamp is the simplest light in Blender, because it can't generate any shadow. This makes it's controls very simple. In fact, the only controls available are the basics, which we have already described.

When we use this kind of lamp, it generates an illumination that simulates a cloudy sky—a diffuse illumination with no shadows and a well spread illumination. If you want to add light energy to a scene, with a constant grade, this is the right option.

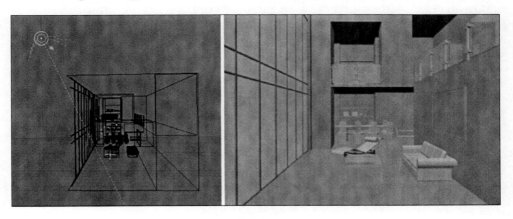

Sun

As the name suggests, this light tries to simulate direct sunlight. After placing the lamp, we can control the direction of the light. Just select the lamp, rotate the object, and aim the line to the place that must receive light.

There are only two extra options for this lamp, which are the **ray traced shadows** button **(Ray shadow)**, and the option to turn on the creation of **shadows (shadow only)**.

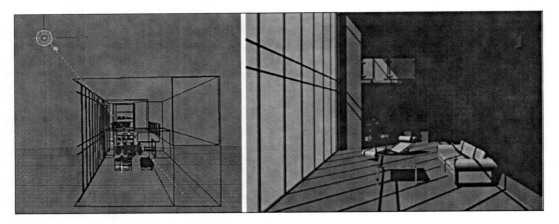

For external scenes, this is the best choice to simulate sun light, even when we use an external renderer. We use it a lot to create sun light for interior scenes as well. It's very easy to set up, so you can use it a lot.

Lamp

This is a lamp that works like a point of light, which can cast light energy from its center to all sides. Although there aren't any new options for this lamp, there is an interesting thing about it, related to distance. We can control the distance with a radius, so it doesn't work like a directional light. Just place it at a point, and it will illuminate the area around it.

The best application for this lamp is in dark corners that need extra light. Since this is the only lamp which is not directional in Blender, every time we need a light that illuminates the surrounding area, choose the **Lamp type**.

Area

This type of lamp consists of a plane that can generate light. It's perfect to fit it at a window or door, through which light should pass. As it is a directional light, we can change the target, select the lamp, and rotate it with the *R* key. Place the line that represents the target on which you want the light energy to be cast.

When we choose this type of lamp, there are some options related to area lamps only. The first one can set the size for this lamp. To change the size, we use the selector indicated in the following image:

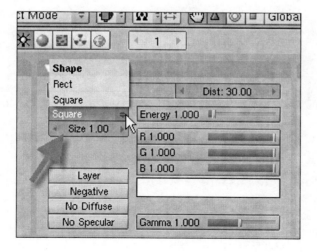

Besides the size, we can also change the quality of the shadow. This is set up using the samples option. With more samples, we have better shadows at the cost of more render time.

Spot

Just as the name suggests, this lamp creates a spot of light. This is perfect to represent a wide range of light sources, with conical shapes. And this is a directional light source, which allows us to point it at the objects or areas that should receive light.

Compared with the other light types, the spot is by far the most complex lamp type in Blender. We have a lot of options for shadows and volumetric lights.

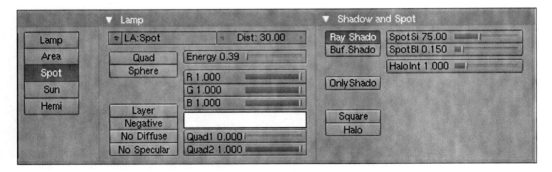

Let's see how we can use each option to interact with our scenes and produce better lights:

- **Ray Shadow**: With this type of shadow, we can create a well defined and accurate shadow. The shadow will have a well defined border, which is perfect to simulate artificial light sources in open spaces. This happens because in open spaces, we don't have surfaces to bounce the light rays and create a fuzzy shadow. To use this type of shadow, just press this button.

- **Buf. Shadow**: The other option is to generate shadows with a Shadow Buffer. This type of shadow is not as accurate as the **raytraced** type, but is a lot faster. We can set up the quality level of this shadow with the **ShadowBufferSize** option. A bigger value will result in a better shadow. Most times we use the shadow buffer to generate shadows, because with this, it is possible to create **fuzzy shadows**, which are generated in closed environments by the light rays bouncing off walls and other surfaces.

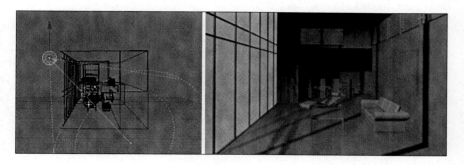

- **Square**: The spot lamp has a circular projection shape, which can be switched to a square projection with this option.
- **Halo**: And with this option, we can create **volumetric light** to give a more dramatic look to any environment. For instance, if we have a church model and want to create a light that comes in through a big window, but want to show the light rays coming through the window, this is the right option.

Volumetric Shadows

As we said, the option to generate volumetric shadows is the **Halo** button. Since it has a lot of options to be set up, let's see how it works with a church model. The first thing to do is place a **Spot Lamp** pointing to the interior of the scene. Set up the camera view to visualize the window inside the environment.

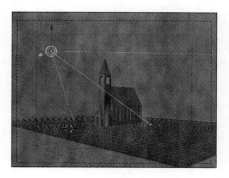

Now, let's turn on the halo option on and set up a few of it's parameters. Let's see how they work:

- **Samples**: With this option, we can adjust the number of samples used to generate the volume of light. Higher values create better lights, but increase the render time.

- **Halo Step**: This option controls the sampling frequency. With values above zero, the light rays will be interrupted if they find an obstacle in their way.

- **Bias**: This option sets the shadow bias to avoid artefacts generated by the shadow calculation.

- **Soft**: Here, we can decide how soft the borders of the light projection should be. Higher values generate softer projections, but with a longer render time.

The disadvantage in using volumetric light is that almost every parameter or option increases the render time. If your scene is complex, be careful about the type of light that is required.

See how the volume light gives a more dramatic look to the render in the following image:

 Camera View and Volume light

If you set up a spot lamp to generate volumetric light but nothing is happening at the render, try to change the **camera view**, since it's a key point in the generation of this effect. Sometimes, a simple rotation is enough to make the effect stronger for a particular view.

Soft Shadows

All light types in Blender, except the Hemi Lamp, can generate soft shadows, which is a feature added in the 2.46 release.

These soft shadows can be set up in a small menu, available for all lamp types. Prior to the release of Blender 2.46, only the Area Lamp could generate this kind of shadow. Now, even a light type such as the Sun Lamp can generate these shadows. It works by simulation the existence of an Area Lamp, only for shadow casting purposes.

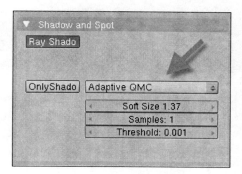

In the first combo box, we can choose the method used to generate the shadows. The **Adaptive QMC** is the fastest for detailed scenes. With **Adaptive QMC**, the samples used to generate shadows are created incrementally to fit the scene best.

The following are some options available to us:

- **Soft Size**: With this option, we can change the size of the area lamp considered to generate shadows.
- **Samples**: Increase this value to make the shadows look better. But, higher values make the render time longer.
- **Threshold**: This value controls the size of the shadow. If we increase the value of the threshold, fewer samples will be calculated for the shadow, thereby making it noisy.

Lighting Exercise

Now that we know about the light types in Blender, we can do an exercise to see how a light setup is done entirely with the standard lights in Blender. For this exercise, the scene used will be the solarium used for most of the examples in this chapter.

The model is quite simple, and consists of an apartment, with very big windows.

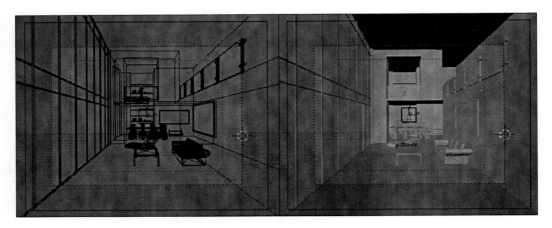

Before we do anything, let's plan how we can add the light to the scene. Since the environment has big windows, and the image will be simulating daylight, most of the light energy will enter the environment through the windows. Sunlight will be the main light source, and the only **shadow casting light**.

With that in mind, we can plan the lighting for our scene. The camera position is defined and represented by the previous image. The sunlight will be represented by a **Sun Lamp**, placed behind the camera.

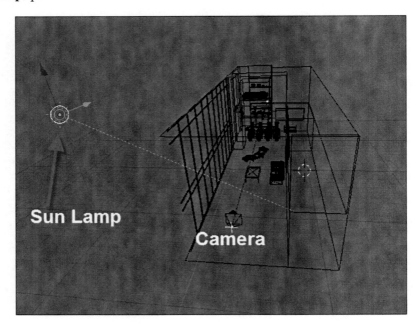

This Lamp is set up with energy of 0.30, and a slight yellow color. The **Ray Shadow** button is turned on to make this light cast shadows.

If we render the scene now, the image will show some areas with a **weak light energy,** and some completely dark. We have to simulate the light energy that comes in from the big windows. To do that, the **Area Lamp** is the best option.

With an Area Lamp, we can place the **light emitter** to fit the area of the window. Just create the lamp and change the area light shape to **Rect**. And then use **SizeX** and **SizeY** to change the size of the lamp without changing the energy. If you don't want to face troubles with the energy of this light type, avoid the scale transformation to change the size of the **Area Lamp**.

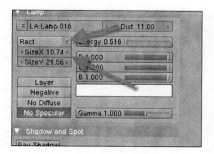

Let the shadows be turned off for this lamp and place it in a position that fits the **window size**. Remember to point the light towards the **interior**.

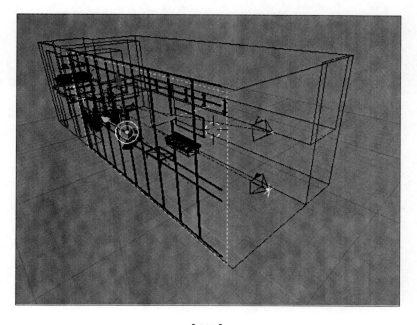

Place another lamp on the other side. It will add light energy from both sides where a big window would let the sky light come into the scene.

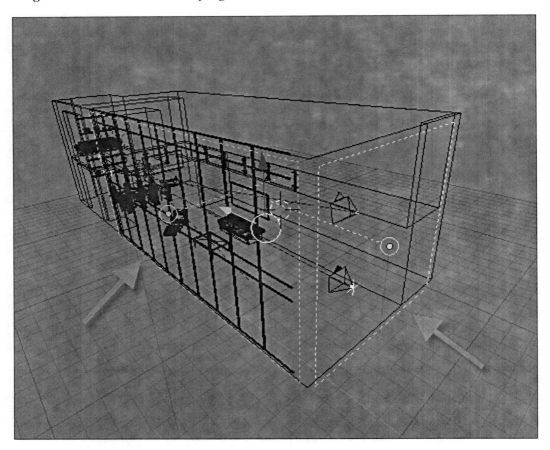

Both lights should be set up to have an energy of 0.50. If we render the scene, we will see the following image:

The light is starting to look good, but it requires more energy to get better. We have two choices — the first one is to increase the energy for all the lamps, and the second is to change the **exposure** for the scene.

Let's use the exposure, since it will enable us to quickly increase the energy and make the scene brighter. The controller for the exposure settings is located in the panel called **World buttons**.

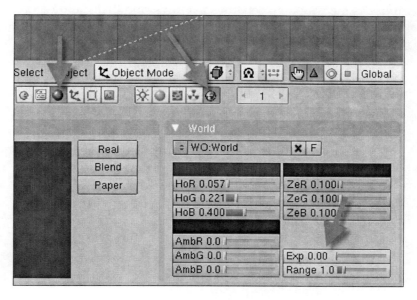

There, we will find the **Exp slider**. If we change this **slider** to something like 0.60, we will make the image more sensitive to light energy, and the overall **rendering brighter**.

Summary

In this chapter, we have learned how the light system of Blender works, and when we must use a particular light type. Besides that, we also saw that all light types share common parameters such as energy and influence area. What makes every light type unique is the way they generate shadows, and their unidirectional or directional nature, which makes our job easier in some cases.

11
Radiosity and Ambient Occlusion

In the last chapter, we learned how to use lights in Blender. Now it's time to learn how the advanced lighting features of Blender work. The advanced lighting of Blender is based on two main techniques, Radiosity and Ambient Occlusion. Both techniques give us better results for lighting environments, with less planning and light sources. But this comes with longer render times, because all the effort will be during processing time.

Which one of these methods is the best? When should we use Ambient Occlusion and Radiosity? To answer these questions we have to look at how they work.

Global Illumination

When we use a standard method of illumination, light sources emit rays that stop when they hit a surface. And that's it—when the light ray finds a surface it simply stops. If a surface is not touched by light rays, it will be a black surface in the render. We have to set up the lights and their position around an object or scene to distribute light sources and ensure that all surfaces get the right amount of light rays. This setup is the key to good lighting. But it requires a lot of work, and sometimes a bit of artistic touch, to set up a scene. Most people doesn't have this kind of artistic feeling, or even the patience to stay focused on a single scene for a long time, leave alone adjusting lights for a long time.

To aid these people, there is a method to distribute light energy through an environment called Global Illumination. This method is based on the bouncing of light energy at the surfaces of an environment, which is what happens in the real world. The light rays don't die when they hit a surface; they bounce and reflect, illuminating large areas just with this bouncing action. Depending on the extent of bouncing, a single light ray can illuminate a lot of surface, with its bouncing energy.

Besides the simple bouncing, there are some physical aspects of light and materials such as the light or surface color that can influence the result. The lighting produced by a white light source is, of course, white. But when this light hits a red wall, the bouncing light will be red. With a standard light setup, we will have to add a red light near this wall, to simulate the emission of red light energy. But a Global Illumination system can do that automatically, avoiding a complex setup in big scenes.

It looks like a Global Illumination system is the best thing for us, right? Well, before we start using this kind of light system, there are a few points that need to be clarified. Even if it looks easy to use, don't expect to create a scene without any kind of setup. It does require some setup, but the setup will depend on the method and renderer used.

Sometimes, setting up a scene with a Global Illumination method can become even more complex depending on the number of parameters and area that must be illuminated. Another important thing is that the amount of processing power required can impede the process in some old computers. To build a good lighting for a scene, the process is based on complex mathematical calculations that determine the direction, amount, strength, and other aspects of light bouncing.

This means that a Global Illumination method requires strong hardware with a lot of RAM memory and a good processor if we want lower render times. Otherwise, it will result in a long render.

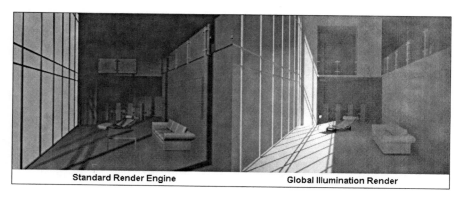

Standard Render Engine	Global Illumination Render

The **bottom line** is that with a **Global Illumination system**, we have a simpler setup of lights to achieve good illumination. But the render times are longer.

With this in mind, we can say that both **Radiosity and Ambient Occlusion** are methods of **Global Illumination**. We can't call **Ambient Occlusion** a full **GI method**, but it works with the same concept, with a longer render time for better illumination.

Besides the use of **Radiosity and Ambient Occlusion**, we can use a **GI method** with an external renderer such as **YafRay**. We will learn how to use **YafRay** in the next chapter.

Radiosity

Using radiosity we can generate a good light for animations and games, because most of the illumination is processed just once, and stored like some kind of paint on the surfaces. Where can we use Radiosity? In Blender, this kind of Global Illumination is mostly used for interactive presentations, created with the **Blender Game Engine**.

Another interesting thing about Radiosity is that we don't use lamps to generate light for our environments. In this system, we must use an object called an **emitter** to generate light rays.

The way to create these so called **emitters** is to change the **Emit properties** on the **Materials panel**. For instance, if we want to create a plane that generates light energy for **Radiosity**, we must apply a material to the plane, change the color of the material to match the light color, and then increase the **Emit property**. The **Emit option** works just like the Energy for lamps, with higher values generating a brighter illumination.

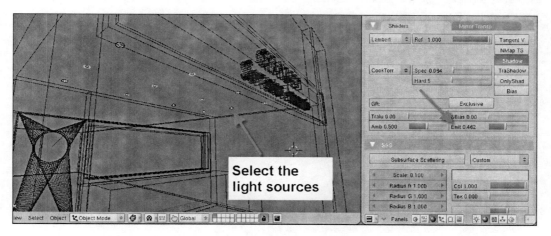

Let's see an example with a simple room. Just place the emitting object where you want the light to be placed. If the project requires more than one light, duplicate the object until you get the right number. When they are placed at the right positions, apply or create the material with the **Emit property** adjusted to something bigger than zero.

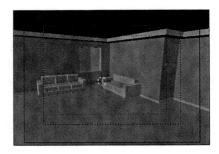

Before we start to actually do the **Radiosity illumination**, there is something we have to double-check with all the objects involved with the scene. The **Normals** of all faces must point towards the camera. If any **normal** is pointing away from the camera, the surface will look black. To check and assure yourself that all **Normals** are pointing in the right direction, just select all the objects in **edit mode** and in the **Editing panel** click the **Draw Normals button**. It will make the **Normals** appear like small lines coming from the centre of all the faces.

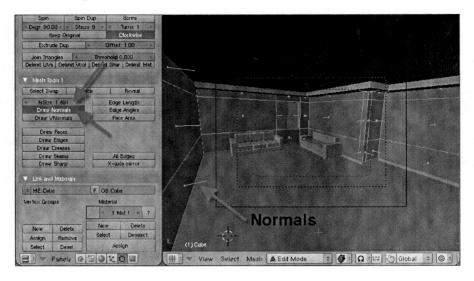

To change their direction, use the **Flip Normals button** on the **Mesh tools menu**. Or select all faces, and press *CTRL+N* to recalculate all Normals on the outside direction of all faces.

When all **Normals** are pointing in the right direction, we can start to simulate the **Radiosity solution**. To do that, open the **Radiosity Buttons** option. There, we will find all buttons and options related to Radiosity.

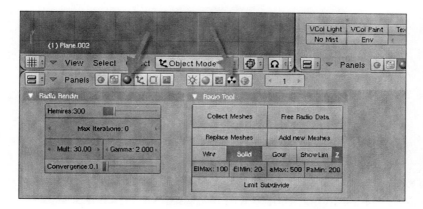

The process of generating illumination is simple. Just select all objects in **edit mode** and press the **Collect Meshes button**. When we hit this button, all **meshes** will be converted temporarily to **Patchs**, which are the objects manipulated by the Radiosity engine.

Make sure you have the **view mode** configured to **Shaded**, to view all the details of the illumination. To start the calculation, just press the **Go Button**. It will start the process, and will continue the calculation forever. To make it stop, just press the *Esc* Key.

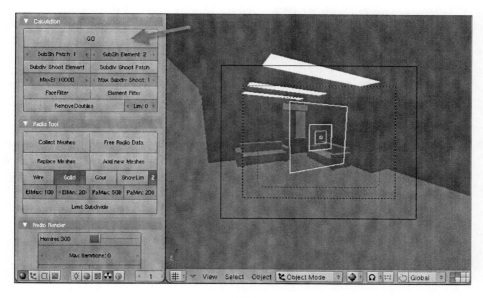

Now, we have an image, with some light information stamped on all surfaces. Since the light is stamped with the default settings, we can see a lot of pixels on all the surfaces. To make the lighting smoother, just click the **Gour** button.

After we make the light distribution with the Radiosity, it's not possible to change anything in the scene. If you need to change something, press the **Free Radio Data** button to make all objects editable again.

If we really want to have control over **Radiosity**, we must learn a few commands and know what their controls do:

- **Max Iterations**: With this option, we can set up the number of iterations the Radiosity solution should run. The default value is zero, but we can set it to a specific value. If it's set to zero, we will have to manually stop the calculation by pressing the *ESC* key.

- **Hemires**: This is a value that determines the quality of the Radiosity. If you need better light distribution or smoother shadows, increase this value.

- **Convergence**: When we start the Radiosity solution, there will always be some portion of unshot light energy in the scene. This parameter can set up the minimum value, before the solution stops for this unshot energy.

- **Mult**: This option sets the multiplier factor for the light energy. Higher values will generate a brighter scene.

- **Add new Meshes**: Press this button to generate a new **Mesh object**, with the color information from the Radiosity solution. The new mesh will have a material with the light information ready to be rendered. And we will be able to change the colors with the **Vertex Paint tool.**

- **Replace Meshes**: This option does exactly the same thing as **Add New Meshes**. The only difference is that it replaces the original objects with the new and illuminated meshes generated by the Radiosity solution.

- **Go**: With this button, we can start the Radiosity calculation.

As we can see, the Radiosity option is best suited for interactive visualizations, but not for printed presentations or video. For those, the best choice is to use **Ambient Occlusion** or another Global Ilumination tool. The main reason is the quality of shadows and the overall surface smoothing, which is a bit crisp with Radiosity.

One thing you have to be careful about with Radiosity—always try to set up and adjust the color of your materials. Their color defines almost all the reflections and soft shadows generated by light bouncing at surfaces.

To use the Radiosity for rendering, just press the **Radio button** on the **scene panel**. It will ensure that the Radiosity information is considered for the final render. If you leave this button turned on, you will not have to calculate the Radiosity again. For instance, to render an animation, you wouldn't have to change anything. The Radiosity will be calculated automatically for each new render.

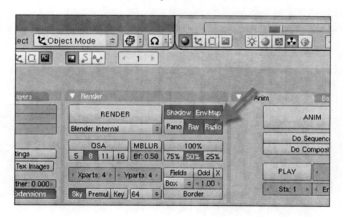

Vertex Paint

If you are not happy with the Radiosity solution generated by Blender, there is an interesting way to improve the lights and shadows generated by the calculation. Since the information for the Radiosity is stamped on all surfaces as vertex colors, we can literally paint these colors if want to improve the solution.

To do that, just select the model and enter the **Vertex Paint mode**.

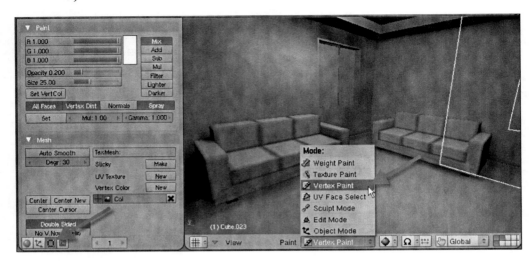

At the **Editing panel** paint the **vertex of the model** by choosing from the available tools. For instance, if the shadows of a scene are not so good, or need a bit more color, just select the desired color from the selector, and adjust the opacity and size of the brush.

Hold and drag the **mouse cursor** over the faces that you wish to paint. It will add the color information to the faces.

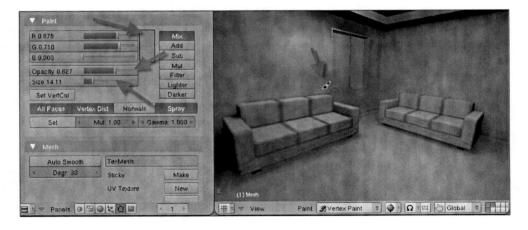

Use it as much as possible to improve the lighting. By the end, we will have a scene prepared for interactive visualization. If you want to use Radiosity to light a scene for print, remember that your scene may need a lot of work and adjustments to present a good light.

Ambient Occlusion

Ambient Occlusion is the best way to simulate a Global Illumination environment for architectural visualization, without the use of any external renderer in Blender. It works like this—when we turn on the Ambient Occlusion option, the background of the scene will randomly cast **light rays** to the centre of the scene. When a **light ray** hits a surface, it stops. It will make objects near each other block the rays that would hit each other, causing the **casting of shadows**. The surfaces will be stained with the shadows, which will give the effect of a Global Illumination render.

It will give us a better lighting, and of course a longer render time for any scene. To use this process, we just have to set up the **Ambient Occlusion menu**, located on the **World panel**.

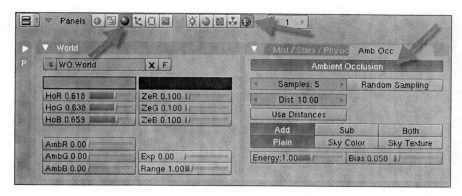

The menu is very simple, with few parameters. There is a big button called **Ambient Occlusion**, which turns on the Occlusion effect.

When the button is turned on, we have to set up a few parameters. Most of them relate directly to the **Occlusion effect**. All images generated by the **Ambient Occlusion** have a common characteristic, that is, the noisy aspect of the images. This aspect of the images can increase or reduce their quality, and also increase the render time. With less noise in the image, we get better quality and longer render time.

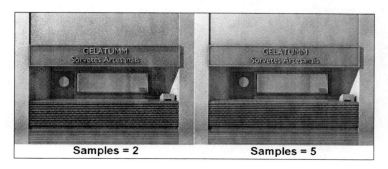

Samples = 2   Samples = 5

The main parameter of **Ambient Occlusion**, which controls the level of noise for the render, is **Samples**. The value of **Samples** always starts with 5, but we can increase this number up to 16, which gives the best quality. Very rarely, do projects require a number higher than 10 for **Samples**. This setup already results in a very good **render quality**.

For testing purposes, we can use a samples value of 2 or 3. This will result in a very **grainy image**, but in a very fast render time.

Let's see how the other parameters for the **Ambient Occlusion menu** work:

- **Random Sampling**: When we push this button, the samples will be cast in a random manner. This will cause a render with even more noise.
- **Dist**: With this parameter, we can set how far the light rays are cast. If we set up the Dist with a high value, it will make the light go far, resulting in a brighter scene.
- **Use Distances**: Setting up a distance for the light rays is not enough to make them work. To use distances, we have to turn on this button. When the button is turned on, surfaces located far from the light source will be less illuminated.
- **Add**: With this option, we can determine the light energy that will be added to the scene.
- **Sub**: Here, we can set up the Occlusion to remove light energy from the scene. If this button is turned on, remember to place a lamp at the scene, or the render will result in a black image. This option is good for night scenes and environments that require a lot of shadows.
- **Both**: Here, we can choose the **Occlusion to Add and Remove light energy** from the scene.
- **Plain**: The three buttons placed at the bottom of the menu determine the color of the light. With this option, we can choose white for the **Light rays**. In most cases this is the best choice for the Ambient Occlusion, which reproduces most of the light sources, such as the sun or artificial lamps. Choose this option, unless the project requires a different light source.
- **Sky Color**: If a white light source is not enough for your project, we can set up the **Ambient Occlusion** to use the Sky Color. This is the color used at the background. If you want to simulate a clear sky, try setting up light blue as the background colour. For alien environments, say Mars, try using a red background.

- **Sky Texture**: To use something more complex as the light color, like a texture, we can use this option.

- **Energy**: Here, we can set up the intensity with which the light rays hit the environment. It works exactly like the energy parameter for the lamps. Higher values result in a brighter scene.

- **Bias**: With Bias, we can set up a limit for smoothed surfaces to show even grainier environment.

It's all about finding the right set up for a scene. So let's see how we can set up both indoor and outdoor scenes.

Outdoor Scene

When we have to light an **outdoor scene**, the setup will be extremely simple, with only a few lights. In most cases, we will need only two main light sources — one to simulate the sunlight, and the other, a small fill light. The fill light will make the darker areas of surfaces a bit brighter, because the sunlight will hit the surfaces only from one side.

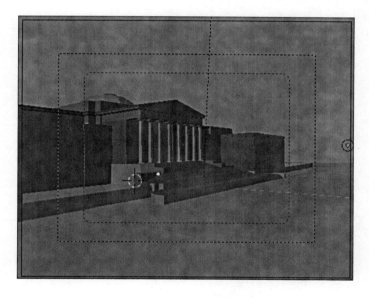

Take a look at the example scene; it has a small model of a museum. What we have to do with this scene to light it is to place a **Sun Lamp** right at the position of the Sun and then place a lamp or hemi on the opposite side, to make it work like a fill light.

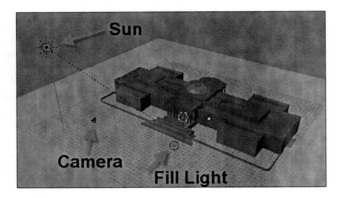

Remember that the position of the light will depend a lot on the **camera view**. That is why we always have to decide where the camera will be, before placing the **light points**. When the lights are placed, just run a small setup through the **Ambient Occlusion options**.

AO for Outdoor scenes

This is the scenario where the setup for **Ambient Occlusion** will be easier. The only care we have to take is to choose the **camera position**, before doing anything else. If your scene has any special requirements, say a specific position of the sun, or a specific time of the year, the position of the lights may require some changes.

Indoor Scene

An indoor scene is a bit more complex to set up, because the lights may react to several surfaces and factors. Just as in the outdoor scenes, we have to determine where the camera will be placed, before starting to work on the light. When the camera is placed, we must answer a few questions to set up all the light sources for the scene.

- How do the colors of the surfaces interact with the light?
- Is the main light source for the scene a natural light or is it artificial?
- From where is the sun coming into the scene?
- How strong are the artificial light sources? And how many of them are placed at the scene.
- How do the windows and doors interact with the light sources?
- Is there any piece of furniture with material that can change the way a light source works?
- How big is the scene?

If we can answer those questions, the setup of all the lights will be a lot easier. But what if we can't? Well, the answers for those questions should be in your project, if it is already complete. What I meant is, look up the answers before you start to test the light. You should use a 3D environment such as Blender to test some concepts. But these concepts require a minimum level of planning. Otherwise, it will turn out to be more like a guessing process. And believe me when I say this, this kind of process can and will consume a lot of time.

Take a look at this scene. The lights are placed in a way to simulate the sunlight coming from a window.

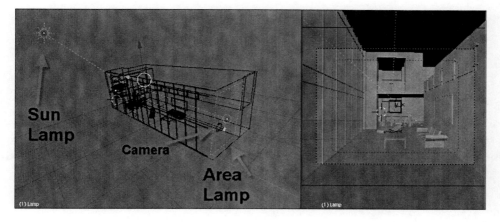

When we take a look at the setup for the **Ambient Occlusion** and the lamp, we can see that a lot of adjustments are required to **fit the size of the scene**.

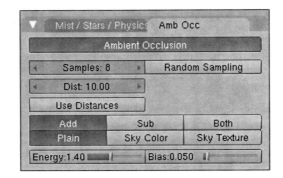

Measures and light

Always try to use the same measurements for all the scenes. It will make the **light setup** process a lot simpler. If you always use the same units when the lights need to be placed, you will get to know the right values for energy and the **Ambient Occlusion settings**.

Working with interior light is a very complex subject in architectural visualization. To successfully reproduce the light for an interior scene, you should start with observing light conditions in closed rooms. With these observations, you will be able to reproduce the light by adding lamps with a small amount of energy.

A good exercise would be to find some good tutorials or images of interior scenes, even if they're created with another 3D software and recreat them with Blender. Since it's a general subject in architectural visualization, you will be able to reproduce these tutorials in Blender.

If you want to try the results of the Global Illumination solution, just go to the next chapter, where we will learn to use YafRay.

Summary

In this chapter, we have learned how to use the Radiosity and Ambient Occlusion options to create a better illumination for our scenes.

With the Radiosity options, we could generate a lightweight solution to create shadows and interactions between elements. The light is distributed at the scene following a physics-based energy distribution, with the light rays bouncing at the objects' faces.

Even through it is a great solution, the illumination generated with the tool is used mainly for interactive animations.

For more sophisticated illuminations, there is the Ambient Occlusion option. With this tool, we can simulate a global illumination environment to create a smooth light solution.

12

Global Illumination with YafRay

What is YafRay? It is an external render, which works well with Blender. Actually it's the external software that presents the best integration with Blender. We can even call YafRay directly from the Blender interface. With YafRay, we can use some tools and features that aren't available with the default Blender renderer such as Global Illumination and a very fast ray tracing. There are some other effects that we can do with YafRay, such as caustics, which we can't do easily with Blender.

In the last two chapters, we learned the tools and techniques to illuminate our scenes with a wide range of options. When we use YafRay and its Global Illumination rendering system, we can see the light rays emitted by lamps bounce at the surfaces of our models. However, using YafRay comes with a price, which is that the consumption of resources from the computer is higher. So, if you base all renderings in a Global Illumination solution, be ready for long render times.

In this chapter, we will take a look at some examples of renderings created with YafRay, like the ones shown in the following images:

These are good examples of what we can do with Blender and YafRay. We will look at how each scene should be set up to create these images, in detail.

The integration of Blender and YafRay is very good. It's actually the best external renderer to use with Blender. Since it's an external renderer, the first thing we have to do to use YafRay is to visit the official website and download a copy of YafRay.

Installing YafRay

When we get to the **YafRay** website (`http://www.yafray.org`), there will be a download area, where we can choose to download a copy of **YafRay** compatible with our operating system. Don't worry. They have almost all major operatiing systems, such as Windows, Linux, and Mac OS X.

YafRay is a command-line renderer, which can be used only at the command line. To make things a lot easier, there is a way to call YafRay from the Blender interface. But if you want to try, we will take a look at some options available only in YafRay from the command line.

Blender and YafRay

To use YafRay with Blender, we have two options. The first and the more complex option involves exporting our scene to the XML file format, and rendering this file with **YafRay** through a command-line environment. The second option is quicker and easier, since it uses a menu integrated with the Blender interface.

On the **Scene Panel**, we can find a combo box that allows us to choose the render engine used to process the scene.

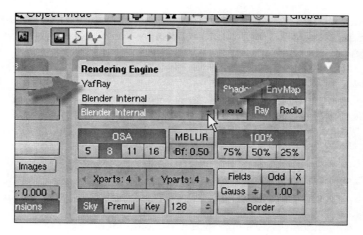

Of course, to use **YafRay**, we must choose this option in the **combo box**. When we do that, every time a scene is rendered, it will be exported to **YafRay** and rendered.

A few other things happen when we change the main render in this menu. Two new menus appear to let us set up **YafRay**. We can see these new menus to the right. They are the **YafRay** and **YafRay GI menus**.

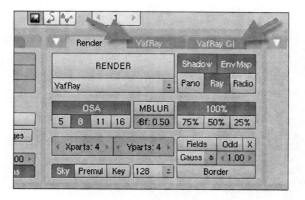

And that's not everything; a few other things also happen. Since the **YafRay** renderer provides some extra features not available in Blender, new options will appear on the **Materials panel** and **Lamps panel**.

Is there any difference between choosing **YafRay** to render from the Blender interface and using it through the command line? Unfortunately there is. The integration between Blender and **YafRay** is not perfect. There are a few options available in **YafRay** that can be used only if we render through the command line. But don't worry, almost everything we need for architectural visualization can be used using only the options available at the Blender interface.

And what about render times? The rule here still remains—since it uses a lot of ray tracing and a Global Illumination engine, scenes rendered with YafRay take a long time to render, depending on the setup. To be honest, be ready to wait for two to four hours to render a complex scene. And when I mean complex, imagine a scene with a lot of details, furniture, textures, and light sources.

Remember to install

It's really important to check if **YafRay** is installed on your system, before you use it. When we install Blender, the option to choose YafRay as the renderer is available by default. But that doesn't mean it's already installed.

YafRay Setup

Now that we already know how to get started, let's see how to set up **YafRay**. All setting up is done with the two menus that appear when we choose **YafRay** as our renderer. They are called **YafRay** and **YafRay GI**.

The first one, called **YafRay**, is used to adjust the overall parameters of the render.

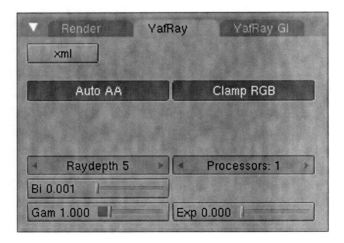

Here is what we can do with some of the parameters:

- **XML**: With this button turned on, we will export our scene to the **XML file format**. If the button is turned on, we won't be able to see the render progress in the render window. The image will appear only with the finished render. When the button is turned off, we will be able to see the render progress. Besides that, there is a little trick we can do with this button to export our scene to the **XML file format**. The trick is to turn on the button, and when the render starts, just press the *ESC* key. It will cancel the render, but an **XML file** of our scene will be available in the same folder where it is saved. This file can be used with the command-line options of **YafRay**.

- **Auto AA**: With this button, we can choose to use the anti-aliasing of Blender, or manually set up the **AA** options with **YafRay**. If the button is turned on, the options in the render menu of Blender will be used. When we turn the button off, some new parameters will be available.

  - **AA Samples**: This option will determine how many samples will be used for the anti-aliasing process. Higher values will result in better images, but with longer render times.

  - **AA Passes**: Besides the samples, we have to set up how many passes will be used in the render, for the anti-aliasing process. Again, higher values will result in better renders, but higher render times.

  - **Psz**: Here, we have the pixel size for the anti-aliasing filter.

  - **Thr**: This is the threshold for the anti-aliasing.

- **Raydepth**: This option is very important, especially if our scene has some glass or transparent material. Every time we render a scene, the light rays will bounce and reflect at surfaces. If we want these light rays to penetrate transparent objects, we must set up the distance the ray can go. With a small **raydepth**, some of our transparent objects may present black surfaces, because the light rays couldn't reach those surfaces. If this happens, just increase the value of the **raydepth** to make the light get there.

- **Processors**: This option lets us choose how many processors will be used for rendering. If your computer has more than one processor, choose how many you would like to use here.

- **Bi**: Some of your objects will cast shadows on themselves. With the bias, we can control and even avoid these shadows.

- **Gam**: Some scenes require a bit of a gamma correction to make the colors look more uniform. If you don't want to work on image processing software, but right at the rendering process, this parameter lets you control the correction. With a value of one, there won't be any correction. Increase the value to make all the colors at the render look more uniform.

- **Exp**: Here, we have the exposure settings for the scene. If you know something about photography, this option will be familiar. With the exposure, we can set up how much light energy will interact with the scene. The default value for the exposure is zero, and if we increase the value, our scene will look brighter. Use this option with caution, because high exposure levels can make all the colors at the scene look a bit washed out.

It's a lot of information to set up for every new scene. In practice we won't use all those parameters for every render. The most commonly used are the **XML**, **Raydepth** and **Exp** parameters. Sometimes we use **Auto AA** to make test renders, but that's all. If you want to get started, just focus on how these most commonly used parameters work, and then take some time to study the others. We never know when a scene will require fine tuning of some of them.

YafRay GI Setup

This is the most important menu of **YafRay**. If you just choose the render, but don't set up the GI, nothing will happen to your scene. Only a black scene will be rendered. The **YafRay GI menu** holds all the information about how the light will behave at your scene.

The first thing we have to notice is that **YafRay** uses two methods to render and determine how light will behave at the scene. We can choose those methods on this menu.

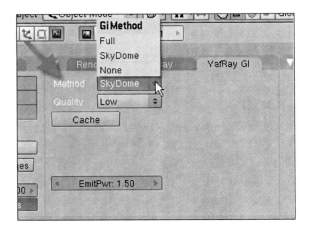

The methods are called **SkyDome** and **Full**. With **SkyDome** we have the simplest **GI method**, which looks like the Ambient Occlusion method. This method makes the background of the scene cast ray lights. The main use of the **SkyDome method** is in external scenes, and for quick renders.

With the other method, called **Full**, we have the most complex **GI effect**. This method makes the light rays really bounce at the surfaces, generating a very realistic render. We can use it for both interior and external scenes. Though you can benefit from the realistic effect, expect a long render time.

SkyDome

When should we use **SkyDome**? If your scene is simple, and doesn't require complex interactions between surfaces for a good illumination like an interior scene, **SkyDome** is the best choice.

After we choose the **SkyDome method**, there are a few more parameters we need to set up to render a scene. All those parameters are available for the **Full method** as well. The first one is the quality.

- **Quality**: With this option, we can choose the level of quality for our render. If we choose the **Low quality**, our render will be completed very quickly, but the image will present a lot of noise. With the **Best** quality, there won't be any noise in the render, but the render time is a lot longer. In most scenes, a **Medium** quality is enough. It's always a good practice to test the settings to find the best quality level for your scene.

- Cache: Here, we have a very important option, which can save some time during the render. When we render anything with **YafRay**, the background casts the light rays, which are sometimes cast at the same pixel more than once. It consumes render time and makes the overall process slower. When we turn the **Cache option** on, the information about how many pixels have already received light rays can be stored.

    ◦ **ShadQu**: With this option, we can set up the shadow quality of the render. Keep it under .95, and with low values, we have a better shadow.

    ◦ **Prec**: Here, we can set up the maximum number of pixels without samples. If you want more quality, use low values, but it will increase the render time. Use this parameter very carefully, because it's not easy to see the difference visually between renders that use 5 or 10. But the render time can be really different between them.

    ◦ **Ref**: This parameter sets up the threshold for the shadow quality.

- **Emitpwr:** Since the background is a light source, with this parameter we can set up how strong the background light energy is.

Lighting with SkyDome

Now that we know how the **SkyDome method** works, let's see how we can light a scene, and set up the light to render it with **YafRay**. The first thing we have to ask ourselves to start the process is—what are the main light sources?

With **YafRay** we have a few more options:

- We have small light sources such as a lamp.
- We can use the background to emit light.
- We can also use the light that bounces at surfaces.

Let's take a look at our test scene. It's a building, with an external environment.

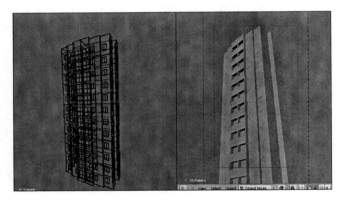

This a common light setup for architecture visualization. The light of this environment is provided by the sunlight, which will be represented using the **YafRay SkyDome**.

To light this environment, we will be using:

- The environment background, which generates light with the SkyDome method.
- A Sun Lamp to simulate the sun.

The first thing to do is to set up the background color and the **SkyDome**.

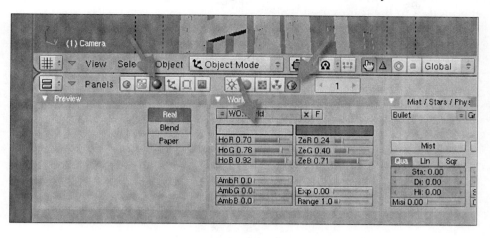

On the **World** menu we can choose a light blue color, to simulate the sky color. Since it will generate light, the color we pick for the background will determine the feel of the environment.

The next step is the **YafRay setup**. Choose the **Method SkyDome**, and then set **Emitpwr** to 1.0. Just to make a quick test, leave the quality at **Medium**.

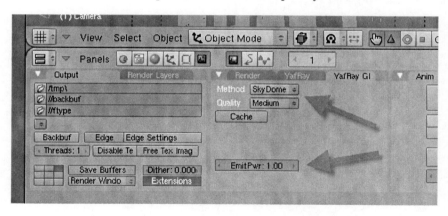

Remember that all those parameters and values can change, especially if the scale of the project is different.

With everything setup, let's make a test render. When we press *F12*, the render will be generated as in the following image.

As we can see, the background is generating light, but not enough to illuminate the entire scene. To make the scene looks better, we can add a **Sun Lamp**.

Place the **Sun Lamp** pointing at the building and turn on the **Ray Shadow button**. It will make the **Lamp** generate shadows.

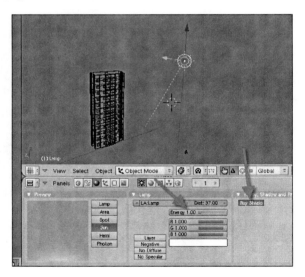

Now, we can hit *F12* and wait a few moments for the render to finish.

As we can see, the **SkyDome Method** is good for external scenes, but it requires some extra light to generate enough light energy. If we use only the background to illuminate it, the scene will look dark.

Full

Even through we get incredible results with **SkyDome**, we can make our renders better using the **Full** method. This method is the best choice for complex interior scenes, and renders the required effects, to like caustics. When we choose **Full**, some new options appear along with the parameters available for the **SkyDome**.

Before we start to use the **Full method**, let's take a look at how those new parameters work.

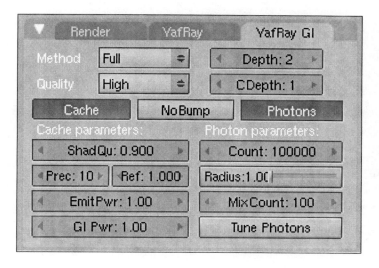

The first two parameters that show up, when we choose the **Full method** are:

- **Depth**: This number specifies how many bounces a light ray will have. For instance, we have an object made of some kind of transparent material, say glass. With this option, we can determine how many times a light ray will bounce, before it stops being cast.

- **CDepth**: Here, we have the same option. But there is a difference, in that this option does not influence the visible light. It uses only the light used to create caustics.

When should we use these options? If you have a scene, where something has a glass material and the interior of this object is not well illuminated, you can improve it by increasing the value of **Depth**. And, if something has to produce caustics, but nothing is happening, we can increase the value of **CDepth** too.

With the **Photons button**, we can turn on the use of **Photons** calculation. This helps to increase the accuracy of the Global Illumination calculation to create more realistic scenes.

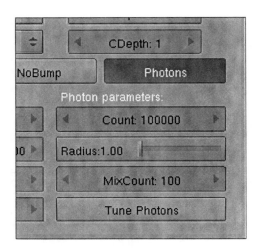

For indoor scenes, where the light source is small, say a window or a small lamp, the use of **Photons** helps YafRay make a better Global Illumination calculation. A small light source generates a noisy image.

With **Photons**, we can make the light rays leave a mark on the surfaces when they bounce. The collection of marks left by the **Photons** is called a photonmap. Since the **Photons** are cast by the light sources, they will generate a very realistic effect for any scene.

The **Photons menu** has a few options to set up; let's see how they work:

- **Count**: This value determines the total number of **Photons** at the scene. A big number of **Photons** can create more details for the lighting. But try not to increase it a lot, because a big number of **Photons** can increase the render time of the scene. It's a bit hard to determine the right number of **Photons** for a scene, because of the differences in scale and light setup. The key to make a good scene here is testing different setups, starting with low values.
- **Radius**: Using this value, we can determine the radius that YafRay should search for **Photons** to blur. A blurred photonmap will make your scene better with smoother illumination.
- **MixCount**: Here, we can set up the number of **Photons** to mix.
- **Tune Photons**: This is a simple option. If this button is turned on, we will be able to see the **Photons** as small dots during the render process. It would be useful for us in fine tuning the **Photons** parameters to best suite our scene.

To finish all the options from the **Full method**, we have the **GI Pwr**, located right below the **EmitPWR**. This option sets up the strength of the global illumination. It can affect our scenes by making more light energy be reflected on all surfaces of a scene. High values make our scene look brighter, while lower values can make a scene look a little darker, and even weaken the global illumination feel. To find the right value for your scene, it's important to test it again. Try to find a value that makes the light distribution of your scene look good.

Interior Light with the Full Method

All those parameters look awesome, but how can we set up an interior scene to make the light realistic using the **Full method**? That's what we are going to see now. Let's take a look at an interior scene and try to find the best way to light it.

The scene is a **dining room**, a very small environment with a lot of objects. As part of the planning, this scene should get most of the light energy from the only window available in the room.

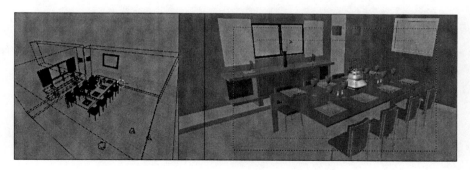

Scenes of this kind require a few light sources, which get repeated in most interior scenes. First, we have to set up a light source to simulate the sun, which can be achieved using a **Sun Lamp**. This lamp type is compatible with YafRay and gives us good light, to simulate the strong illumination that comes from the sun.

We can place the light in such a way that the target line goes through the window.

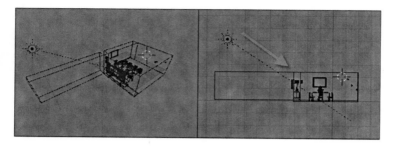

The next step is to add a light source, at the side of the window, to simulate the reflection of the sunlight on the wall. In theory, the sunlight should bounce off all surfaces inside the room. But it would take too long for the rays to actually bounce off in all directions and from all surfaces, and generate a realistic effect. In these kinds of scenes, we can add some extra light sources to help the Global Illumination, and decrease the **Depth of the ray** bouncing. This can be achieved with a **Lamp light** that will cast light rays in all directions.

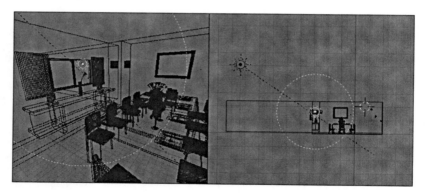

With all lights placed, it's time to set up **YafRay**. Choose the **Full method**, and then these options:

- **Depth**: Here we choose a value of 5 to make sure that the light rays penetrate the glasses and other transparent surfaces.

- **CDepth**: In this scene, we won't need any caustics effect. So, a value of 1 will be enough.

- **Photons**: Turn the **Photons** on, to help with the illumination.

- **Count**: The **Photons** count here has to be huge to make the light look good. After a lot of testing, I came up with the value of 1500000. There is no math involved. It's only a matter of testing the render with low settings, and trying to find the best fit.

- **Radius**: Here, we have the same thing. For this scene, a value of 40 is the best option. What happens if we use lower values? Values below 40, make the scene look noisy.

- **MixCount**: A value of 100 for this option works just fine.

- **GI Pwr**: Since this scene requires a lot of light, bounced from all surfaces, it would be good to increase the GI power as much as possible. A value of 7.50 will make all the surfaces reflect a lot of light energy. This way we will have a very bright scene. It's important to increase the **Emit PWR** as well, to make the background of the scene emit light energy.

Again, there is no magic here, but a lot of testing and the right positioning of light sources. Try to plan the places where the light energy will come into your environment. This will give you a good idea as to where the light sources should be placed.

To make some tests, choose **Low quality** to reduce the render time. The scene won't look good, but it will give us a good idea of the light setup. If you think any adjustments are required, make the changes and then test it again.

When you feel that the light looks good, try increasing the quality and wait for the render to finish. After a few minutes or hours, you will have a scene like this:

YafRay Materials

Besides the render options, when we choose to render a scene with YafRay, a few more options will be available or changed on some of **Blender's panels**. One of the panels that suffer a few changes is the **Materials panel**, especially the **Mirror Transp menu**.

When we choose **YafRay**, the menu will be reorganized, but the options remain the same. The good thing about this change is that a few presets become available.

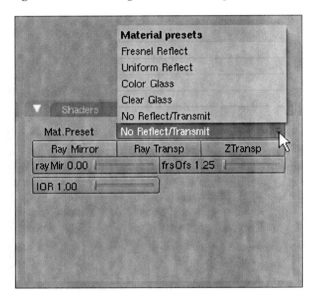

If you want to speed up the setup for any material with advanced reflections, these new presets can help.

YafRay Lights

Along with the materials, when we choose **YafRay** as renderer, some of the Blender lamps also gain some new options. Also a new lamp type appears. This new lamp type is called **Photon**, and its main function is to emit photons for caustics! Expect that, no light energy is generated from this lamp type.

Let's see how it works, if we have a scene with a transparent object, and a **Photon lamp type** placed as in the following image.

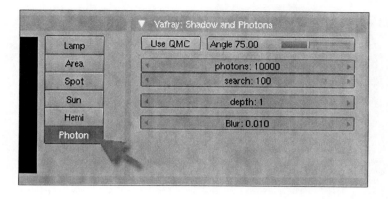

It can be any kind of object, such as a crystal glass. If we render the image with the proper settings, we get a light dispersion causing the caustics effect.

Here are the settings used:

- **Photons**: We can determine how many photons are cast by the lamp. For this scene, the Photons are set to 4000000.
- **Search**: This is the maximum number of photons that should be blurred. The default value is fine for this example.
- **Depth**: Like the **CDepth**, here we can set up the maximum bouncing level for the photons. If you don't see anything in the rendering, try increasing this value. Since the model has some level of complexity, a value higher than 2 or so will be the best choice here. For this scene, a value of 8 will make the photons go through the glass material.
- **Blur**: With the blur, we can blend the small dots of light generated by the caustics effect. An amount of 0.2 of Blur will work fine for this example.

Along with the **Lamp settings**, here are the **YafRay GI settings**:

- **CDepth**: For this particular scene, a value of 6 will work fine for the rendering. If you don't see any small spots on the final rendering, try increasing this value.
- **Quality**: High
- **Photons**: 1000000

And for the final render, we will have this kind of image.

Use this feature with caution, because the render time can grow rapidly with the use of caustics.

Use caustics with caution

When you try to get the caustics effect, try to go easy on the settings and always save your scene. If you increase the settings too much, your render can literally crash Blender, or the render time can get really long!

Another feature that shows up in the **Lamp settings** is the glow option. With this, we can make a light glow, and make it appear like a globe of light in the render. There are a few options available to set up this glow.

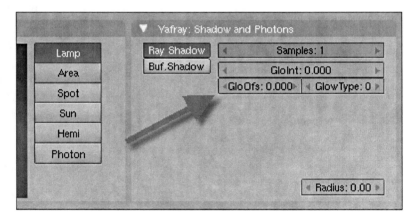

- **Samples**: Here, we can set up the quality of the shadow generated by the Ray tracing process.
- **GloInt**: This option sets up the intensity of the glow.
- **GloOfs**: With this option, we can set up the size of the glow.
- **GlowType**: Here, we can choose the type of the glow.

Besides the set up of all the parameters, we always have to follow a rule to make the glow appear in the rendering. A plane or surface always has to be placed behind the light source, to make the glow happen. If you set up all the parameters for a lamp, and it doesn't show up at the render, the first thing you should check for is whether the lamp has a background surface.

Let's look at this example scene, where we have a lamp and a wall. Take a look at the left side image. We have the image rendered without the **glow option enabled**. And on the right, we have the same lamp with the **glow enabled**.

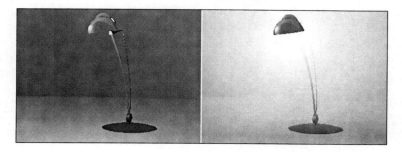

If you have a scene where the glow is important to show the light source, use this feature to achieve the effect.

Summary

We have learned in this chapter how to improve our images with the advanced features offered by YafRay. With these features, we can produce images using global illumination options such as photons and light reflection on surfaces.

Here is the list of subjects learned in this chapter:

- Choosing YafRay as the render engine for Blender
- Setting up the basic parameters of YafRay
- Using the YafRay GI settings
- Setting up a scene using the SkyDome method of YafRay
- Setting up a scene using the Full GI method of YafRay
- Working with the special options available for lamps in YafRay

13
Animation for Architectural Visualization

From the beginning of the book till now, we have only worked with static images. But Blender offers us much more than static images, if we start to work with its animation features. Show a project with an animation and you make a very strong impression on any person, especially in the area of marketing. And Blender can offer us an extra feature, which no other 3D package can; that is interactive animation. Yes! With the integrated Blender Game Engine, we can create interactive animations to allow the people who validate your project to walk into all environments and have a full virtual experience of your project.

This is a great feature and tool for anyone working with architectural projects. Besides that, we have the standard features in Blender to work with linear animations. So, let's get started with the animation basics and go further into how to make small movies of your projects.

Animation

When we have a project and have to show it to someone with an animation, the best solution to produce this animation is a walkthrough. This is a very simple type of animation, where we have to work only with the camera position. In this animation, the camera goes through the entire project, simulating a walk into the building or environment.

Since we work only with the camera, there won't be any requirement to learn or work with more advanced animation features, such as armatures or bones, which are used to make character animations.

However, before we produce any animation, we have to take some time to prepare and plan all the steps to avoid any troubles or reworking. The planning of an animation can really save you a lot of time, and if well executed, can even show you how to improve or even abort your animation.

Planning the Animation

The first point to plan for the animation is to make a small storyboard, or to trace the path of the walkthrough where the camera should pass. It's important to know exactly what you want to show in the animation, because as you will see, the required time to build an animation and the long render times makes animation a very expensive type of media for presenting a project.

After identifying the path for the camera movement, the next step is to identify the places where the camera should stop or turn around to show a particular area of the project.

Storyboarding can be done on paper or any type of media where you can easily make notes. Although a storyboard is helpful, it's not essential to make a storyboard for an animation aimed at architectural visualization.

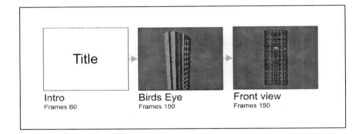

Animatic

The basic planning of an animation is to determine exactly what you need to show, for your client and the development team in the office. But, there is something that can't be predicted from the planning done with a storyboard or 2D project—the timing for the animation.

Besides the technical challenge, setting up the right timing for the animation can be a very difficult task. A very common mistake that inexperienced artists make is that they try to guess the right timing from the **3D View** and not in the rendered animation. Sometimes, the artist setting up the animation waits for hours to finish the render to discover that the timing is not right. The animation is either too slow or too fast.

Don't be afraid to spend a lot of time fine tuning the animation. It's perfectly normal and will probably happen to you. Find the right timing, as the animation can take a long time, even more than the light setup. Just as in light setup, with proper practice, you will start finding the solution for the timing quickly.

A good solution to avoid this kind of mistake is to make an animatic! An animatic is a very simple type of animation, exactly the same animation that you will create for the animation, but with simpler shapes, lights, and textures. The objective here is to validate only the timing; no other visual aids are required.

Here are a few tips on how to build an animatic:

- Replace all models on the scene with primitive shapes such as cubes.
- Remove or decrease the light quality.
- Don't use global illumination.
- The animation for the camera should be exactly the same as the final render.
- Remove all textures or advanced materials from the objects, such as ray-traced reflections.

With these guidelines, a very simple animation will be created. Besides the simplicity, there is another important thing about the animatic. The render time required to make one is very short.

Since it's short, if the animation requires any type of adjustment, you will be able to make the camera move faster or slower and validate it again with the same speed. And for the final render, there is chance that everything will work exactly the way you want.

A great way to create an animatic is with the **Render this window button**. It's located right next to the **Layers manage buttons**. If we hold down the *CTRL* key and press this button, a very simple render will be generated; the *CTRL* makes Blender render an animation.

The animation will be generated with the same view type as the object shown in the **3D View**. For instance, if we set up the object to be displayed as wireframes, the **render window** will be generated like this:

Save time with planning

Some people think that creating pre-production animations or plans is a waste of time and they go straight to the animation production. But the whole point of preparation is exactly to save time, and not be surprised after a long render with a bad camera move, or too slow a movement. Always pass through this preparation, and there is a big chance that you won't have to rework the animation ever again.

Animation and Frames

How does an animation work? Before we start to create animations with Blender, let's understand how the process of creating a linear animation works. The result of an animation created with Blender is a video file, such as an AVI or MOV file. For interactive animations, we will have an executable file.

To make a video file, a lot of still images are rendered and placed in order. That's the reason which makes an animation time consuming. If we think that one single **frame** can take something like thirty minutes to render, an animation with fifty frames can take something like twenty five hours to render! Now, do you understand why it's so important to plan the animation?

How many **frames** are required to make an animation? It depends! In most cases, for a smooth animation, we use a rate of **twenty four frames** per second. That's the **Frame rate**.

Here is a list of common **Frame rates** used for animation:

Animation type	Frame rate (FPS)
CG Animation	30 FPS
Film	24 FPS
Animatic	10 FPS

Keyframes

If we want to create any kind of animation, we must add and manipulate **keyframes** in Blender. To understand what a **keyframe** is, we have to think about how the animation is formed. All animation is made of a series of frames, rendered in order to create a motion image. When a series of images are played at a rate of **twenty four frames per second,** we will have the impression of motion.

With the **keyframes,** we can set up the properties of an object at a specific point in the animation. For instance, we can set up a camera at the entrance of a house at frame 1 and then outside of the house, a hundred meters away at **frame 400.** What will happen when we hit play? Since the camera is placed in different **positions and frames,** the animation will automatically move the camera between the two positions.

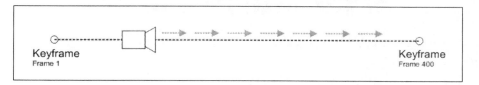

Keyframe
Frame 1

Keyframe
Frame 400

We won't have to do anything. It will all be handled by Blender. All we have to do is to set up where the **keyframes** should be, and the properties of the object. For us, the **main properties** that we have to set up are the position, rotation, and the scale of objects.

> **Interactive Animation**
>
> For interactive animation, it won't be necessary to set up **keyframes**, since all animation will be interactive. Since it is interactive, the user will decide where the animation should go and what the camera should see.

Creating Keyframes

To create **keyframes** in Blender, we have to select the object that will receive the **keyframe**, and press the *I* key. When we do that in the 3D View, a menu will appear for us to choose the proper **keyframe type**.

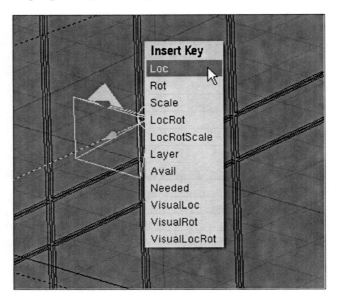

For each type of property there is a specific **keyframe**. Let's see what some of them mean:

- **Loc**: Keyframe for position
- **Rot**: Keyframe for rotation
- **Scale**: Keyframe for scale
- **Layer**: Keyframe for layers

There are some options that blend different **keyframes** as shortcuts to mark properties for **Loc**, **Rot**, and **Scale** at the same time. For instance, if we choose the "**LocRot**" option, a keyframe for the position and rotation will be added.

Before we add a **keyframe** for an object, we have to place the playback head at the desired frame where the **keyframe** should be placed. To do that, just use the navigator indicated in the following image:

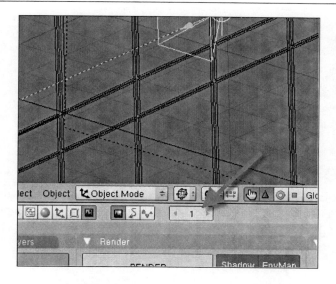

For instance, if we want to add a **keyframe** for an object exactly in frame 10, then we have to move the playback head to this position. To move it, just click and drag the number, or click once and type the number of the frame.

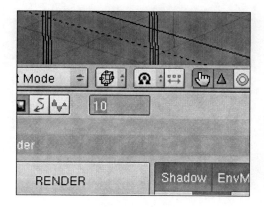

When the playback head is in the right position, just press the *I* key and choose the **keyframe type**. Always remember to place the frame before adding the **keyframe**, because it can alter the animation or the property of your object. A very common mistake is the addition of **keyframes** without changing the position of the animation. It will cause the keyframes to be added at the same position, which will not make an animation.

For a camera animation, always use this sequence to add **keyframes**:

- Place the playback head at the right position.
- The second step is to edit and adjust the object. For instance, alter the size, position, or orientation of the object.
- After the previous two steps, add the keyframe to the object to build the animation.

Timeline

There is a window called **Timeline**, which was created to help with the animation process. With this window, we can easily add, move, and change the timing of an animation. To make the process easier, we can open and adjust the window to make it appear on the interface, in a horizontal way.

The organization of the **Timeline** is very simple, as the following image shows us:

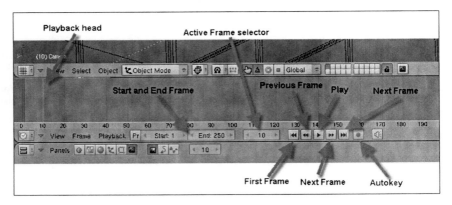

- **Start**: With this option, we can set up the frame where the animation will start.

- **End**: Here we can set up the frame where the animation will end.

- **Play**: Just hit this button to start the animation.

- **Next frame / Previous frame**: These buttons allow us to navigate through the animation, frame by frame.

- **First frame / Last frame**: If we have to jump to the beginning or end of the animation, we can use these two buttons.

- **Automatically insert keyframes**: Here we have one of the most useful options for the timeline. When this button is turned on, the **keyframes** will be added automatically when we change some property of an object.

Use the **Auto-key option** to make animations faster. Just turn it on, and make the required changes to an object. For instance, place the playback head at the required frame, and then change the property of the object. The **keyframe** will be added automatically. For the next **keyframe**, change the frame to the next position and then change the property of the object again.

With this sequence, you will create a complex animation in a short time. Always use this window to help in the process. But even with this window, we will have to make some adjustments later, because the motion or sequences won't always be created the way we want.

Managing Keyframes

Sometimes we may want to manage the **keyframes** used to build an animation, to move, erase, or duplicate them. To do that, we can use a window called the **NLA Editor**. There we can select each keyframe and do almost anything that we can do in the 3D View with 3D objects. For instance, we can move, rotate, and erase a **keyframe**.

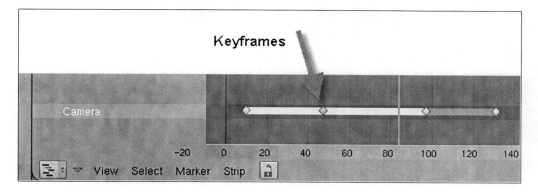

The process of doing that is very simple, and uses the same shortcut keys used for the 3D view. Of course, the only thing that we can't do in the **NLA editor** is a rotation.

- Right click: Select a **keyframe**. If you want to select **multiple keyframes**, just hold the *SHIFT* key while you click over the **keyframes**.
- G: With this key, we can move the keyframes.
- S: If we select one or more keyframes, we can scale them with this shortcut.
- X: Just select the keyframes that you don't want anymore and press X or *Del* to erase them.

IPO Curves

When we edit our animations, sometimes we will have to fine-tune the motion or adjust the rotation speed of the camera. The nature of the motion generated by **keyframes** is based on curves, and not on straight lines. If we want to edit this kind of animation, we have to use a special kind of window called the **IPO curve editor**. With this window, we can have total control over **keyframes** and the curves over time, because we see the animation in a graphical environment.

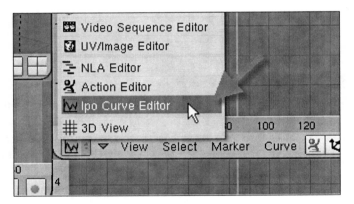

This editor allows us to choose several animation channels, which contain their own curve types. All those channels are placed on the right side, and we can add curves and **keyframes** to almost any property of an object. To select a channel, just click with the right mouse button, over the name of the **channel**, and the curves for this property will be shown on the **curve editor**.

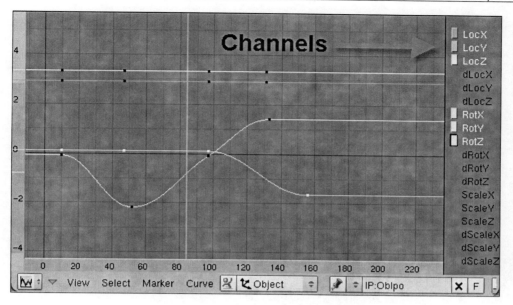

The curve is shown with the display of time on the horizontal, and the property value on the **vertical axis**. For instance, when we select the **LocX channel**, the curve for the motion of an object will be shown with the frames on the horizontal and the location on the **x-axis** in the **vertical axis**.

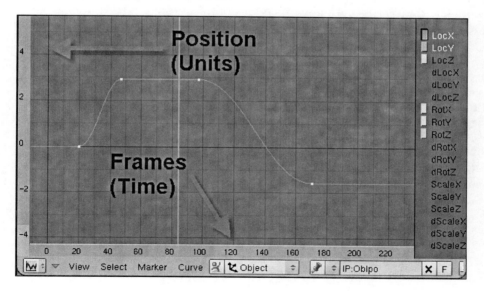

Showing multiple curves
If you want to show more than one curve, just hold the *SHIFT* key while you click on the **channels' names**.

Well, if we want to add new points to the curve, just hold the *CTRL* key and left-click on the place where you want the new point to be added. We can add as many new points as we want.

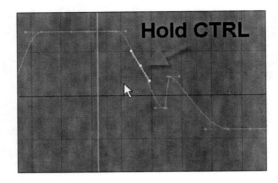

Editing the Curves

To edit a curve, we may enter an **Edit mode** for the **selected curves**. If we select a channel, and press the *TAB* key, the nodes of the curve will be shown as **Bezier nodes**, and we will be able to move and edit the curves. Only one curve can be edited at a time. If you have multiple channels selected, only the last selected active curve will be edited.

The curve can be edited with the same shortcuts used to edit objects. With the *G*, *R*, and the *S* keys, we can move, rotate, and scale the curve points. Hold the **CTRL key** here to add more points.

If you need more precision, such as putting a node at a specific position, press the *N* key to open a **property menu**. It will allow us to place a node at a specific position on the curve editor.

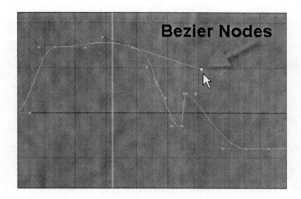

Using Curves

You may be asking yourself why you should use these curves. Well, there are a lot of uses for these curves. An animation may require a more sophisticated movement, rather than a simple linear translation. If we want to add some ease in or ease out to the movement, we have to use **curves**.

Let's look at an example, Take a look at this **curve**, for a **linear motion**:

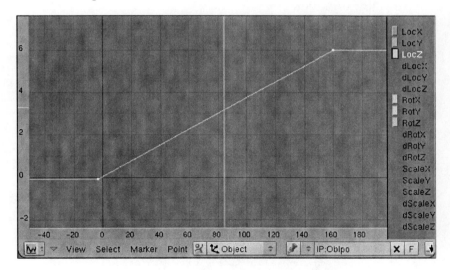

This **curve** will generate a linear motion, with no acceleration or changes in the motion. If you ever saw any type of animation, you will understand that this kind of motion is very artificial and doesn't give any natural feel to the animation. We have to add some easing for the movement. This can be done with the **curves**.

If we change the **curve**, it will look like the following one:

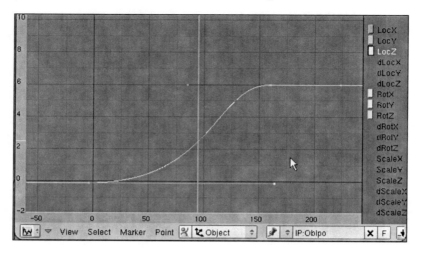

So, the motion of the object or camera will gradually decrease at the end of the animation. It's an effect called ease out, which gives the sensation that the camera is slowing down its motion, as it gets closer to the destination. It's a more natural feeling than just a linear motion.

Animating a Camera

The most common animation we create for architecture is a camera animation, which consists of the movement of a camera to show a building. To create an animation like this, we must have at least one building and one camera to start.

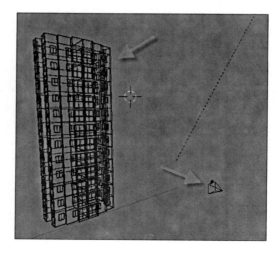

Place the **camera** where you want the animation to start and add a keyframe. If the **camera** will only translate, add a Loc keyframe.

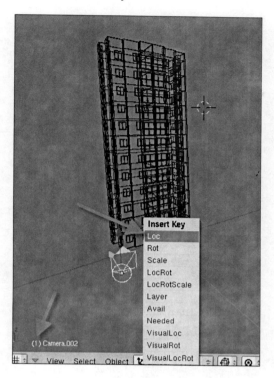

Change the current frame to the next keyframe position. If the **camera** translation requires 2 seconds, use 60 frames to get to keyframe 2. So, change the current frame to 60 and place the camera where you want, and add another **Loc** keyframe.

And it's done! Just place the mouse over the **3D View** and press *CTRL+ALT+A* to play the animation.

Adding a Target

Animating the camera may be a difficult task without the use of a target object, especially if the camera has to be aimed at a specific part of the project. In Blender, we can add an Empty object as the target for the camera, and make the camera always look at this object.

Add an object called Empty from the **tool box**. Then, select the camera first, and the empty object later. When the two of them are selected, press *CTRL+T* to add a track to constrain the camera.

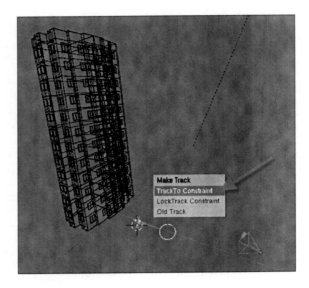

It will always make the camera look at the empty object. Now, we can animate and manipulate the camera in all directions, and it will keep looking at the empty object.

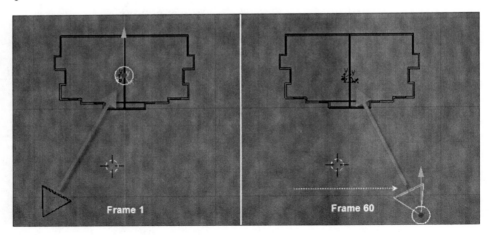

This tool works for all objects, and we can use it every time we need the camera to be aimed in any direction.

Rendering Animation

The main purpose of making an animation is to create a video file, which requires a different approach to rendering the file. Before anything else, we have to know how many **frames** will be rendered to create the video. It's important, because Blender can only render animations with a predefined number of **frames**. To set up the **start and end frames** of an animation, we can use either the **Timeline** or the **Anim menu** on the **Scene panel**.

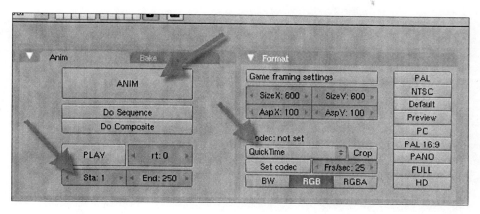

When we set up the start and end frames, the next step is to choose the file type. For most animations we choose the AVI or MOV file formats. If you want to output the animation in a video format, with a high quality, choose the MOV format. Besides the format, we have to choose the compression format for the video as well.

What's the best compression type? The focus of this book is not to describe how to compress video, but to choose some popular compressors.

- MOV files: For this kind of file, choose the H.264 or H.263 compression types. If you want to create a video file with the highest quality, for post-production, just choose none to create a video with no compression. It will generate a huge file, but with no loss of quality.

- AVI files: With this file type, we can choose three different options for the AVI. The first one is called AVI Codec, which allows us to choose a compression for the video. It's very useful if you want to publish the video over the Internet. Just choose Xvid or DivX for a good compression rate. The next type is the AVI Jpeg, which stores the files as a sequence of JPEG images. The compression is very good and it preserves the file quality. This type of file is mostly used to play animations inside Blender, in the Video Sequencer editor. The last one is AVI Raw, used for files destined for post-production since it doesn't compress the video file.

After the file type is selected, the last step is to press the **Anim button**. When this button is pressed, Blender will render the animation with all the frames that we set up.

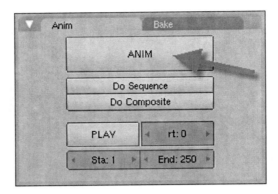

If you want to control where the animation file is being saved, we can alter the default folder where Blender saves this file. Just select the place where you want to save them in the place indicated the following image:

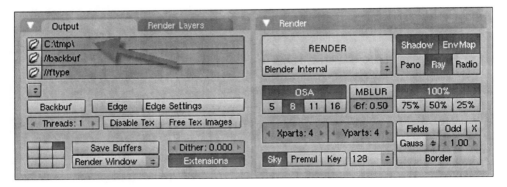

Video Sequence Editor

When we finish a project for an animation, sometimes the result is a set of video files. For each scene or shot, we render a new video file. Unless we want to select those files and play them individually, the overall project should be presented as a single piece. For that, we have to merge all the video files into a single presentation.

For this task, Blender has a tremendous advantage, since it has a built-in **video sequence editor** or **sequencer**, which allows us to edit and merge these files without the need of **video editing software**.

To open the **video sequencer** we select it in the **Window Type selector**.

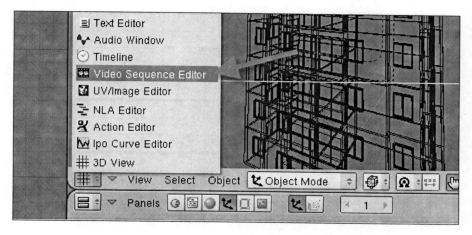

Editing Video Files

Now that we know how to open this window, let's add and edit video files to finish our animation. For instance, we have an animation made up of three video files, and we want to merge all those files into a single sequence.

In this window, we can mix other types of media with the video files. The most common are audio files for soundtracks and still images. With image files, we can create slideshows of renderings, adding a soundtrack and making a high quality presentation for our projects.

Let's take a look at how it works. Right after we open the editor, the next step is to add media to edit. This is done using the **Add option** in the menu.

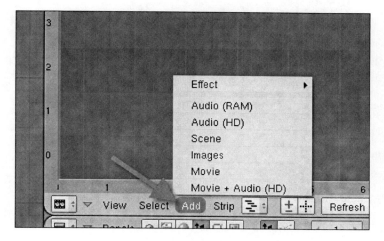

Here are descriptions of the media types we can use:

- **Movie**: With this option, we can select **movie** files such as AVI and MOV.

- **Audio**: Here, we can choose **Audio** files. For instance, we can choose a WAV file to add a soundtrack.

- **Scene**: If you have separated your animation into scenes, in the same Blender file, it will be possible to join them in the **Sequencer**. Just choose this option, and then pick the scene by name. At the end, we will be able to render all the scenes as a single animation.

- **Effect**: Along with the media types, we can choose a few effects to make our animation look more interesting. For instance, we can add a PNG image over an animation, and make the background of the image transparent.

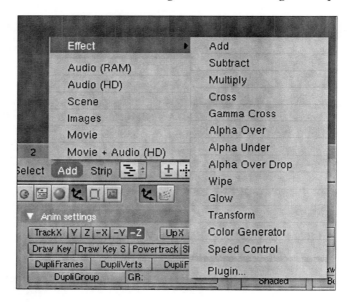

When we add a media type, say a movie, into the sequencer, it's called a strip. Right after choosing the file or scene, we will have to place the strip in the sequencer. To transform a strip, we use the same shortcuts we use in the **3D View**. For instance, we can move a strip with the G Key. We can also use the other shortcuts to:

- **Select**
- **Transform**
- **Erase**
- **Edit**

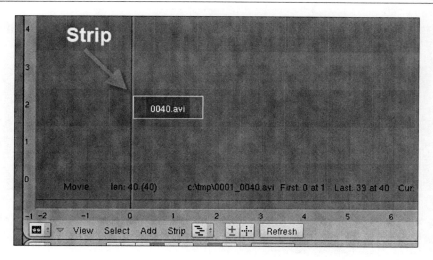

Just like a 3D model, we can edit a strip. This is used to set up the timing for an image, since a movie already has a defined timing. It works like this; just right-click on a **strip** to select it, and then right-click again on the left or right arrows of the **strip.** When one of the arrows is selected, just press the *G* key and move the mouse to change the timing of the **strip.**

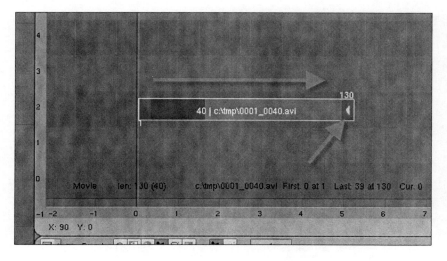

With the left mouse button, we can change the location of the playback head. This playback head is used to place the animation at a certain frame. If you want to split a movie into two or more parts, you use this playback head too.

Select the **strip** and place the playback head where you want to cut the movie, and press the K key. It splits the movie into two parts.

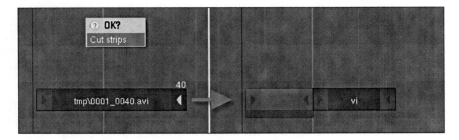

On the left side of the sequencer, we can see a few numbers, which are related to the channels of the editor. They work like layers, where we can place a movie or an image in front of or behind another media file.

Preview the Video

We can see a preview of the video while we edit the **strips**. For that, open a new division in the interface and choose the **Video Sequence Editor**. Then, we can choose the **preview option** in the header. Now, we won't see the layers of the sequencer, but a preview of the current edition.

Effects

Now that we know how the sequencer works, we can edit our previous animation and make it look like a single file. And to make things even better, let's add a watermark at the top of the video.

The watermark image has to be in an image format that supports alpha channels. For instance, we can use PNG or TGA files. For this example, we use a PNG file, which is added in a **channel** above the video file. When it's placed, select both strips and add an **Alpha Under effect**.

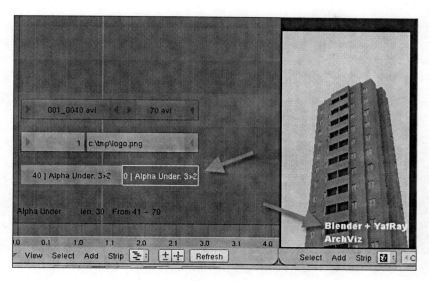

Other great effects for the sequencer are Glow and Wipe. The first one makes the image brighter and the last one creates a wipe effect for slideshows and transitions. If you want to see extra options for those effects, just press the *N* key to open the properties options.

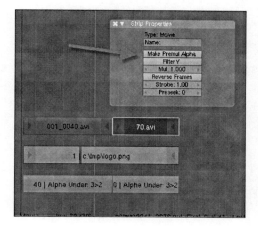

The video sequencer is really simple to use, but gives Blender a unique power to edit and manipulate video files that almost no other package has.

Meta Strip

When we work with several strips in a project, a good practice to follow is to organize our workspace to group all strips together. This way, we won't get lost in a mess of video files. The group of strips is called a **Meta Strip** in Blender, and to create one, just select more than one strip and press the *M* key.

The difference between a **Meta Strip** and a normal strip is that we don't visualize all the strips of videos, but just a single block.

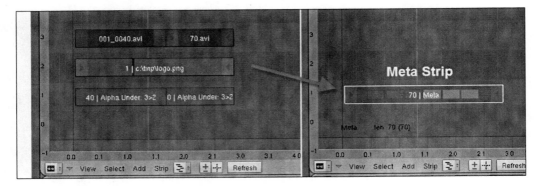

But, if you need to edit a strip from a meta strip, press the *TAB* key. It works just like the switch between **object** and **edit modes**.

Exporting the Video from the Sequencer

To export the sequence to a video file, we only have to turn on the **Do Sequence button**, right below the **Anim button**. If this option is turned on, the **Sequence** will be rendered when we press the **Anim Button**.

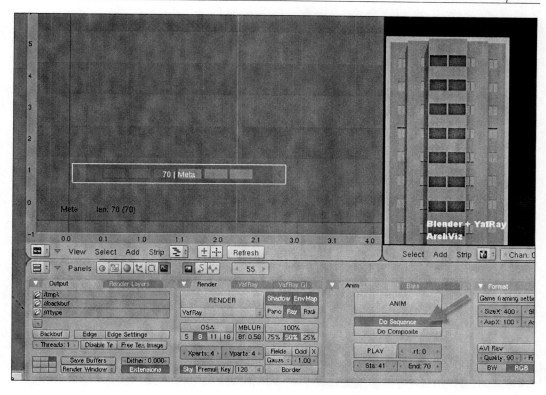

Interactive Animation

The difference between a regular animation, created for a video file, and an interactive animation is that here, we don't have to set up keyframes. The goal here is to create something like a simple game, where someone will walk through and even interact with a virtual environment.

Most 3D suites can't create this kind of simulation by themselves, but Blender can! It's because Blender has a Game Engine, which allows us to use physics simulations and of course, create games.

For Architectural Visualization, it's very useful to create an interactive walkthrough for a project. It's extremely simple to build this simulation, because it involves only the animation of the camera, and not characters, or complex interactions. So, all we have to do is prepare the environment, textures, and lights. Then we set up the camera movements to respond to keyboard commands.

And guess what? We can do all that, without a programming language using logic brick.

> **Test drive the Game Engine**
> To call the game engine, just press the *P* key. If you do that without the proper setup of the scene, everything will look simpler and the animation won't start. Just press *ESC* to exit the game engine.

Logic Bricks

These so called logic bricks are small menus, located in the logic panel. To open this panel, just press F4 or use the button with a small "Pac-man" icon. This panel gathers all options related to game engine manipulation in Blender. The use of these bricks is simple. We just have to choose some options and parameters and then connect the bricks, with a simple drag and drop action.

Before we start to work with the bricks, let's understand the different types of bricks and how they behave. There are three types of bricks called sensors, controllers, and actuators.

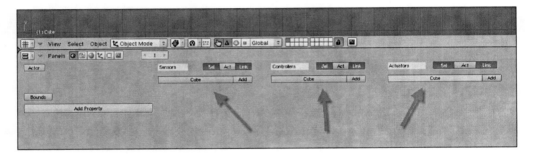

Sensors

This type of logic brick is used to gather information from the keyboard, mouse, or the scene. For instance, if a user inadvertently presses a key on the keyboard, or two different objects collide on the scene, something may happen. Or even, something may happen to an object forever, without the intervention from the user or anything else.

Well, with this brick, we can send messages to the Actuators every time a specific event happens.

Controllers

Here, we have a brick that controls how the action, required from the sensor, must be applied. We can use an expression, python script, or simple logic controllers such as OR and AND. Mostly, we use the OR and AND controllers.

Actuators

With this logic brick, we will actually say what object, or what action must be executed when the sensor brick sends the "signal". There are a lot of different options here to move an object, apply torque, change visibility, call a sound file, and much more.

For us, there are some particular useful actions. Actuators do the action for the interactive animation. The sensor identifies a specific event, and with the Actuator, we can set up the object to move, jump, or play a sound file.

Walkthrough

Now that we know what every type of logic brick does, let's start to build our own interactive animation. Before we start, we must do a few things to prepare the environment. These two steps will guarantee the quality and accuracy of our scene.

- To set up the light for the scene, we have to use Radiosity to make shadows and simulate some kind of Global Illumination, as described in Chapter 11.
- As for the textures, all of them have to use UV Mapping to be shown in the Game Engine as described in Chapters 8 and 9.

If you have textured your scene for rendering, you will probably have to work on the textures again. It's a completely different production environment and it's very hard to re-use textures and lighting for the game engine. If you want to test the textures, just try to visualize them with the textured mode in the Blender 3D View. If a texture doesn't show up there, it won't appear in the Game Engine either.

Well, when the light and textures are all set up, we can go work on the interaction. The first thing to do is place the camera at the starting point. If you don't have one, create the camera and right-click on the camera to select it.

When the camera is selected, go to the **logic panel** and add a **sensor brick**. Choose the **keyboard type** of sensor for this object.

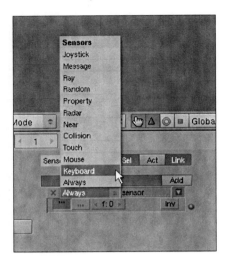

Right after choosing this brick type, we have to set up the key that will act as a trigger for this sensor. To do that, press the button placed right next to the **Key** option. When you press this button, a message, "**Press a key**", will appear. Then, press a key on the keyboard.

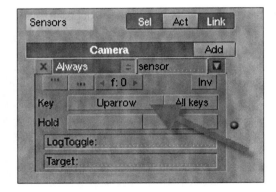

For instance, if we press the **up arrow**, a message shows that this key was selected. After that, add a controller brick, and choose the AND type. It will connect the trigger that we set up with the sensor brick to the actuator. When the user presses the **up arrow**, we want the camera to move forward. So, we have to add an actuator brick and choose the **Motion** option.

This actuator presents us with six types of actions available to choose from. We will use the **dLoc** and the **dRot**, which will change the position and the rotation of the object respectively.

There are three columns, to alter the values for the **x, y, or z axis** respectively. In our scene, to move the camera forward, a positive value in the **y axis** is required. So, we alter the value in the **dLoc line**. In the second column, change the value till it reaches 0.20.

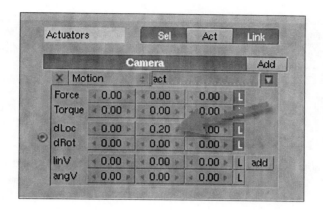

How do we know if it works? Press the *0* key to see the active camera, and then press *P*. It will start the game engine. If everything was done correctly, when we press the **up arrow** key, the camera will move forward. Repeat the same steps to create the actions to move the camera backwards, and to the sides. We can also set up the camera to rotate when the user presses the right or left keys. This way, the view will always be pointed to the front.

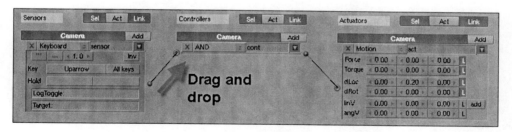

If your scene is big, it may be a good idea to set up the camera to look up or down. This way, the user will be able to move and explore your scene more naturally. Just add some values to the **dRot line**.

As you can see, it's simple to create a walkthrough animation with Blender. When we show a project with this kind of animation, the audience will have the feel of being in the real scene and controlling what they want to see, and not just seeing what you want to show them. If you have the chance, always use this type of animation; it's worth the setup time.

Walkthrough template

The Blender Foundation has a template for the walkthrough animation, available for anyone to download. This template has all the actions for the camera, already set up and configured. All we have to do is to place the scene, and use the camera. It may require some adjustments, because of the scale. If you want to try it, visit this link:
`http://www.blender.org/education-help/tutorials/`
`tutorial-folder/3d-walkthrough/`

Export Walkthrough

When the animation is ready, we may create a standalone application to distribute on a CD/DVD-ROM or just make it available on the Internet. To do that, you have to pack all the textures in the scene, or they won't be shown in the animation. When everything is set up, just use the **File menu** and choose the **Save Runtime** option.

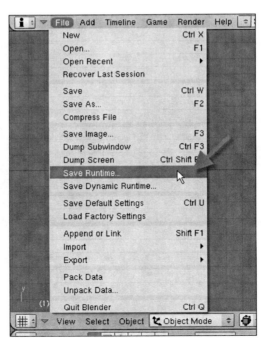

And it's only that! This option will create a standalone application, created especially for the system that you are using. For instance, a standalone application will be created for a Blender running on a Windows system.

Take Blender with you!

Since Blender is open source, and can be executed without an installation, it'd be a idea to take a copy of Blender together with the original file when you have to make a presentation. It will help avoid issues related to compatibility or missing files.

Summary

This chapter presents the techniques and tools used to create an animation in Blender. The focus was on camera animation, which required a lot less work than character animation, but not less adjustments.

Here is a list of the subjects learned in this chapter:

- What animation is, and how to plan the process to avoid problems and issues during the creation of the animation
- The different types of planning required for animation, such as animatic and storyboards
- The different types of keyframes in Blender, and how to use them to make animations
- How to set up the animation with three special windows in Blender: Timeline, NLA Editor, and the IPO Curve Editor
- How to create interactive animations and make a standalone application

14
Post-Production with GIMP

What would happen, if you found out that your render, which took so many hours, didn't look the way you want? In this kind of situation, probably one of two things will happen. The first option would be adjust the model or the problematic setup, and render again. The second one, which will be the subject of this chapter, is to take the rendered image and edit it into some image processor software, such as GIMP. Of course, the second option is always the best choice in these situations, especially when the render time is long.

With software such as GIMP, or Photoshop, we can make adjustments to images, which would require a new render, with just a few mouse clicks. If the bricks of a wall don't get the right brightness, or the color balance is different, just select the area and edit it.

Well, that's just one case. There are a lot of advantages to using GIMP. If you manage to work with render passes, an image editor is important to gather all images together and build the final composition.

GIMP Interface

Before anything else, let's take a look at GIMP and its interface. It's important to know a few basics about it, even if the focus here is not to teach how to use all features of GIMP, but just the main tools and tasks related to post-production work.

The interface is made out of different windows; each window has holds, tools, and options to edit or organize the image. Here is a list of the main windows in GIMP:

- **Tool option dialog**: This menu holds the main options for GIMP, such as the **File** menu, and the main tools such as selection and painting tools.
- **Image Window**: Here, we have the canvas of the image, which has the actual composition. When we do any kind of adjustment, it's here that we will see the results. Most of the color controls are placed in this window tool.

- **Layers dialog**: As the name suggests, here, we find options related to layers.

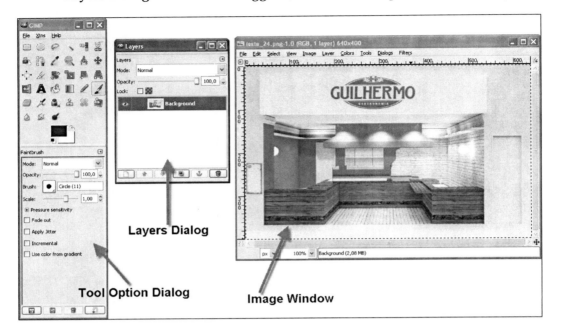

- **Layers Dialog**
- **Tool Option Dialog**
- **Image Window**

Selection Tools

Now that we know how the interface works, it's time to learn a bit about selection. If the adjustments have to be made to the entire image, then the process is easier. We won't have to select anything. But, if only a small part or one object of the image requires adjustments, we will have to select it, and apply the adjustments.

With the selection tools available in GIMP, things will be a lot easier. Here is a brief list of all the tools:

- **Rectangle/Ellipse selection tool**: Here, we have tools to select areas with regular shapes.
- **Free select tool**: This is also called the lasso tool in other image editing software.
- **Select by Color tool**: With this tool, we can select a single color from the area of an image. For instance, click over the area you wish to select, and all the pixels with the same color will be selected.
- **Fuzzy selection tool**: This works much like the Select by Color, which allows us to select pixels with the same color. The difference is that with this tool, only a continuous area is selected.

- **Foreground select tool**: Here, we can select an object or area, with the objective of splitting an image into layers. The selection process involves two parts. First, we use the free select tool, and then paint the selection to fine-tune.

- **Path select tool**: If your selection must be realized with precision, this is the best option. Here we can draw with a Bezier curve to mark the area that should be selected. Since these curves are actually vectors, the lines can be adjusted easily to fit an object or area.

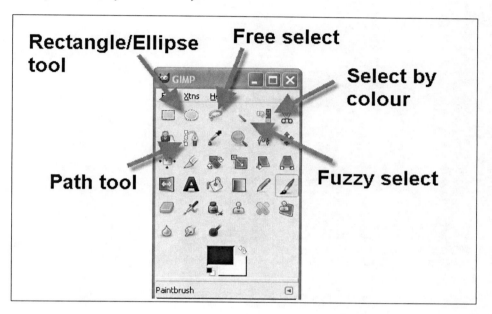

Selecting Regular Shapes

Instead of going through each tool, let's analyze the types of selection that you will have to make. The simplest and the easiest type is the selection based on regular shapes, such as squares, circles, and polygons.

We will use an image as an example, to make selections on regular shapes located there. First, we will try to make two selections, one with a **rectangular shape,** and the other with an **elliptical shape**. This can be done using the **Rectangle and Elliptical selection tools**.

When the proper icon is selected, just click and drag over the image to select it. For the first area, we want to select the sign, which has a rectangular shape. And after that, select the logo on the same sign, which has an **elliptical shape**.

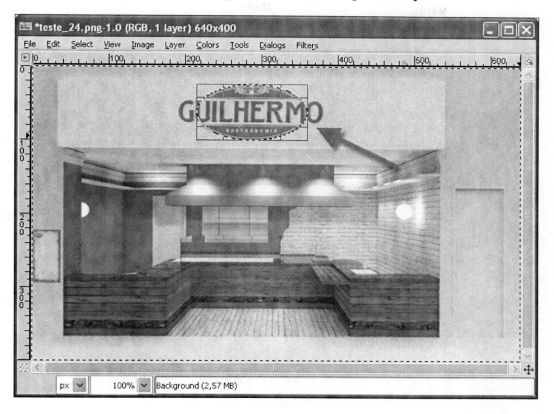

To select a regular shape, just press the *SHIFT* key while you drag the mouse. It will make the shape of the selection become regular.

If the shape to be selected requires an irregular shape, we can use the **Path tool**. For instance, let's select the plane which has a more irregular shape. Activate the path tool and click once at each vertex of the shape. Every time you click, a small black dot will appear to mark the point.

When all the points are marked, just press the **Selection from path** option to make it turn into a selection. You don't have to close the path; just mark all the points and the tool will complete the shape for you.

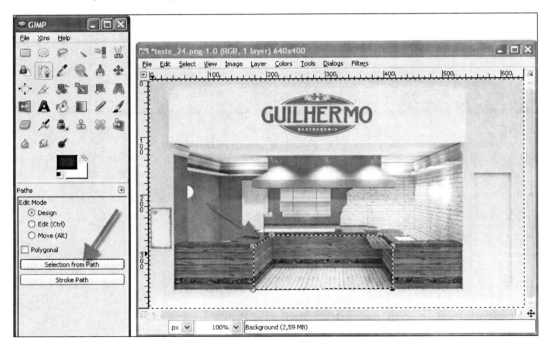

If something needs to be curved, just click over the line, and drag the mouse. It will turn the line into a curve. Along with the curve, some control points will appear for the selected curve. Use these points to fine-tune the path, and create a shape that fits your area or object. It's possible to add more points by just pressing the *CTRL* key and clicking over a line.

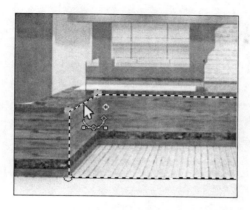

Complex Selections

It's possible to add or remove a part of the selection, for instance, when the area to be selected will be best selected by two circles or small squares. We can add new parts to the selection by holding the *CTRL* key while we drag the mouse. To remove a part, just press the *SHIFT* key.

Selecting by Color

If we have a large area to be selected, with a single or prominent color, there are a few tools that can help us select those areas easily. We have the fuzzy select, and select by color. The first one can select a single area and add all pixels with a similar tone to the selection, but never outside the area. For instance, if we have a white wall, and click on it with this tool turned on, all white pixels from that wall will be selected.

If we have another white wall on the same image, but in a different location of the rendered image, the other wall will not be selected. The other tool called **select by color**, works in a very similar way, but with it, all the pixels with the same color are selected.

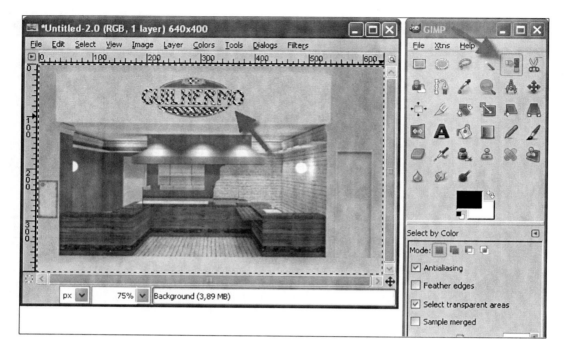

Looking back at the wall example now, if we have three walls with white pixels, all these walls will be added to the selection, together with all other elements or areas that contains white pixels. Therefore, we have to be careful when and where we use this tool. Sometimes, it's a lot easier to use the **path tool**, instead of the **fuzzy or color select**. Use it only if you have an area with a solid color, which will make the process easier, and the adjustments for the selection very quick to implement.

Quickly Undo a Selection

If you want to remove a selection, always use the *CTRL+SHIFT+A* shortcut. When we press this combination of keys, any active selection will be undone.

Color Adjustment

Now that we know how to select just a small portion of our images, we can edit and adjust the color of the rendered images. If a part of the image is selected, when we activate the color tools, only the selected part will be affected. To change all pixels in an image, just use the tools without selecting anything.

To see the options for colors, we have to use a menu called **Colors**, located in the canvas window.

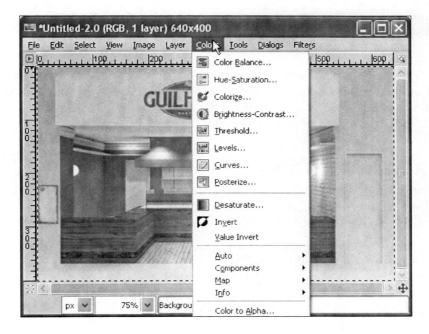

There are a lot of options to choose, but not every one of them is useful for us. Just a few of them are really helpful in editing an image.

Let's see what we can do with them.

Color Balance

Sometimes when an image is rendered, we miss some tones or the image don't give the desired feel that is required for the scene. For instance, if we work on a scene of a room illumined by sunlight, all the room should have a warm feeling. This can be accomplished if the image has a lot of yellow and red pixels, but not too many. If you find that the setup with the Blender lamps is too hard, or time consuming, you can try to adjust it with GIMP!

With the **Color Balance** option, we can make adjustments to an image to make it look warm or cold. Just call the menu option, and a dialog box will appear.

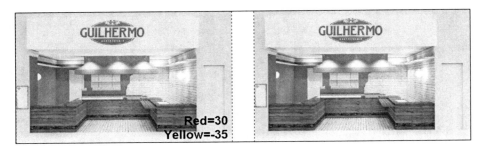

Use the sliders to adjust the amount of each color that will be added or removed from the image. Another great use of that feature, if a color is not right or the light reflection is wrong, is that we can remove the main tones by say increasing the amount of Blue to remove the Yellow pixels.

Hue and Saturation

If the color balance is not the problem, then we can try the **Hue and Saturation menu**, which allows us to adjust the saturation of the overall image, or just a primary color. To use this feature, access the **Hue-Saturation menu**, below the color balance.

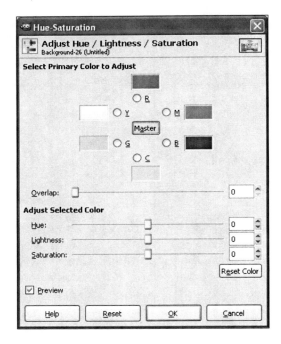

In the menu, we can choose to adjust only one of the primary colors, or the master channel, which contains all the primary colors.

The most useful adjustments for us here will be the saturation and light sliders. With the first one, we can change the level of **Saturation** of colors. A highly saturated image has vivid colors, and a low level of saturation makes the colors look greyer.

We can use this option to improve our prints! For instance, if your printer makes your image look dark with a high load of black ink, then we can increase the saturation to make the image look more vivid with a low amount of black.

Together with the **saturation option**, we can use the **Lightness** slider to make the colors of the image tend to white or black. Always use it with the **saturation option**, and make a lot of tests to find out the best setup for your image.

Take a look at the difference between the two images edited and fine-tuned on **Saturation**.

Saturation =70   **Saturation=-30**

Color Enhance

There is an option that allows us to make a quick adjustment for color. On the colors menu, choose the **Auto option**, and then choose **Color Enhance** to automatically enhance and make all the colors in your image look better. If you don't want to make tests and tryouts, this is a good shortcut for color adjustment.

Color Level

Just as in digital photography, we can use the color levels to adjust our image. For that, we will work with the channels of RGB color (Red, Green, and Blue). It's possible as well to work with the master channel, which has a mix of all those colors.

Before anything else, we have to access the **Levels menu**.

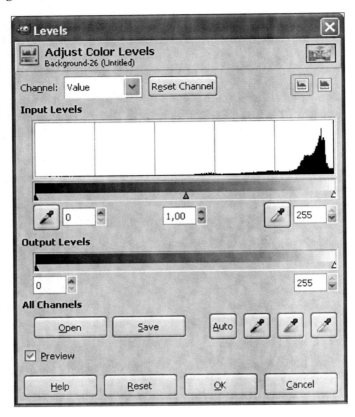

The menu is very simple to use; we can choose the channel to be edited and work with the sliders to fine-tune the levels. **Levels** deal with how much white or black colors we have on the image. All the levels range from 0 to 255, with 0 for black, and 255 for the white color.

To make things easier, we can pick some white and black pixels to make the editing work better.

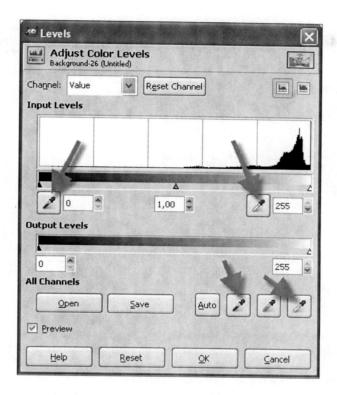

Try to find a good balance between the two opposites, which would make a good image. If you are working on a series of images, and all of them could use the same adjustments for the color level, there are **Open** and **Save buttons** to save the adjustments, and use them again with another image.

Layers

Along with the color adjustments, we can use layers to split the image, and work on the composition of the elements. Sometimes, we will have to add a background, or simply split the image into layers to fine-tune the colors in a specific area.

To work with layers, we have to use the **Layers menu**.

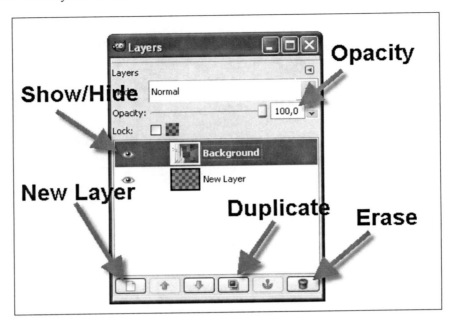

If we create a new layer, pressing the corresponding button, an empty layer will be created above the image. To locate it below, just click on it and drag the layer down.

Another good practice is to duplicate the main layers before you work on some adjustment. This way, no mistake will be applied to the duplicates, and the original layers will remain untouched. We can also hide a layer to see only the layer that needs to be edited. To do that, click on the eye icon on the left side of the menu.

Create a New Layer

To create a new Layer, just press the button indicated in the last image. But, this new Layer will be empty. If you want to add any graphic content to this new layer, just use the painting tools or paste something.

Create a New Layer from a Selection

Another way to create a new layer, is just to select an area of the image using a selection tool, then just copy and paste it. Yes, use *CTRL+C*, and then *CTRL+V*, or simply the Edit menu.

Adding a Background Image

If you create an external image, you will probably need to add a background. It can be a picture of a sunny sky, or simply a photo of the actual location where the building will be created.

To do that, we have to open the rendered image, and select the parts that will be erased. In this case, the parts excluded are the ones representing the window. Use the regular selection tools to select the window, and then use the **Select menu** to choose **Invert**. It will select everything, except the window area. Now, to copy the image, press the *CTRL+C* keys.

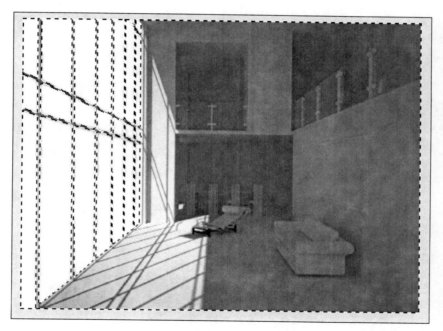

Open the image that is in the background and leave it open. Now, press the *CTRL+V* keys to paste the image.

And that's it! After the image is placed, you may have to make color adjustments to fit the levels, and balance the photo and the rendered image. If a layer is selected, the color adjustments will be applied only to that layer.

Fixing Errors

What if something is rendered at the wrong location, or a part of the geometry is not right? If we don't want to render the image again, we will have to edit the image in order to fix the error. To do that, we have two incredible tools available in GIMP. The first one is called the **clone tool**, and the other, the **heal tool**.

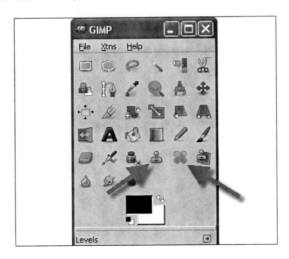

With the **clone tool**, we can clone some pixels over selected areas. The process is quite simple. After activating the tool, we have to hold the *SHIFT* key and click the area to be cloned. This will give us the source of the pixels. Then, we have to click and drag over the area that should be overlapped by the cloned pixels.

Here is an example, where we clone an area of the image to fix an erroneous geometry.

The **heal tool** works similarly, but in a much smarter way. The pixels here are not simply copied, but they are analyzed and only the required pixels are changed.

This tool was developed to adjust photos. But for us, it would be especially useful to change and fix small spots in textures. For instance, if a textured surface is rendered with small defects, use the **heal tool** to remove them.

To use this tool, we have to follow the same steps as for the **clone tool**. When the tool is activated, press the *CTRL* key to mark an area as the source. Then, click and drag the mouse over the area that should be healed.

Watermark

The best way to protect your work and to show everybody who is responsible for a particular image is with a watermark. To add a watermark in GIMP we have to use the text tool and the layers controls.

Let's see how to add a simple watermark to an image. The first thing to do is choose the text. For this example, the text is "Allan Brito".

So, we select the **text tool** and click on the image. It will open a dialog box, where we should type the text.

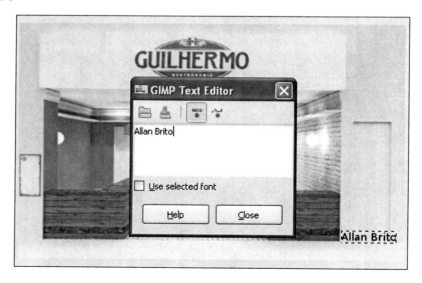

If you want to change the font and size of the text, just use the **property menu** in the main window.

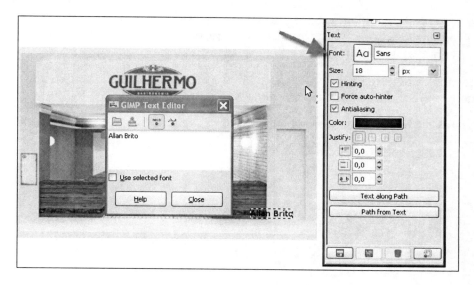

Now, we can make the text transparent. To do it, just select the **text layer** and decrease the **opacity**.

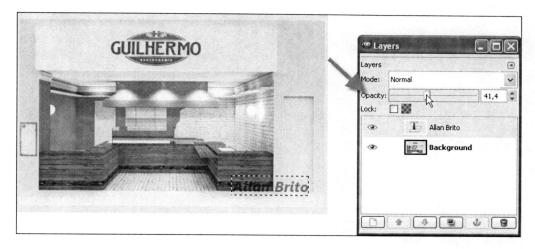

And then you will have a **watermark**, which will show everybody that you are the author of the image and prevent unauthorized copies of your work.

Summary

In this chapter, we didn't work with Blender, but learned how to make your life easier, avoiding the long render times in Blender, and switching to GIMP for the post-production process. Now, you know that some adjustments can be done in GIMP with a lot less effort than in Blender, especially for color correction.

Besides the color correction, we can even make improvements on erroneous geometry with the clone and heal tools.

Well, here is a list of what we have learned in this chapter:

- Using GIMP tools to make color corrections
- Correcting errors caused by displaced geometry, with the clone and heal tools
- Using layers to composite the image with real photos
- Adding text to the rendered images
- Adding watermarks to the images to protect your work

Index

Symbols

Render Levels 62
subdivision 62

sun
about 210
ray traced shadows button 210
shadows button 210

symmetry, modeling
center point, moving 99, 100

T

timeline window, animation
Auto-key option 265
organizing 264

textures
control panel 181
types 177

texture library
about 178
websites, texture downloading 178

textures
adding 179
applying 178
bitmap textures 178
buttons 183, 184
clouds and wood texture, using 181
clouds texture, addting 181
control panel 181
mapping 184
overview 177
procedural textures 177
Reload button 183
setting up 182
texture controls 180
type, choosing 180
types 177
UV mapping 187
wood texture, addition 181

types, objects
curve 37
mesh 37
meta 38
surface 38

U

unfolded mesh
align X/align Y tool 199

creating 198
exporting 200
layout, setting up 200
Pin tool 199
shortcuts, using 198
weld tool 199

unfolded model
about 197
editing 198
unfolded mesh 198
unwrap option 198

UV mapping
about 187, 193
ArchiMap UV Projection Unwrapper, using 191
creating 194
flat layout, creating 190
flat layout, setting up parameters 190
good Seam, features 196
Mark Seam option used 195
model, marking 195
model, unfolding 197
need for 194
seams, marking the model with 188, 189
Seam, removing 196
scripts, unwrapping 191, 202
texture image, creating 187
UV layout, creating 192

V

visualization tools, Blender
3D modelling 8
3D rendering 8
CAD 8
image processing 9
presentation 9

video sequencer editor
about 274
Alpha under effect, adding 279
media types 276
meta strip 280
opening 275
strip, editing 278
strip, editing from meta strip 280
strip, transforming 276
video, adding 275

video, editing 275
video, exporting from sequence 280
video, previewing 278
watermark image effect 278, 279
working 275
volumetric shadow, spot
disadvantages 214
halo button used 213
parameters, setting up 214

W

watermark
adding 307
adding to GIMP 306
window, modeling
Array modifier used 127
Bridge Faces/Edge-Loops, accessing 124
cube, creating 115
Double-hung sash window 114
faces, extruding 117
middle faces, connecting with Bridge
  Faces/Edge-Loops Script 118
mirror modifier, applying 128
preparing 113
subdivision modeling used 115-121
types 113
view, changing 125-127
window frame, building 122
windows, Blender
Action Editor 17
active window 20, 21
active windows 36
audio window 17
Buttons Window 17
File Browser 16
function 16
Header 19, 20
Header, adding 20
Header, removing 20
horizontal division 18
Image Browser 16
IPO Curve Editor 17, 20
merging 18, 19, 36
multiple windows 18
NLA Editor 17
Node Editor 17

Outliner 17
scripts window 16
Text Editor 17, 20
timeline 17
user preferences 17
UV/Image Editor 17
vertical division 18
video sequence editor 17
wireframe materials 174

Y

YafRay
GI setup 242
parameters 241
render times 240
setup 240
using with Blender 238
Yafray
about 237
examples 237
installing 238
light 252
materials 252
setting up 239
YafRay GI setup
about 242
full method 247
SkyDome method 243
Yafray light
about 252
glow, setting up 254
glow option 254
settings 253
Yafray materials 252
YafRay setup 240

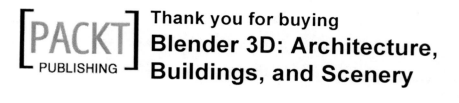

Thank you for buying
Blender 3D: Architecture, Buildings, and Scenery

Packt Open Source Project Royalties

When we sell a book written on an Open Source project, we pay a royalty directly to that project. Therefore by purchasing Blender 3D: Architecture, Buildings, and Scenery, Packt will have given some of the money received to the Blender Project.

In the long term, we see ourselves and you—customers and readers of our books—as part of the Open Source ecosystem, providing sustainable revenue for the projects we publish on. Our aim at Packt is to establish publishing royalties as an essential part of the service and support a business model that sustains Open Source.

If you're working with an Open Source project that you would like us to publish on, and subsequently pay royalties to, please get in touch with us.

Writing for Packt

We welcome all inquiries from people who are interested in authoring. Book proposals should be sent to authors@packtpub.com. If your book idea is still at an early stage and you would like to discuss it first before writing a formal book proposal, contact us; one of our commissioning editors will get in touch with you.

We're not just looking for published authors; if you have strong technical skills but no writing experience, our experienced editors can help you develop a writing career, or simply get some additional reward for your expertise.

About Packt Publishing

Packt, pronounced 'packed', published its first book "Mastering phpMyAdmin for Effective MySQL Management" in April 2004 and subsequently continued to specialize in publishing highly focused books on specific technologies and solutions.

Our books and publications share the experiences of your fellow IT professionals in adapting and customizing today's systems, applications, and frameworks. Our solution-based books give you the knowledge and power to customize the software and technologies you're using to get the job done. Packt books are more specific and less general than the IT books you have seen in the past. Our unique business model allows us to bring you more focused information, giving you more of what you need to know, and less of what you don't.

Packt is a modern, yet unique publishing company, which focuses on producing quality, cutting-edge books for communities of developers, administrators, and newbies alike. For more information, please visit our website: www.PacktPub.com.

PUBLISHING

ImageMagick Tricks

Web Image Effects from the Command Line and PHP

Unleash the power of ImageMagick with this fast, friendly tutorial and tips guide

Sohail Salehi

ImageMagick Tricks

ISBN: 1-904811-86-8   Paperback: 230 pages

Unleash the power of ImageMagick with this fast, friendly tutorial and tips guide

1. Complete tutorial and a gallery of tricks and techniques

2. Create impressive image manipulations and animations on-the-fly from the command line or within your programs

3. Complete PHP-based sample applications show how to use ImageMagick to add pizzazz your web site

---

Learning VirtualDub

The complete guide to capturing, processing, and encoding digital video

Georgios Diamantopoulos Sohail Salehi John Buechler

Learning VirtualDub

ISBN: 1-904811-35-3   Paperback: 196 pages

Get started fast, then master the advanced features of VirtualDub, the leading free Open Source video capture and processing tool

1. Capture and process broadcast, digital, home, streaming video

2. Cut, paste and edit ads, trailers, clips

3. Demos and walkthroughs of processing sample videos

4. Written by video and VirtualDub enthusiasts and experts

Please check **www.PacktPub.com** for information on our titles

GDI+ Application Custom Controls with Visual C# 2005

ISBN: 1-904811-60-4   Paperback: 272 pages

A fast-paced example-driven tutorial to building custom controls using Visual C# 2005 Express Edition and .NET 2.0

1. Learn about custom controls and the GDI+

2. Walks through great examples like PieChart control

3. Customize and develop your own controls

Learning the Yahoo! User Interface library

ISBN: 978-1-847192-32-5   Paperback: 380 pages

Develop your next generation web applications with the YUI JavaScript development library

1. Improve your coding and productivity with the YUI Library

2. Gain a thorough understanding of the YUI tools

3. Learn from detailed examples for common tasks

Please check **www.PacktPub.com** for information on our titles

Printed in the United States
132525LV00003B/14/P

9 781847 193674